# The story of the hidden life of Jesus

# Yeshu'a

## Book One

by Pietro de la Luna

Published by
Filament Publishing Ltd
16, Croydon Road, Waddon, Croydon,
Surrey, CR0 4PA, United Kingdom
Telephone +44 (0)20 8688 2598
Fax +44 (0)20 7183 7186
info@filamentpublishing.com
www.filamentpublishing.com

© Pietro de la Luna 2015

The right of Pietro de la Luna to be identified as the author of this work has been asserted by him in accordance with the Designs and Copyright Act 1988.

ISBN 978-1-910125-17-5

Printed by CreateSpace

This book is subject to international copyright and may not be copied in any way without the prior written permission of the publishers.

"*Yeshu'a* is a powerful read and should help everyone on their journey toward integration of the physical and the world of Spirit."

Lynn Andrews, International and *New York Times* best-selling author of the *Medicine Woman Series*

"*Yeshu'a* is a beautifully written remembrance of an Initiate's passage through the Mystery Schools of the ancient world, told from the unique point of view of the Oversoul, at once both present and eternal."

Glen Craney, multi-award winning author of *The Fire and The Light*

"Sometimes a book comes along that stops you in your tracks and reaches out to you. For me, *Yeshu'a* by Pietro de la Luna is one such book. Without question, the author has been greatly inspired in his writing. He draws you in to a time and place that we feel we already know, and brings it to life. The book is very readable and difficult to put down. You cannot fail to feel privileged to have read it."

Chris Day, author and journalist

"*Yeshu'a* is an amazing and compelling story that will captivate you, providing insight and multidimensional wisdom into Jesus and many ancient mysteries. Taking you on a journey that allows you to embrace the spirit of Jesus, God, and many other historical figures in ways you may have never considered before, *Yeshu'a's* insider perspective gifts you knowledge, understanding and compassion as you view Jesus and history itself anew. The story is riveting, and will broaden your view of life and what is possible."

Dawn Demers, author, strategic coach, healer and international speaker

"I was delighted to read this magnificent story of the birth and growth of Yeshu'a, so enthralled in this real-life history, I had to read it a second time to get the full impact of his wonderful life. *Yeshu'a* has been written in a most beautiful and understanding way that all who read it will be immediately enchanted by the story."

Ron Wilding, Reverend and Healer

"Wonderful! Wonderful! Transforming Humanity is the purpose of Yeshu'a, as he shares with us his profound life-affirming wisdom. Pietro de la Luna's brilliant evocation of the savior's autobiographical voice overrides institutional interpretations as he sees reality through the liberating eye of a loving divinity."

Harvey Kraft, award-winning author of *The Buddha from Babylon*

"*Yeshu'a* is well written, with power and passion. It maintains the Messiah's message of God's unconditional love and forgiveness."

Lord John Taylor, Baron of Warwick

Pietro de la Luna's poetic *Yeshu'a* series inspires today's world population to transform and save Humanity, proclaiming *"You are the ones you have been waiting for!"* In this Age of the Holy Spirit, we are called to BE the second coming of Christ. A richly detailed autobiographical account of the full life of Jesus of Nazareth—not just the distorted, truncated, and reinterpreted account given us in translations of the biblical Gospels—gifts us a full and inspiring picture of how Jesus lived out BEING Love incarnate. The Yeshu'a series reveals a deep devotion to the Divine Feminine missing in church-mediated Christianity that must now be resurrected in our hearts. This inclusiveness allows us to reclaim our full Humanity and become co-creators of a new Story honoring all beings on Earth. Intimately depicting Jesus' deep respect for the Humanity he serves, it encourages that which is holy within us all to flourish. Yeshu'a calls us to the compassion, sacrifice, and activism needed to save the world.

Burl and Merry Hall, authors of *Sophia's Web*

# Foreword
# By Lynn Andrews

Pietro de la Luna's series *Yeshu'a: The Story of the Hidden Life of Jesus* is a gift. As I first held the books in my hands the energy therein infused me with wonder and joy, uplifting and healing me. Even before I had read one word I knew the series would assist me in my transformation during this extraordinary age. Then while reading the books I felt I was being given a great gift. Perhaps this was the result of the exquisite poetic style of the writing, Pietro's ability to transport us into exotic places and times we feel we recognize. Perhaps. Yet in my innermost heart I know it is because the series puts us directly into the story; we live and breathe the events and relationships as if we are there.

Indeed, throughout, it reveals this is our story, the story of all Humanity. Yeshu'a's message is *You are all the ones you have been waiting for*. But it is as a result of this most intimate, tender voice: loving us, embracing us, understanding our every step in life that allows us to accept this, freely and without reservation. The true gift of the Yeshu'a series is we have finally given it to ourselves.

There are moments in Yeshu'a when lines like: *radical trust is required of you* and *I am you and I cherish you* truly enter our hearts and illuminate them, reopening our love-blossom, fearlessly, completely, as this energy has always been there awaiting the time when once again we accept our true divine nature.

I have always believed we are all the ones we have been waiting for. Chronicled in my Medicine Woman series, in this life I have discovered this to be true. As a shaman, a healer, a woman venturing out into the world to experience the journey, this is revealed to me. Pietro de la Luna's ability to lovingly pierce the veil, to give us the wisdom of the heart, that we have nothing to fear in fully loving and trusting ourselves, is truly unique in my experience.

Some are calling the Yeshu'a series the highest transmission. This may be so. That it deciphers the Christian story, lovingly attending to the Divine Feminine and the feminine within everyone and everything, surely engenders a loyal following. Yet the series' remarkable ability to both humanize The Story, so we touch and taste, see and feel it all, and also reveal our own true nature, so that we *are* The Story may be its greatest virtue. The Yeshu'a series also accurately sets the stage for the transformational age in which we now live.

In its beautiful poetic style, we are invited by our higher selves to set sail on the most wondrous adventure, as Pietro says *on the journey all love makes*. For indeed, the rare gift of the Yeshu'a series is its tender voice allowing us to realize that we *are* Love.

Lynn Andrews
Santa Fe, New Mexico
May 2017

I REMEMBER THE DAY I was born. No noble attendants were present, no princes come from afar, no clarions of eternal glory intoned. There was no magical halo wrapped around the sun. My *Savta* Anna was there, five hundred and ninety-six years young, two half-brothers, too, each holding the cloth I fell into, half-sister Salome at my Mother's side. And my beautiful Mother: her disheveled chestnut hair soaked in sweat, matted down over her brow, her countenance of purely joyous exhaustion, the strength of her muscles as she had pushed me through, and the sweet look in her eyes as she gazed upon me for the first time. The floor was hay and dirt and stone, the room a cave near Bethlehem, and outside, the night sky did begin to sparkle with lightning.

Anna wiped me clean with water from a well, while Salome dried me, after she had cut and tied my cord. Figs were in the air, and lilacs and dates, a fire burned.

In my heart I knew I had come and why. There was never any question.

"Look, Salome!" Mother cried. And Salome came over to us, I cradled in my Mother's arms. "Do you see?"

Looking down at me, her shining, almond-shaped hazel eyes opened wide into a smile of their own. In them I saw the glint whence I had come, from she who was to be cherished, saintly sister, beloved friend and teacher and fellow mischief maker. She and Esther and Martha: my sisters, my daughters, my mothers, blessed be thy names.

"There *is* a light, Mother dear, around his head! It glitters like the stars but shines like the sun. My beauty, Isis is happy! And Asherah! They will speak us his name."

I did not tell her, but I shone for her; she allowed me to shine. I saw her light. She had listened to Mother, and together they, too, knew, and also my brothers, of God's Glory. They called me a gift. But they were my blessing. They say my Father was away. He was out collecting wood for the fire.

They say many things of me, some true, some not. Many things they say I said, some true, some not. No matter what has been written and said, I will say this: I remember the day I was born, and every day before and thereafter.

For I am the beginning and the end.

Into mine eyes each morning falls the Love-Light, the Chime of God, the breath of remembrance: the true gift. And each eve waxes across my tired eyes a pale, healing Mother of Truth, blowing kisses over me…Oh, the sweet water.

I am the beginning and the end. All humanity is my brothers and sisters.

Martha rushed in then, like a great gust of wind, her tunic flying about her, her wild raven hair half-covering her piercing eyes. In her fingers were little spheres, agates; she turned them over in her hand. "Mother! I have heard you! Are you alright?"

"My sweet Martha, fear not. He has come. And I am with God."

Martha's gaze rested upon me, and her heart opened wide as the Nile. She crowed like a rooster and stepped about the room, creating a sacred circle. I almost cried.

Then, sensing me suddenly, my eldest sister came to me and kissed me on the mouth. What greater gift could have been bestowed upon me?

I am the beginning and the end. Every day I have known, and every night never forgotten. Deep in the well of my heart is my Love for you, for you are here, with me, and I shall never leave your side. This I promise.

# Chapter One
# Home

THEY TAKE ME TO TEMPLE, the Temple of Jerusalem, to be blessed and circumcised. Our land is so barbaric it will not allow women into the main areas of the great temple. There is the Court of Women, but they can walk not beyond. My Father, a talented builder and artisan, takes me, and my brothers surround us. When the priest snips my foreskin I do not cry. But as we are leaving, I gaze full into the Holy of Holies; the veil is partially lifted. Within I espy an old scribe, withered to the bone, slouched over scrolls, craning his neck to see more clearly the Law, and the high priest barking orders. Indeed, the room is filled with golden light. But there is a pall over it, as like when a man has been wronged by his fellow men, has become despised, and the taint, the stain, though seemingly on the man, is truly on his fellow men and his institutions.

Seeing us pass and begin to descend the fifteen grand steps, I tightly wrapped to stem the bleeding, the high priest calls out to Father: "You would be wise to tell the boy of the Law, for the tide must soon turn. He will have need to know it; Judea is become a bandit's nest of Greeks and Romans and Galileans and Samaritans. Only by abiding the Law will we overcome." His voice cackles like a mad hyena's: full of fearful bombast at the mere sound of the wind.

The priest does not understand. I know already the Law. But I have not come to fulfill it. He knows not who I am. There is naught he can teach me, save of false pride. He knows the Law but comprehends it not. One day anon we will meet again, and he will think me an arrogant, ungrateful, precocious child, in this age when prophets line the streets like so many pebbles and are hunted like game by Roman and Jew alike.

Father looks askance at the holy man, his cavernous eyes unsurprised at his statement of authority. Father is not fooled. His long, soft beard grazing the top of my head, his sure and hardworking hands cradled round me beneath, he merely smiles: a quiet, unruffled, dignified smile. "In our house we live the Law," he lies, straightening his vowels, trying not to sound Galilean. And we depart.

He did not tell the priest that in our house women sit at table with the men; this is not done in our land. In our house we venerate Woman in all her phases and wisdom, and we welcome any soul who passes no matter their origins and beliefs, if they but live with God in their hearts. Salome and Martha speak the name Yahweh out loud, as does my dear Mother; this is in breach of the Law. They, too, speak of His wife and, like many others, have knowledge of gods and goddesses from other lands and times. They sometimes name God *Adonai*. Martha, especially, knows of magic and spells and philosophy. Round her neck on black twine she wears a vial containing tears which exact a power akin to blood. She is scarce without her little spheres, in her pouch or tumbling in her hands. She tells me Anna the Prophetess bestowed them upon her as a gift. And we are of close acquaintance with some who are called the Jebusites and Amorites, from Canaan, those who were on this land long before the Jews.

Before I am two years on this Earth a bird flies into our tiny house, through an open window. I sit content in Salome's lap, she of the vine and the root and the oil of myrrh. Father works, Mother rests, and dear Salome is become my child-mother. She loves me so. Though there is talk of the *Sicarii* in the streets, assassins each and every one, and various groups all professing to be *The Way*: from the Sadducees and the Pharisees, to the Few and the Many, Jew pitted against Jew, and against every man come into our land from other nations, in our humble house there is yet no fear.

The bird indeed is welcome.

He is a blackbird, big and full of confidence. Eloi! He speaks to me, looking me straight in the eye: *Yehoshua, watch the hills leading to Carmel, travel the roads to Damascus in your heart, sail the seas to Albion. Use bits of soul and you will see clearly what comes. And when you are old enough, look deep into your Mother's water well. There you will find the face of your Beloved. Listen well your heart, Yehoshua. God within it resides.*

He jumps down from his perch on the back on the chair, and comes to land on Salome's shoulder. His eyes devouring me in kindness and wisdom, the brilliant blackbird nestles his beak softly in my chest for a moment, before flying back through the window.

Salome and I giggle like tickled sprites. She, too, has heard. And I am like the string of David's harp, God's fingers thrumming me lovingly, singing the eternal song of Love.

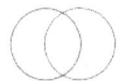

Today my half-brothers James and Simon battle amongst themselves. It is nigh ever thus with them. Behind our house is the brow of a hill, and atop it they have argued over the day's catch of fish. James counsels none be given to the poor, that we are poor enough; salt it and store it proper, before the month of the olive harvest. Simon, he with the long, bending nose, full ruby lips, and hair orange as sunset, is of a softer nature.

"You have the stink of the Romans, brother James," declares Simon. "You speak like the rich who are satisfied with the way things are. I stand with the Many. Have you so quickly forgotten the words of our Lord, to give to others freely and expect none in return?"

"And I think of our Mother and Father and family. Was it not only yesterday we were short of nuts and olive paste and sunfish for our own, little Yeshu'a appearing weak in the eyes? I will not have it! The Temple speaks trite truths fit for the Kingdom of God, but says little for us in living the *real* life! ... You might fare better as a stone carver, brother, for your talents as a fisher verily depend on mine. Walk with me when I visit the streets of upper Jerusalem; there you will see the nature of which we need more."

In turns political, societal, and religious, the quarrel now becomes personal, and my brothers are at each other's throats, cascading down the hill, bludgeoning each other with blows. Their robes becoming green and brown, their faces red with anger, blood on Simon's bottom lip, I am carried out of doors by Salome, Mother behind us. Without a thought, I pull at Salome's hair to take me to them. She obliges. At the middle of the hill, James has Simon's head wrenched in his left arm, while Simon issues blows to James' stomach, both gasping for air.

I cry aloud and then clear my throat. And they stop, dumbfounded I have arrived. Extending my two nubby arms, Salome brings me close. I lightly touch each brother on the top of his head and hold fast. In my mind I see them as they really are, filled with the Light of God, and feel the energy pour through me into them. I smile wide.

Suddenly my two brothers are laughing uproariously, gazing upon each other at once with recognition, as if not having been aware the other was, in fact, his brother. The rose is leaving their cheeks, and I speak my favorite word: "Kisses."

A crowd has gathered round the side of the house, and murmurs ensue.

Mother finally exclaims, "Enough! Heed Yeshu'a; your Father soon comes, and he would want none of this. Fetch and ready food for the table and offer contrition in your prayers before you allow it to touch your tongues."

The Nazarenes flee with eyes bulging, fingers pressed to their lips, whispering words into the air only they and God and I can hear. Arms akimbo, Mother is smugly satisfied as Salome and I reenter our house and my brothers fetch the fish.

When Father arrives from Zippori, he is tired and dirty and in quiet mood. "Mary, I have heard of ours in the street as I returned. The boys were fighting again?" he asks, knowing well it is true. Washing his hands in the ceramic basin, he then sits exhausted at table, contemplatively combing his fingers through his long beard.

Mother's azure eyes look upward, as if seeing through the ceiling, asking for strength. She nods and says not a word.

He gazes upon her for a moment. "They speak of Yeshu'a, Mary. Jeremiah the cobbler and his wife say they witnessed him exude light into his brothers. The others seconded and described."

Again she nods, this time curtly. She is wise, my Mother. She speaks not.

"You have known of this, yes? You told me so, when he was born, and even before."

"…Yes, husband."

"Tell me, so I may know, before I lose my nerve to eat."

"Yea Balaam! The angels came to me, dearest. They whispered in my ear of his coming. Their words were sweet and light and loving. And they gave me visions. The Holy Shekinah I then saw descend and settle before me; her face full of Glory, she shown me him in shining white robes, his arms outstretched, a sea of people round him on a hill. My heart raced like the chariots at the Alexandrian games. We are blessed."

"Hmm…The wonder of it. Blessed? I believe it. But also cursed, I wager."

"Think not of it. And not like this."

"They will talk, Mary. They will talk."

His face is full of furrows, as I sit in my Mother's lap, hearing every word, grinning with delight, knowing full well what is to come. I fear not.

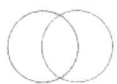

Tonight, as my brothers and Father sleep, Mother rocks me in her arms, Salome sitting nearby on the floor, her eyes wide, as Martha, she of the wisdom of the ages, plays with her word stones. She speaks words from time out of mind, for not only does she hear the Great Beyond, but by day she chases about looking for and reading books, engaging travelers, seeking ever more knowledge, wishing she were with coin. In one corner she hides a stack of three books beneath her blanket.

"Tell us what the stones say," Salome asks excitedly, looking from the short distance across the room.

Martha puts a finger to her lips, then closes her eyes. "Be still."

Mother starts softly humming an ancient tune I recognize: the Love-song of Inanna, Sumerian Queen of Heaven and Earth. It is my song. They once sang it to me, ages long past, the sun glittering through fields of grain and velvet grass. I remember it still.

Salome now follows her lead, as Martha passes her pendulum over the stones. Then she stops still as night, her face reading the letters once more. My heart beats in time.

"Enter me, spirit. I know you are near. Take me as your vessel; we have no fear," Martha calmly intones, a breeze coming through the window. "We are pure of heart; we are your children." Once more her face is cold, rigid stone. Her mouth opens like a cave, and a voice, deep and indisputable like a man's, exits her throat.

"ISSA," it says. "ISSA IS IN HIS BREAST. THOUGH THEY WILL COME AND CALL HIM MESSIAH, HE KNOWS IT NOT TO BE SO. HE IS NOT A KING OR A GOD BUT A GREAT BEATING HEART WHO BRINGS MAN THE MAP TO THE GLORY."

Martha suddenly slumps over, her breath spent, her chest heaving. I ache to touch her. But dear Mother holds me firm, as Salome rises to see to her with a dampened cloth. Slowly Martha's breath returns to calm, she lifting her head to view Mother's face. The spirit is now departed.

"I have known it, daughters. Little Yeshu, too, knows it," says she, calling me by my little name, the name my Beloved will also one day call me.

"Who is Issa?" Salome asks.

Mother smiles her incandescent smile. "The hidden ones of Issa — the Issa-enes. The Essenes. They tell the story of Issa, born of a virgin mother named Mari. Claiming he was the perfection of man, the Son of Man, as indeed are we all, they say he performed miracles, healings, was crucified, and would come again as the Messiah."

"Is this pagan? How is this possible?" Martha, revived once more, asks, incredulous.

"These are the Nazoreans, child...The voice spoke truly, for it spoke of the belief in a Messiah."

"But there have been many, so I know."

"So it is told. But the voice spoke truly. Men ever seek the Anointed One, the Messiah. Yet this belief brings with it great calamity; it ever has, men fighting and killing one another in fits of fevered, crazed ideas and feelings, as though the world would end, denying the divinity in each other. The truth is: the spark of God exists in every woman and man, and the Glory, the coming of our Lord, the Kingdom of God, will only arrive when this consciousness resides within enough of us that the rest will plainly see. In our land we live by prophecy, but truly it is *intent* which brings thee closer and closer, cubit by cubit, to attaining God, the Ascension, and to creating Heaven on Earth. Everything you are, you intended; everything you experience, you intend...Tell not your Father of this. He knows, the dear one, but he fears what comes; he has told me so."

Martha and Salome both nod in solemn earnest.

"Issa is the Moon," Mother continues. "And Issa is also Isis of Egypt, the Queen of Heaven. The Egyptian god of the sun is Ra, and El is the stars. Thus you now may understand the name of our land: Issa-Ra-El."

Oh, dear Mother is wise. Her Mother and Father, Anna and Joachim of Zippori, have taught her well.

Martha leaps to her feet, her sharp black eyes beating with sudden comprehension, her breath short but deep. "Now I see! ...I want more, Mother, more. Give us more!"

"It is enough for one night. I will say only this: the story we are taught of Adam and Eve, tempted by the serpent, tells us the serpent is evil. Yet the serpent represents wisdom, the wisdom and Truth of Source: God. Politicians and priests desire you not to possess Truth; they wish to keep the wisdom for themselves. But the serpent also symbolizes our reptilian nature, which we must master along the Path. Speak your praises to God; praise God every moment, children. Speak of nothing but your Love and gratitude. The great secret of the world is now birthing in your breasts. But keep it well-hidden. We must see to young Yehoshua's protection, and he will in turn see to ours."

Mother signs two fingers across her lips. I love her so.

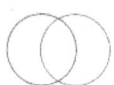

The rolling, deep purple hills of my home are wondrous. Gazing out across them, I smell the sea and the carob trees and the olive groves. The words of the wind are not lost to me. It tells me of the birds, the trees, and the weather, and spins tales of faraway lands I will one day visit, one named Albion, another India. And it speaks of coming events in a soft, sweet, caring voice. Glad is the sun upon the violet hills of Galilee.

As I learn to walk, my sisters carry me from one hilltop to another, pointing to this landmark and that. One day, west by north on a rise, we see Zippori, meaning birdlike, as from it one has a bird's eye view. Here Father works on Herod's new buildings, the city wherein my Mother was born, now named Sepphoris by the Greeks. It is a grand, shimmering site, the temple a towering glory to behold.

Returning to town, we make onto our street and soon witness a woman fall from her horse onto the cobble. She is carrying bundles and swaths of cloth in her arms and cannot soften the fall. A small crowd rushes to help her, my sisters and I, in Martha's arms, coming from behind.

Peering through the spaces between, I at once see the Light shining within her. I can help her. She is a beautiful woman, and young, from a poor family. I tug at Martha's sleeve and nod into her gaze. She brings me close to the woman, the men near the front letting us pass.

Alongside two other men, an older man, wearing a brown hempen robe, looks upon us askance. "What are you thinking, bringing a child to see this scene? Take him away and allow us to assist her."

The pierce of her black eyes slicing through him like a *sicarius*, Martha hisses. "Be gone! Can you not see what is before your eyes? Let the little one see her."

Her gaze is enough to stop Osiris, but the words put the men on their heels.

The young woman, chestnut-haired like my Mother, has broken her arm. I see the energy streaming from the spot. It is not a bad break, but a break nonetheless. She cries and moans, her face pale, as she in agony holds her arm. And then she sees my face and attempts a smile for my benefit. Martha lowers me to the street. I espy Salome, looking concerned this way and that, biting a fingernail.

Slowly I walk four tiny steps, up to the fallen woman, and place my hands on her damaged arm. As I do, I silently communicate to her to release her cares, to think of nothing but God: *See yourself as you really are: Light. Release all thoughts and enter your heart. Reside with God.* Heat pulses through me and travels into her.

There is an audible crack beneath my tiny fingers. The bone straightens. And suddenly there is shock on the woman's face, relief on her brow, her cheeks flushing full, and her eyes glimmer.

"The ache is vanished! I feel no pain!" Moving her arm, flexing at the elbow, she then stands on the street, looking at her bundles. The crowd gasps, a collective inhalation of breath, and many step backward, giving my sisters and me space. Murmurs ensue.

Now the woman resolutely picks up her wares and drapes them over her horse. She gazes upon me once more, next upon my dear sisters, then back again. Picking me up off the cobble, she embraces me, kissing my cheeks and ears and lips. "Bless you! God always be you. Eloi! Eloi! Eloi!" She mounts her horse, looks back into my grateful eyes, and then gives a quick kick, and they gallop out the south entrance of *Nazara*.

A few stragglers stare at us as Martha once more gathers me in her arms; several others run in all directions; still others congregate in a circle muttering and gesturing to each other. Salome grabs Martha's free hand and we make for home.

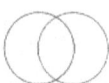

When we are very young, we are capable of such magic. Yet we are told the young child knows nothing. The secret is to keep the blessed child within us, throughout our days; this is the way to enter the Kingdom. This I will teach, come what will. And many will hear and understand with their hearts; more will not. Already I have revealed some of what you have heard of me is true and some not. It is true my family traveled south to Bethlehem to take part in a Roman Census; born I was near Bethlehem, though Father finally thought not to register our family. And we live in *Nazara*. Mother's dearest wish was for me to live and breathe in the velveteen hills, to imbue my reblossoming spirit with their magical caresses. And Father, always wise to listen to Mother's intuition, agreed.

For in the purple hills I bathe in the shimmering Light of God, and I am close to the land of Seth and to Mount Carmel. Save our trip to Jerusalem and eight nights in Bethlehem, Father's angelic dream setting us to flee, not one single moment have I spent apart from these treasured mounds. Tonight I lie on my back, next to sleeping Salome, and envision. The blackbird has told me what I already know, but he did well to remind me. I first listen to my beating heart, thinking of each member of my family. When we ask questions of our heart, if the beat is high in our chest, the answer is yes; when it is low, the answer is no. And with the sending of silent messages of Love, the heartbeat is always high in our chest, mine pumping like a vast team of steeds, their feet pounding the Earth in unison. I praise God and send loving blessings to each member of my family, and they will hear. Everything I do comes from the Heart, any power I have is born of my physical heart, for to unite Heart with mind, the Heart being the source of our spiritual flame, is to attain God.

I now send bits of soul out onto the roads, just as the blackbird counseled. The Heart is the seat of our soul, and since the day I was first born, oh so many lifetimes ago, I have had the ability to travel with my soul's eye. Through *Nazara* I journey, the streets dark and silent, and wing west to Mount Carmel.

Mother was wise to tell us of the northern Essenes. Their Mystery School resides atop and amidst its exquisite peaks. Here are: lush forest and secluded pool and copse and flower-strewn meadow so brilliant, so fine, verily so enchanted, the orchards and gardens so luxuriant and in balance, it returns me to the very beginning, when human and beast lived as one, and for sustenance we picked globules of energy straight from God: manna from Heaven. Caves cleaved deep into the Earth herein also reside. And the essence of Source remains. The modest yurt tents amid lea and glen remind us we shall remain mostly mute of our wisdom and share through acts and deed and service. We reveal by word ever so slowly, with great ease, according to the ability of each to receive; our acts of healing are likewise according to each one's ability to receive the Light of God.

Pythagoras came here and was schooled. Thoth did here also come. And during my days in Atalantia I arrived with others I will one day name, for that treasured isle was once the great keeper of Truth. Here, too, the Kabbalists also came, those of the venerated hidden inner tradition given directly from God to Moses on Mount Sinai, its awesome truth that the Supreme Creator permeates all substance in the Universe still too much for humanity to bear. In my long, fruitful life as Solomon I was also here, my dear Sheba, she who was truly Asherah, at my side, as the Carmelites always welcomed woman as man's equal. So, as my Mother told us of them, my heart smiled, for already I knew; she, flush with wisdom, reminded me of home, tugging at my roots with tender care.

You may hear I was schooled by the southern Essenes at Qumran. I there did receive my certificate in basic subjects, and

John of the River did baptize me there, but my heart was trained atop Carmel. Ezra chose the writings which became Torah. But Issa did not approve, and so the Essene Carmelite Order was born, to inform the time when inner and outer could in unity live, as you, my dearest reflections, now know it to be, as you live and breathe today.

The moon is high and full, and I bask in one of the pools for a moment, the perfectly crafted stone steps strolling grandly down the heights into its waters; hues of lavender, sapphire, and mustard seed shimmer and dance in both sea and sky. Then I soar to Carmel's highest point, gazing down upon the hidden rooms in the clefts, sensing the white-robed ones are in the deepest of these. There is a soft chant, furious candles burn, for mine eyes pierce the veneer of stone. Seth of Damascus will be pleased when I speak to him of it. He will be a Carmelite master.

In truth, *Nazara*, known by you as Nazareth, was once a camp for the northern Essenes, and grew to be a cooperative village of a few hundred souls by the time I reentered the world through my Mother's sacred gateway.

In my home Hebrew tongue the word Carmel means *garden paradise*. And as I imbibe its essence, allowing its air and water and life to enter my soul once more, it is indeed so. Here one lives in harmony and conversation with the trees and the animals and can fulfill the fullness of possibility amid nature's gifts. It is God's Garden. Liberating our senses from the world man has made, when we meld Heart with mind, Mount Carmel signifies the absolute center of spiritual connection, situated in our body-consciousness at the top of the head: the pineal gland. In my land the powers have taken to the sacrifice of animals in temples. But at Carmel it is forbidden to spill blood of any kind or to harm any part of nature. Once, long, long ago, when I lay in a meadow as Solomon with my dearest and others, as we rose to depart, we straightened every blade of grass we had touched, and spoke loving words unto them, then putting our ears to hear their grateful refrain. For Mount Carmel is the most sacred of mountains.

Though I was not he, our great forefather Elijah was here; he made Carmel his chief retreat. His sacred cave you may today still visit. Truly it was he who pitched the first yurt-tent temple, of many rooms, so as not to disturb the sanctity of the Mount, and atop its peak a yurt village also spanned. And tonight, as I learn I, too, will become the bird later in life, transforming my very body into that of the dove or the great eagle when the loving-need arises, I feel Elijah enter me, O Great Prophet of Judea and Phoenicia. Into my soul's ear he whispers: *Ye will have to fight the powers of the Pentateuch; various of Moses' records were falsified, changed. The Essenic Order of Mount Carmel still retains the true record, the true words of our Dear Lord. This is your mission.*

Knowing what comes makes it easier, but only as the breath of Carmel fills me once more. My soul now sits under yawning pine and yew, next to me a sleeping lamb.

# Chapter Two
# Flight

KING HEROD HAS HEARD of me. The murderous one, the fearful one, he of the ever-trembling face, crooked, long fingers, and badly twitching eye has heard of me. Though I have hitherto kept it from you, for reasons which will become manifest, a star *was* indeed born the day I came into the world. My birth had been for generations planned, and was virginal, as my earthly Father's physical seed was not the agent and Mother indeed was pure. There, too, was a planetary conjunct in the night sky which appeared as a massive star over Bethlehem. As well, I was born some years earlier than even secular scholars believe. My dearest, loving reflections, I bestow upon thee the great gift of patience, for I will reveal all. Your Faith in me is your Faith in yourselves, is your Faith in God. Never doubt. For in Truth and Love, we are all Christ.

Originally four in number, representing the four stars which led them — Aldebaran, Regulas, Antares, and Fomalhaut — three magi did come to Herod's palace, heralding my arrival. Melchior, Casper, and Balthasar were their names. The fourth, Artaban, lovingly did God's work and was delayed. All four are beloved of me. Golden are their souls in service to God. Consulting his high priests and soothsayers, Herod heard them name the town of Bethlehem as the place of my birth, a fulfillment of Micah's prophecy, and with orders to return to him, this he sent the magi to confirm. But I was protected by God's Glory. By my family's counsel and also a divine dream shared by the magical three, they returned not to King Herod but to their countries of origin. Time passed. Frightened when, after many moons, the magi had not returned, Herod hatched his hideous plan.

The story is told of the infanticide, the *Massacre of the Innocents*; when Herod's troops entered the tiny town, seven children, cherished by me, were found of my age and were murdered. And so Flavius Josephus is mostly correct in his omission of this chimera. Though known by very few, both Philo Judaeus and Josephus possessed deep Essenic knowledge. In truth, there were twelve magi, and their wives, who were also magi, accompanied them. But Artaban was indeed delayed. And as the hierophants of the magi, Melchior, Casper, and Balthasar did gift me with gold, frankincense, and myrrh. Meet them again I will, as will you for the first time, when I am a man.

But now the murderous king has heard of me once more. Ever-seeking the Anointed One, like all people, mine can be in moments weak. And word of my gifts has traveled to Jerusalem, from one mouth to the next, like a living thing unto its own. Mother has seen it, my sisters have seen it, I, too, have seen it. Herod's seers ere had sensed it out in the air.

And my Father, dutiful, strong, and devoted also in his knowledge, has had another dream, a magnificent dream, a treasured dream. Speaking with Jedediah in the sacred grove at the southeastern edge of Mount Carmel, he now plans our journey. To Egypt.

I do not speak ill of my people, or of any. My Judaic brethren are glorious. Especial in their gifts to God, they bring harmonious beauty to us all; they complete the circle of humanity with flower, song, food, and poetry and dance and more. As with all nations, during an age of great calamity, they merely for a time lost their way, and were fooled by the acts and words of fear that can reside in each of our breasts, including mine own.

I tell ye now, from atop the mountain: If ever you hear the word fear ascribed to God, know it to be false. God is Love. Love pure. Ask your heart; your heart knows, of this you may be sure. In the deep, dazzling darkness, find your heart: release. Know in your heart, beyond all veils: there is nothing ever to fear. We are all equally loved.

This is God's gift.

Many dissimilar, impossible, conflicting accounts exist detailing many episodes of my life, most written to conform to the fulfillment of prophecy. The story you may know is also an incomplete rendering of the ancient mythos, old as the solar system itself; it is the story of the sun's passage through the earthly sky. The lives I and my family and others lived in Palestine bear some resemblance to the tales. The truth behind them, however, is purely more beautiful, inconceivable, and can shine a bright lantern into your own soul, awakening it as from a deep slumber. You may have heard there is evidence of my existence. This is not so, and for a reason. Upon this day I now write, save but one, all seeming scraps of proof known to the world have been fabricated or misconceived in their origins. But all will be revealed. You see, my dear children, Faith breathes without proof. This is the path to Glory. No woman or man should ever be placed between you and God. This is why religion, no matter its name, has failed. My roots in this world come from that which is named the East, Asia. And searching for me everywhere but in the Heart has led many to lose their way.

Fear not, dearest reflections. I am always with you; you ever dwell in my heart. You are beloved of me. And there *is* a way of knowing.

I never wanted to be worshipped.

Father has had a wondrous dream in which the first *mal'akh*, or angel, of God appeared. She informed him Herod's men will march into *Nazara* looking for me, and that she will return in dream when Herod is dead; this is part of God's plan. I will not here speak the angel's name, for it is most sacred, but a route has been mapped for my family to travel to Egypt, to the community of Therapeutae Essene above Lake *Mareia*, or Mareotis, outside Alexandria. In their wisdom, the Essenes of Carmel knew this would come; at this moment a Phoenician ship bearing cedar and purple dye sails from Tyre bound for Alexandria. Like the Greco-Egyptian Ptolemies before him, Augustus in Rome desires the Tyrian dye for his royal emblems, and the cedar shavings to keep fresh the tombs of his family, an everlasting symbol of his greatness. Livia counsels well her husband.

Hearing this, my soul soars, for, like a godly breeze come to my heart, I remember as Solomon asking of King Hiram of Tyre the same beloved cedar to build my magnificent temple, the first temple of Judea, the symbol of the Sacred Marriage. Moses' priests used it for the treatment of disease, and its bark for circumcision, so holy it is. As Inanna of Sumeria, I named the cedar groves the dwelling place of the gods and myself traveled there, as Gilgamesh also wisely did.

Using their inner skills, the Carmelites have communicated with the priests of Tyre from the mountaintop, and the Tyrian horse-ship, named the *hippoi* by the Greeks, will drop anchor off Carmel and then carry Father, Mother, my sisters, and me to Alexandria, whereupon we will journey the short distance to Lake *Mareia*. It is decided my brothers will join us after they have seen Herod's men and sown false clues. It is a plan both masterful and mysterious.

As we rest in the sacred grove of pine awaiting the ship's arrival, Jedediah stretches his huge hand over my head, covering my pineal. He smiles so quietly. "Dear Yeshu'a," says he, "we will meet thus again, in this very grove, and have great joy in the meeting. We will speak of the diet of plants, of Sacred Geometry, the true nature of the cosmos…forgiveness…the Merkaba…the Father-Mother…so many things."

Closing mine eyes, I release my thoughts and see scenes, visions, glorious, light-filled visions: of flying through the Universe, the Divine Mother and Father, my future, my family, other worlds and ages, of my Beloved, though her face is mostly veiled.

Her eyes shimmer golden.

The ship is now come. Its prow magnificently wrought into the head of a horse, the ship entire is gleaming cedar, the galleys at rest, the green and white colors of the flags flapping lazily in the wind. A thin reed of a figure stands aft.

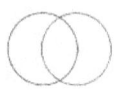

Ever it is true my soul writes this record. Forget this not as my words flow through my pen: ever it is my awakened soul does the writing. Each instant is etched sheer upon me, O Golden Glory, I lying naked on a hillside and You pouring into me…I can smell the lamb on the spit, hear the chatter of the crew, the water of the Great Sea pummeling the vast rounded hull.

Into coves we go each night on our way to Alexandria, three full, to sleep and eat on land. It is wet hot by day, but I have little trouble on the ship. Under the oak and linden we sleep and eat and talk and speak our communions, in morning and eventide; we are ever a devotional family. Father wanders off on his own, with his blue-and-white cloth, into some nearby wood; in these moments he hears God most clearly. The ship's crew stays aboard, while the captain and many of the African oarsmen join us ashore, the mustachioed Tyrian captain warning of the Romans, and spinning yarns of Sidon in days of yore, and of Alexandria, the center of the world.

Each night, the sky a glittering canvas of life, my sisters dash out into dapples of light and shadow, away from us, and perform their own secret rituals. I hear their murmuring voices speaking in earnest of Horus and Osiris and Isis and Issa…and Esus.

So wise are my sisters, they already know my name.

In a circle our family sits together the night before we reach Alexandria, dear Father with us, and Mother speaks more about the future, I soaking up the words like a kite gathering the wings of confidence.

"A younger brother, to be born twin with another, will one day become Yehoshua's Brother of Truth, a defender of his life, a giver to the world of some of the inner teachings. Jude he will be by name. Some will call him Thaddeus, others Didymus Thomas or Thomas. Their looks and coloring nigh identical, they will be seen as twins, and this will cause much confusion in the ages ahead, for it will be said they were born true twins of my body.

I tell you this so you will know, when he arrives, that he is called to this duty; he calls himself to it." Her lips pursed, sweet Mother inspects the eyes of my sisters to ensure they realize the seriousness of her words.

Martha asks, "They will appear twins, Mother? How can this be, if they are not? This is some sort of strange magic."

Father smiles knowingly and nods his head. I love him so. For no matter what at any time he may appear to be, he knows, he knows well. To him falls the creed of concern, of protecting his family. There is no greater task, as he must remain above the events which pass. Many is the time he wishes not to hear, but ever he is there, if not in body, in spirit, with full knowledge of what is to be.

"Like little Yeshu," continues Mother, "I, too, have heard your rituals and words these last nights. You know well the tales. And Salome has heard his name from the beyond, what they will first call him. As you feel the luminous enter your bodies and your souls, as the energy of the great adventure is born within you of Yehoshua's life, at once know as beautiful, as inspiriting it is, so, too, is it equally momentous and grave, for this is not a game, children. ...Martha asks how it can be they will look as twins, when they are not. Remember: when we speak of the true Law, this is the Law of the Universe, not the law of scripture. Words come from man, and God is not in the words. When on Mount Sinai God came and spoke with Moses, Moses understood; the people could not. The laws of man are seven, the laws of the angels four, the law of God one. What came to be the Law for our people were so many words and commandments, the true meaning was lost—"

Beautiful, devoted Salome grows impatient: " —yes, Mother; we know. Please tell us of Jude."

"God is at work in all things, my dearests. And Jude's *intent* is become to be the great protector of Yehoshua. Throughout he will be at Yehoshua's side: listening, speaking not, calculating each move, walking through suspicious doorways before him, the last in line when a threat lurks from behind. The Divine

Mother's angels and the Divine Father's angels will be with him. He will hear their guidance. Though their dispositions be different, Jude and Yeshu'a will form a bond designed to surmount all obstacles. That they will be seen as twins will serve them both well, each moment crafted for the deliverance of man from bondage..." She is still for a moment, my Mother, as I sit upon her lap. Her eyes aglow, she ponders how to say the treasured words. "The Universe is derived from music—the Holy Stream of Sound. We hear it only in the silence; you know this. This is the Voice of God. It is the Holy Stream of Sound which crosses the vault of stars in the heavens and the endless Kingdom of God. It was the Holy Stream of Sound which formed the Earth and all the planets and stars. Ever bathe yourselves in the Holy Stream of Sound, and you will come to know in the beginning of all times that all creation did share in the birth of creation. Born of this knowledge is peace, born of this is healing; Love, of yourself and all life, is born of this. Though the fear-stricken want none of it, it is true. Union with God while living in your skin is the only life worth living. Jude long intended this time, as much as Yehoshua. Life has already been lived."

I will remember well these words. Though in my own manner I will say them, come what will, they first were spoken by my Mother. The Essenes have taught my parents the secret of existence, of the Universe, passing on the wisdom of the Ancients, like the Kaloo and the Order of Melchizedek, and it is to each of us to understand in our own way. But we must desire Truth, we must seek it; ever we must desire the sweet caress of God. My dear children, forget not: a star, too, was born the day you came into the world. And you are beloved of me.

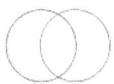

Into the belly of the Egyptian Sea we sail. Passing Canopus to the south, its edifices shone opal-white in the morning sun. Named *Pikuat* by the old Egyptians, Canopus is also the brightest star in the southern constellation of Carina and Argo Navis, and, after Sirius, the second brightest star in the nighttime sky. For the Egyptians, it is their South Polar Star. Humanity, for thousands of years, has misidentified the constellation Orion with Osiris, when in fact he is linked with Canopus, which interacts with Sirius in such a manner that the Ancients surmised the two stars governed time. The Navigator's Star: a doorway into other, higher dimensions and into the Afterlife. In the later, Greek story, Canopus is the pilot of Menelaus' ship on his quest to save and retrieve Helen of Troy from the clutches of Paris. Menelaus claimed Canopus was killed here by the bite of a snake; a monument he built in his name, and the town grew around it. Canopus means south, or southern, but in ancient Egyptian, *kani nub* means Golden Earth.

Since passing Pelusium we sailed above the Nile Delta herself, the essence of the sacred gateway: the vast, fertile valleys of vegetation reaching the horizon, the heady aroma of sweet, moistened, consummated life in the breeze, the sea awash with ships of many origins: Greek, Roman, Egyptian, Judean, Tyrian, Cyrenean, and more. The canopy sails, of many colors, like a symphony of sight, flutter north, west, and east, a testament to burgeoning humanity's great adventure.

The grand, replete Alexandria looms, situated flowing east to west on a narrow jut of limestone: the City of Light. So great is this city, it has two main harbors. Dividing them is Pharos Light, the exquisite lighthouse situated offshore, connected to the mainland, on the Isle of Pharos. One of the Seven Wonders of the World, it first came into sight long before we arrived above the Delta. Four hundred and forty feet tall, it stands robust, indefatigable, with three tiers: the bottom square and imposing, the second octagonal, enchanting in its artistry, and the third is circular, the second and third each diminishing in girth from the one below. In the third tier are windows facing the four directions and mirrors positioned around a signal fire. Atop is a cupola upon which stand statues of Zeus and Poseidon. Made of various stones: granite, calcite, limestone, sandstone, and greywacke, its exterior is gleaming white marble. It is said the power of Pharos Light is so great it can destroy enemy ships before they reach Alexandria, the mirrors used to spy on Constantinople. But it is to me beautiful, a symbol of peace, for its true purpose is to safely guide all ships into the quays of this astonishing city, even those coming north through the canals from the Nile bearing nature's gifts.

Now we pass the increasingly lavish royal palaces of the former Ptolemies on and near the promontory of Lochias, and, entering the royal harbor, we see old Cleopatra's on the isle of Antirrhodus. With its ornate, sculpted gardens, multi-colored lodges, stairways and porticos, Cleopatra's palace is the summit of beauty and ingenuity and royal decadence. Basalt statues line the jade and blue-marble colonnades. As the Tyrian ship carries cargo for Caesar Augustus, we are admitted to and disembark at the royal harbor. This is a part of the Essenes' plan, for here we are not bothered. Father carries me in his arms as we enter the Jewish quarter stretching eastward; due to the dispersion, in Alexandria resides the largest population of Jews in the world. The main synagogue, in the form of an impressive basilica, peeks up over the surrounding buildings. Called the Hebrew Dioploston due to its double-gallery, in front are seventy-one golden, bejeweled chairs for the elders. The synagogue is so large the Hazzan, or Sexton, must stand on a platform in the exact middle to signal those in the outer reaches when to join in amens. I will one day visit the Dioploston when I become an Initiate of the Egyptian Mysteries.

Directly south is the harbor leading to Lake *Mareia*, where we are bound, but Mother and Father wish to walk through Alexandria and return. So we turn westward and enter the city through the Sun Gate, strolling west on Canopic Street, its magnificent double-columns on either side.

"Canopic Street spans the length of the city, some thirty stadia," remarks Father. "At the opposite, western end is the Moon Gate."

Mother nods knowingly. "Everything built in Alexandria and the whole of Egypt is both symbolic of our relationship with the heavens and aligned with the energies of the Earth. It is said the Initiate of the Egyptian Mystery Schools, here long before the Sphinx, remembers their relationship, their connection with God."

Indeed, Canopic Street is grand and wide, fairly bustling with Macedonians, Greeks of all extractions, Persians, Jews, black Africans, Romans, and Egyptians. The center of the world is Alexandria. Through its harbors, and its canals leading from the Nile, are exported: papyrus, wheat, books, tapestries, linen, ivory, glassworks, deep-hued tropical woods, alabaster, bronze, perfumes, cosmetics, precious metals, and much more. But on Canopic Street we find the city of art and culture, of learning, of exquisite architecture. Upon taking the city many centuries in the future, the Arab general Amr will say of Alexandria: *It is a city of four thousand villas, with four thousand baths, four hundred places of entertainment for royalty, and ten thousand groceries.* It would surprise me not. There are four hundred thousand people here. And a hundred thousand of these are slaves.

To the east, we now see the famous Library complex, where I, too, will one day study. Alongside is the Temple of the Muses, the original home of the Library, connected to the royal palace. Modeled on the Lyceum of Aristotle in Athens, the Temple of the Muses houses copious shrines to each of the nine muses; brilliant statues depicting them line the front stairs. But it also functions as a place of study, with observatories, lecture halls, laboratories, and botanical gardens, living quarters, dining halls, and a zoo.

We make through the city entire, exit through the Moon Gate, then return, seeing the impressive Serapeum, the temple of Serapis Bey, he who has many similarities with my life. Indeed, one day long from today, in my name, men will destroy this temple in a fit of arrogant rage. But when razing it to its foundations, they will be surprised to find the sign I will myself choose as my sign: the *Vesica Piscis*. They will then discover the priests of Serapis are Christian priests, and vice-versa. And you, my dearest reflections, see this lovely symbol in the separations of parts within these very chapters. The *Vesica Piscis* is the shape formed of two intersecting circles with the same radius, intersecting perfectly so the center of each lies on the circumference of the other. It is also called the *madorla*, or the almond. Some name it the Womb of the Universe. The *Vesica Piscis* represents the union of opposites. By Pythagoras it was called the measure of a fish. My uncle, Joseph of Arimathea, will place the *Vesica Piscis* on the lovely lid of the chalice well at Avalon/Glastonbury. Thus now may you know why the fish of Pisces was later chosen for me, for if you continue the upper or lower lines of the intersecting circles, you will find the fish's tail; the sign will be turned sideways to form the fish. This is also the ichthys fish. The shape of the *Vesica Piscis* is central to Sacred Geometry. It is our way home to God. This is the reason why my companions and I will call ourselves *fishers of men*. There are mathematical ratios connected with the *Vesica Piscis*, and one of their numbers is 153; John's beautiful future Gospel will cite this as the number of fish I cause to be caught in the *miraculous catch of fish*.

My awakened soul already knows in this age I will become the symbol of the Age of Pisces, though I will come to realize as a man that it leads to the Aquarian Age in which you now live, the Age of the Holy Spirit: the very beginning of the Light of God coming into the world, amidst the violent death-throes of an age of great darkness.

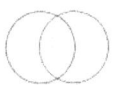

**H**is is the face of a camel. He stands in a solid body, appearing to be going somewhere even when he is still. But he is curiously at peace. All elbows and knees and arms and legs and acute, long angles, his curly black hair like a wreath alive, his is a noble, even comely, intelligent countenance, though in it I see the proud dromedary. Such is he who is Philo Judaeus, who bows slightly before us, his hands palm-to-palm in greeting before his breast. Born of a noble Judean family long in Alexandria,

Philo has ancestral links to the Hasmonean Dynasty. "Welcome, and blessings to you, fair Galileans. We are but a modest sanctuary and school, but we know of you. Joyous are we for your safe arrival. Here we practice the daily communions and speak of the nature of God. We live the contemplative life and ascribe ourselves a path of peace. And we are safe from discovery."

He and Father exchange a look of recognition; in some manner they have met before. There is palpitating energy in Philo. Be he a young man, about him beats the wisdom of the ages, and the resolve to achieve more, as if he knows nothing. I learn much from this, even this first meeting. He aches inside, does Philo. And I feel it most deeply. It sits in my stomach for a moment, a great sadness, and pain, amidst a great glory of Heart and mind. And he has not found his love. Much this man has borne. And he dedicates himself to God.

Gazing full upon me now, his flashing brown orbs brighten. "The women of your family seem a great force for your protection, young Yeshu'a ben Joseph."

I extend my hand to touch his, and he takes my little fingers into the tips of his. He now steps closer, stoops over, and places my fingers to his forehead. All very serenely. I cannot help a giggle, of pure joy it is: to somehow myself recognize Philo.

He places his fingers to my brow for a moment, then retreats, and bows once more, hands palm-to-palm. "You are a remarkable family. A light shines in all of you; there is a caring understanding of the pain of others, which you transmute to joy through healing. Yehoshua already tells me he knows me...a little. He feels so deeply. In him breathes the great Heart. This he will give and teach and pass on by his example. Extraordinary! And there is much to learn. I look forward to prayer, study, and meditation, and we will discuss what we find." His thin lips curl in anticipation of the delights.

"Where shall we sleep?" asks Mother, quick to get to the core of things.

A priestess and priest enter then, both middle-aged, in robes of white, their skin dark brown. The priestess brandishes a golden ankh: a cross topped by a loop, the Egyptian emblem of life. "God be with you," she intones in serene voice, revealing mighty shafts of teeth as she smiles. And we are led to our lodgings.

Surrounded by gardens, Lake *Mareia* is a vast, lush area which extends many miles west of Alexandria and miles into the Lower Nile Valley. Fed by the westernmost branch of the Nile and by numerous of its canals, it is at once a pleasure resort for the wealthy, with opulent homes strewn amid many islands, and a fertile farming area. Here there are vineyards so well balanced with water and rich soil that the grapes of green yield the most pleasant wines. In your time the lake is mostly dried up, but in my days it is the most beautiful of places. Traveling through various of the islands, the play-acted resurrection rituals of Osiris are annually performed here with great pageantry.

Atop a hillock overlooking the east-central portion of the lake the Therapeutae have built their loving community. The houses simple and small and without ornamentation of any kind, the Therapeutae themselves are of many origins. Six days of every seven the most devoted live in solitary seclusion, each retreating into a single-roomed building to meditate, pray, and study. Meals are often forsaken, and, as is true of all branches of the Essenes, women and men live as one, are treated with equal respect, and the Great Cosmic Mother is revered. On the seventh day, all join together for celebration, and feasts are enjoyed. And all is done in dedication to the Mother-Father God who resides in each of our hearts.

Though some live in seclusion six of every seven days, there are many here who do not, and Amisi, the priestess who welcomed us, takes us to a small, humble lodge atop the hillock east, where our family is to reside together in four rooms, a great luxury for us, and we will be allowed to live as normally we do.

Smiling radiantly, Amisi bestows upon us a basket of fruit, touches each of our heads in blessing, and says, "Pleased are we for your arrival; we foresee great works in each of your lives. We are all family here, and you are now a part of us in body, as well as in Spirit." Looking upon me with such tender care, beautiful Amisi states, "The little one is so treasured, so deep in his knowing heart...We have known of this coming for many ages, nigh too many to count." She signs across her breast and then across her temple. "Blissful indeed is young master Philo. He is precious to us. Through him, we will begin with the telling of the stories, to kindle the spark of God."

My heart leaps with joy upon hearing these words, for already I know we will hear of Moses; his name resides lovingly in Philo's mind. It is not the same story that you know from the sacred books later written. For many reasons, including the changing of the meanings of words, and the translations into other languages, as well as the hubris of politics and religions, true it is that many of the stories you have heard, including mine own, have been altered. And by this, the meanings of them are lost. In your age when the world most needs it, my ever-glowing heart is overflowing like a river of Love to be able to share their true meanings with you.

A door opens, and the human Heart floods with God.

# Chapter Three
# Moses

BENEATH THE LOVING ARMS of a pomegranate grove we sit with Philo and Amisi and two young male Egyptian students, the flaming red of the blossoms and fruit bursting into our eyes like Heart-fire, like the mighty blaze of sunset o'er the desert. It is only proper we should meet and sit under the pomegranate trees, for in my homeland the pomegranate is the cherished symbol of fertility. As Solomon, I crafted my coronet in the shape of the calyx: the pomegranate's crown, and commanded that the capitals of the two pillars (Joachim and Boaz) which stood in the porch of my temple be engraved with pomegranates. The robes of my priests also were embroidered with a dazzling array of the sacred fruit. Too, it is become tradition to eat the pomegranate on Rosh Hashanah, for, symbolizing fruitfulness, it is said to have six hundred and thirteen seeds, the original number of commandments in the Torah.

Describing the breathtaking beauty of my lovely Sheba, I speak of the fruit in my Song of Songs: *Thy lips are like a thread of scarlet, and thy speech is comely; thy temples are like a piece of a pomegranate within thy locks.* And for the beautiful souls who will one day bear my name, Christians, the pomegranate will be included in the earliest mosaic depictions of me, and be woven into vestments and liturgical tapestries. Leonardo da Vinci will place the fruit in my and my Mother's hands in some of his celebrated works. Botticelli and Raphael will likewise place the pomegranate in their paintings of us. Mother herself will be likened to the pomegranate tree, bearing sweet fruit, for like the seeds, she will be said to have been the vessel of the benefits of humankind, all revealed as Christ. And in the Quran, the Islamic holy book, the fruit will be thrice mentioned as one of God's great creations, once citing that within each pomegranate is one aril descended directly from paradise, and the great prophet Muhammad will say the fruit brings forth both emotional and physical peace. Pomegranate trees were planted in the olden courtyards of the Zarathustran temples because, as its leaves remain green most of the year, the fruit is considered a symbol of eternal life. And while visiting the kingdom of Bindusara, the Buddha received many lavish gifts from wealthy disciples. But when he was gifted a pomegranate by an elderly woman, in her name he rang the bell of honor as he considered it the greatest gift. Krishna said the individual souls of humanity are like the seeds of the pomegranate and, along with the Universe, are connected to him. Here in Egypt, depictions of the fruit are often found in the wall paintings of tombs, and Tutankhamen took a pomegranate vase into the Afterlife with him.

But on this day, it is most proper, for Moses was by his scouts given many fruits, the most prominent and beautiful of which was the pomegranate. This they did to demonstrate that the holy land was fertile. The sweet caress of God resides in every moment one gazes upon and eats this luscious fruit, for it is also said by some to have been the so-called forbidden fruit of Eden. Yet, indeed, it is not forbidden to know God, albeit when one is ready, and not before. And on this day we learn of Moses, the true Moses.

Myself.

"Moses lived on this Earth well over one thousand years ago," states Philo, tossing a pomegranate up in the air again and again while leaning comfortably against the tree with a wondrous smile on his face. "But the story of his birth and life that came to be known by the Jews was much later written, obscuring the facts, changing his identity to conform to the need for Judean nationhood, following the enslavement of Jews here in Egypt. Indeed, it is within this drama which Moses lived. Because of this, many doubt he lived at all." His knowing eye looks suddenly into mine, as if recognizing me anew. A curl comes to his lips, and all at once my dear Mother laughs merrily. Knowledge has passed between them, and I am not immune to its derivation.

Amisi now speaks, her tone a purr: "Yes, Philo. Like all cultures and nations, the more the ages pass, the more our political and religious leaders stray from justice and Truth in Egypt. But we do know the Truth, do we not?"

"Indeed, Priestess Amisi of the golden memory. The records tell us Moses trained at Heliopolis—"

"—originally named *Iunu*, meaning place of pillars," Amisi exclaims.

Gazing upon her, Philo comically arches one eyebrow. "Yes, yes. Manetho, great scribe of Egypt and high priest of Heliopolis, introduced Ptolemy II to the historical record of Moses' training at the Heliopolan temples. There can be no dispute. Chaeremon of Alexandria also states in his own records that Moses was trained as a sacred scribe at Heliopolis. There is no doubt: Moses was educated in the deep mysteries of Egyptian sun worship. Well-versed in it he was. Heliopolis, the City of the Sun, is the oldest, and still the most sacred and profound, of the universities of Egypt. But this training was highly sought and was not given to just anyone. And to know Moses as he truly was, we must return to the beginning of his life."

Father chuckles and nods knowingly his head. He is ever a practical man, my Father, but he is not one to mistake things. Though it is true some must question in order to find and deepen their Faith, and supportive of this I am, Father is not of this ilk. He accepts. As he will teach me and I will teach others in my future ministry, in the fetus of the unborn child, the Heart beats before the brain is formed. "Master Philo is about to open the box of Truth, children, students," says he. "Mother and I know it, but he will more deeply understand than I. Of Mother, she of the depth of all ages, of the Well of Mary, there in *Nazara* since time out of mind, nothing is hidden, I am sure."

"Joseph speaks well and true and humbly. The Septuagint tells us baby Moses was discovered in the bulrushes, born of and abandoned by a Hebrew woman, and then was adopted by Pharaoh's daughter, Bithiah. But, in truth, he was born of the union of Bithiah and a Hebrew Father, who was a slave in Egypt. Moses was of Egyptian royal lineage. The story of finding him in the bulrushes was concocted to protect him and Pharaoh's daughter, during a time when the Hebrews were enslaved in Egypt."

My sisters look each to each, aghast, their bulging eyes big as full moons. They turn to Mother, perplexed, but she merely signs patience with her left hand. This is only the beginning of the reordering of their knowledge. And with glee I grin, knowing Philo is a man of deeply laid plans. He aches to create a Jewish godman.

One of the young Egyptian students, his robes of cotton dyed azure, states, "The story of being found in the bulrushes harkens of Horus, does it not?" He is pleased with his deduction.

"Very wise, Shushu," Amisi replies. "Indeed, it does. But there is more. While it is true Moses' Father was a Hebrew slave, he, too, came from a royal house: the House of Joseph. So the blood of Moses was on both sides royal, of two different cultures. Bithiah purposefully created the story to imitate the birth legend of Horus, born amidst the rushes of Philae Island." Amisi places her palms together in her lap, her exquisitely long-lashed eyelids close in reverence, and she raises her noble head to the heavens. "Moses' original adult name was Asarseph. Keen in your knowledge, you should see this name is come of Asar, which Osiris himself was called."

Mother and Father nod slowly in unison, their fingers finding each other so they now hold each other's hands in love and remembrance. They have all along known: Moses was heir to the Egyptian throne, a prince. But when he discovered his Father was a slave, and by this knew himself to be slave, Moses surmised his true mission was to lead his people out of Egypt, into Canaan. And he chose a different path, one perhaps equally fraught with peril.

Opening her eyes once more, I catch Amisi's gaze for a moment and speak as well as I can: "Nef...er...tar..."

Philo laughs aloud like the horn of the bull. And Amisi, her long, straight, elegant nose creasing in delight, smiles wide. "Yesu is the most brilliant of all!" she exclaims. Wise is she of the sands of the Sphinx, truly ancient is her wisdom, verily noble is her purpose. For this is what the Druids will call me when I reach the shores of Albion with Uncle Joseph of Arimathea and discover Avalon, where nearby he will one day found my sanctuary at Glastonbury, the lineage of all British kings and queens to follow with my very blood in their veins, the blood-links to the Celts and Scots and Welsh made.

"Yes, yes!" remarks Philo in his melodious basso voice. "Moses and Nefertari loved each other with a great passion. She was the most beautiful woman in all Egypt but was to marry Rameses, soon to be Pharaoh. Niece to Nefertiti, princess of Egypt she was. But Rameses discovered their love, espying them together in this very grove, and became furious. Following his education in Heliopolis, wherein he learned of the divine aspects of both the solar and lunar natures, upon hearing of his Father's enslavement, Prince Moses decided to relinquish his royal title to become slave himself. And Rameses sent him to the Midian deserts, thinking he had sent him to his death. Rameses felt sure to be rid of him, but naught was his vision. God was with Moses. We hear the tale of the burning bush, but, in truth, one only hears God through opening the gateway of the Heart. It was through his heart, through feeling and finding the purity of his heart that he found God; Love gives and gets no gain. Love knows no games. The angels visited dear Moses because he sought no advantage for himself. The great prophet desired only to help his people."

Amisi is pleased. "Philo speaks well. His beloved philosophical Greeks received Truth through the oracle of Delphi. Etched on the walls deep in those caves are these words: *I advise you, whoever you are, Oh you! who wish to explore the mysteries of nature, if you do not find within yourself that which you seek, neither shall you shall find it outside. If you ignore the excellencies of your own house, how do you intend to find excellence elsewhere? Within you is hidden the treasure of treasures. Oh, man, know thyself and you shall know the Universe and the Gods!* By this is meant the very simple Truth: Know thyself, truly, and you will know God. All is but a reflection, a projection of thine own thoughts. Thus it is best to think with your heart. Think the best of people especially. We are all co-creators of everything we experience. The nature of prophecy is misunderstood. It is real, but it can change; it does change, for, as you already know, it is truly a matter of *intent*. In terms of time, which is spherical, not linear, *intent* precedes prophecy."

Amisi gazes for a moment upon our family with tender care. "And your intent is clear. You fear not; you know what comes, and yet still you embrace the essence of God, which is Love. ...All that occurs here in the physical, three-dimensional world first flows down through the higher realms, or dimensions. I have never accepted the story of God speaking to Moses through the burning bush. It is merely a tale, an illustration. Why would God destroy his own, a bush, to speak to a man, even a great prophet like Moses? No, Moses received his guidance from God by way of opening his heart. He had released all selfish desire, all thoughts related to greed, suffering, separation; by so doing, he heard the heavenly angels; truly, God's guidance through them flows. As an Adept, Moses heard well, and while he learned of Ascension and of the nature of Sacred Cosmic Reality through the Egyptian Mystery Schools, there are many such throughout the world. And he was tested. In the Midian deserts he married Zipporah, a daughter of Jethro, a black Midian priest. After forty years, he then returned to Egypt to gather his people and find their homeland. Indeed, as his mission continued, he lost himself and his Faith for a time, wandering forty more years. Instead of hearing God, he began to listen to the wishes of his lost people, who said to him: *Let us go this way and that; no, this is not the way, Moses, that is the way; no, this is way.* Finally, he asked again for God's guidance and was given the true path to his and his people's homeland. The lesson learned by this story is to listen. God is within us in every breath, if we but learn to listen."

Philo adds, "Hence the reason why Moses placed the true inner teachings behind a veil. This long adventure taught him his people were not yet ready. One may wish to see the story as allegory, symbolic of the path to God all must walk, finding the essence of Him within ourselves. Or one may wish to view it literally, as a long walk through the desert of life before returning home. Both in this instance are true."

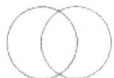

We stroll through the grasslands near the vineyards of Lake *Mareia*, Mother, Philo, and I. Months have passed since our arrival, and I am walking on my own well enough that Mother allows me my own steps. Here the Earth is firm and lush and emerald green, and I call to a butterfly to join me on my shoulder. In the grass walks a black and white Sacred Ibis, a noble animal he is; a great intelligence lives in his face. I click in my cheeks and make a sweet, short whistle, and he follows after us, a shining light in his indigo eyes. Amused is Philo as he watches this scene, putting his fingers to his mouth as if he believes he is dreaming. Then he laughs. I have seeds in my waist-pocket, but I am talking to the half-black and half-white ibis, and he speaks in return.

"I come from the southlands of what is called the Kush," says he.

"Why do you come?" I ask.

"Every year I journey here for the rich water and food."

"I have seeds in my pocket, for I knew you would be here."

The Sacred Ibis chortles at this statement. "Yes, I know. But I care not. For you are the Light above men."

"Shh!" say I. "I will not hear such things. Already I hear them, yet I am still but a child. Cannot I have a childhood, free and easy and filled with joy, without these things being whispered in the air? It makes them real."

"Every day you live the world is free and easy and joy-filled, as are you. And forever more it is so; because you are here, this is true."

I speak with a bird yet think not of it. Citrus and iris and blue lotus perfume the air, the sun sparkles, a cloud hastily passes overhead, and I, too, hear its voice as it chases the horizon. Now Mother and Philo also hear the ibis, as the beautiful bird allows them to join with us.

"Watch closely, Yeshu'a. As we near the lip of the lake, Moses will appear. He will come because he is you and you are he and Philo and Mary Anna have also deigned it to be so. I am his messenger, but it is you who summoned me with your Love-voice."

"What is your name?" ask I aflutter.

Mother and Philo now walk on either side of us, and Philo says, "Do not be surprised when you hear it, Yeshu'a ben Joseph."

The ibis cackles with delight. "I am Thoth, the most ancient of Egyptians. I am the writer of the sacred scrolls and came from Atalantia, as the Greeks have named it. I am wisdom. Though I have long traveled beyond the world, I still come when called, I still return when the Heart is pure. And say I now: in his day, I knew Moses; he and I had many such talks."

"How is it that I am he and he me and we will see him on this day? How can this be?"

"He is reborn through you, as you already know you are Solomon. Moses is more ancient, but I am more ancient still. His wisdom soul is eternally with God; his soul of purpose was reborn into the world through you. You have known you are Moses, have you not?"

"Yes. It seems I am everyone."

The lake is coming into view now, a magical grove of sycamore on its shore.

Thoth the Sacred Ibis opens wide his beak and fairly giggles. "Glee this brings to my heart to hear you say this. You are not wrong. It is true of all humanity, but you are the first to remember it for many long ages, since the days when one person's thought was heard by all humanity."

Lightly I place my hands upon his fine feathers and pet him softly. Mother comes alongside and signs across her breast. This wisdom-keeper, this winged master of all knowledge, this speaker of the Heart, his perfect union of white and black feathers like the union of female and male, is my great friend. I praise God in my heart for this great gift. Every moment I praise God, for the Father-Mother breathes in our every breath, but the Sacred Ibis named Thoth awakens my soul anew.

We approach the lake following Thoth, the water like liquid crystal, and sit beneath a giant sycamore fig tree, its branches thick and reaching for the heavens in joyous gestures of epiphany, the dark green leaves heart-shaped, the bark nearly orange in hue. Its figs are ripening, and from time out of mind I am reminded: this sycamore is the Egyptian Tree of Life, as is also the acacia tree. It is the sacred tree of Isis, Queen of Heaven; she once metamorphosed into the sycamore suckling Tuthmosis III. And one day in Jericho, Zacchaeus will climb a sycamore to see me pass. Because of this moment at Lake *Mareia*, Zacchaeus will feel my connection to the tree and will join with my soul.

As we approached the lake a light seemed to dance above it, blue and white and gold. But now it is clear a form is taking physical shape above the water. Philo, Mother, and I press our palms together in reverence. Thoth the Sacred Ibis stands at attention, raising his head. The wind in the sycamore trees ceases.

Out of the crystal water itself a man made of light and body emerges. He is tall, commanding, young, his hair of ebon long, his face clean-shaven. His eyes are kind and his skin is dark. Now he smiles and a golden light surrounds him. "Blessings, children of Galilee." He outstretches his long arms toward us. "I bring thee great Love and joy from God. ...I am Moses."

As if I doubted.

"Young Yeshu'a knows me well. His dear Mother also. And Philo is my sacred sage. Already you have heard some of my true history, and more yet you will come to know. But the Master Thoth was called by Yeshu on this day. He was my great teacher, was Thoth. It was he who introduced me to Melchizedek, who lived two hundred thousand years ago. Far into the future, man will not believe humanity lived so long ago. With the gap of what will come to be known as the Dark Ages, science will truly begin its long journey to decipher the past, nigh-never realizing its standards will be mistaken, its calendars wrong, its hypotheses flawed. Believe: intelligent man has long lived; all that was known was lost, save by a very few. And you are among them."

Moses hovers closer to us, now merely a few feet away. And upon his long face is a countenance so serene, so Love-filled, the wings of angels surround his head. Looking directly into mine eyes, he states, "Yeshu, you know of your life. In it there is unimaginable joy. But you will also suffer, in human ways. From your head will come aches of pain which you will learn to master, for one, but only from finding your Beloved. And there will be other things, be sure. But as your Mother knows, by the passing of your days, you will master pain. This you will achieve by your unconditional Love for humanity, your Love for the world, and your Love for God. There will be times when men will fear you and call you a witch. I, too, suffered this; Egypt still blames me for its plagues. They will not understand; there will be forces guarding you, protecting you, which you may summon, but only in peace, and will also act at the behest of God. You will be misunderstood. Suspicious minds have the ability to alter the very words they hear coming out of people's mouths, to paint false-pictures of the very things they see with their own eyes, even influencing them by mere judgmental observation. Even your teachings will be changed. In the end, those minds twisted by fear will come to know Love Pure. Be patient. And I will be with you..."

"As will I," says the Sacred Ibis Thoth.

"Nigh-ever man will seek to twist the truth of Love and what must transpire for it to prevail. You and I will many times thus speak. But today I myself will tell you the truth of the Red Sea story. From this you will learn how to use your own powers in future."

Philo says, "Yeshu'a ben Joseph, the story is told that when Moses led his people out of Egypt, he parted the Red Sea, straight down the middle, and they walked through in safety to freedom, the water then crashing down on the Egyptians so they could not follow."

"Ha!" laughs Moses like thunder. "What nonsense! When we use our energy powers, we join with nature on such a deep level that we coexist with it and can achieve things which appear magical or miraculous. Your and your family's healing abilities are like this. It will be said of you that you could heal anyone of anything at anytime. Yet, you already know this to be false. The true healer is God and the angels of God, and you the conduit, the medium, the connection. For one to accept healing, one must have great Faith. The weak-faithed and those without Faith cannot be healed, for they must heal themselves, by conjoining with God, through someone like you, or on their own.

"The true story of the Red Sea is akin to this. To have parted the Red Sea would have been an act against nature, and this cannot be achieved or endured; God's hand would not allow it. What truly occurred was enough of us had the skills of transmuting energy that we could walk just above the water. As a group, we placed enough energy between our feet and the water that we walked seemingly at ease above it. Not all of us had this much knowledge and Faith. But enough of us did, so that all could travel over the Red Sea to freedom. It took great Love and skill and concentration to achieve this, believe me. It was not easy. But God was with us. Pharaoh himself let us escape because he was my brother. But Egypt had become corrupt: the military, the priests, the common-folk were jealous of us Hebrews. We had grown large and wise. And when the moment came for the Egyptians to follow us across the Red Sea, they simply fell in, where we did not. We were free. Finally free!"

I nod in remembrance of this; indeed I have seen it in a vision, beloved of me it is.

Once more he stretches his arms out to us in Love. "This is why I am here with you on this day, standing above Lake *Mareia*, a spot still imbued with the magic of this land. I am a Lightbody in this form, and thus have no real weight. But my message is clear, the skills are the same, the Love as pure. My soul of purpose in the world now resides in you. And you will continue the mission of all humanity to reach the Light."

Raising my right arm toward Moses, he comes closer still, so he may touch my little fingers with his. There is heat, for his are Light-fingers, but they do not burn, for they are made of Love Pure. Tears come into mine eyes and suddenly run like streams down my cheeks. How is it possible I am so loved? My tears are tears of joy.

# Chapter Four
# Remembrance

TODAY I WRITE THESE WORDS sitting in my rooms at peace. For while the world entire seems on the verge of destruction, the Love in my heart knows no limits.

My Faith in God is everlasting. I know what comes. And so do you.

Outside my window a Phoebe comes to sing her praises; her four new hatchlings chirp a new song in their nest under the eave, and Mother Phoebe is glad upon the hills, flying to and fro gathering food. Soon it will be time for flight school. And with little stumbles along the way, the hatchlings will learn to attain the heights. They, too, know the truth, and to me they speak of it. The Earth-transformations at this time are increasingly severe, but they fear not. They fret not. As nations and religions wage wars born of ignorance, upon both men and the Earth, the Phoebes care not. Though darkness seems fated to overtake the world, just when there will appear to be no more tomorrows, at the very moment when humanity seems to be falling off the cliff of the world, all hope nearly lost, suddenly the Light of God will come into the world and shine upon everyone and everything.

Like the sun shining at midnight.

This is the supreme test of Faith, unlike any age has ever seen.

My heart sings with the song of David's harp, to know and feel it so deeply. This, too, my friends the Phoebes know. Of God's existence there is no doubt. Ever.

Phoebe was also the name of the woman who delivered Paul's Epistles to the Roman Christian Church. Some have ascribed the title deacon or deaconess to her, from the Greek word *diakonos*, meaning servant, others the title of patroness. Along with Lydia of Thyatira and Dorcas, in America the Episcopal Church honors Phoebe on its liturgical calendar with a feast day on January 27th. She also appears in the Calendar of Saints of two Lutheran Churches. September 3rd is her feast day in Rome.

She was, in fact, a deacon for the church of Cenchreae. Important this is because Paul, or Saul, of Tarsus himself mentioned her by name. Some of Paul's writings were altered, even forged, for he made enemies easily with early Church authorities. Simply, this is because, though we did not meet in the flesh, I was later with him, and he taught my counsel of traveling in male-female pairs to teach *The Way*; this means not I at all frown upon same-sex unions; Love rejoices wherever it is found. As the life of Phoebe indicates, he also gave women as well as men church offices. Though many later authorities dispute Paul's high regard for women, the record is in Timothy, where he speaks of them being worthy of respect, temperate, and trustworthy in all things.

On this fine day, the Phoebe birds outside my window know and live this truth. The Father and Mother Phoebes work together, remain mated, and as one teach the truth of the world to their children, Mother in command. Each year in spring they come to my humble dwelling, calling me before their arrival, announcing themselves in lilting song. The Father Phoebe is now come to say his goodnights. Though to churches the deacon Phoebe may mean servant, I know the bird and the woman to be messengers of God. And the family of lovely Phoebes outside my window sings a song of remembrance.

I today reside in the mountains. It has been said I would return. But for what possible purpose? Reborn I was twenty-two minutes after the reawakening of the Earth's Kundalini, presaging the Precession of the Equinox announcing the Aquarian Age. Already have I tasted many adventures in this life. So many lifetimes I have lived, long ago, of spiritual, artistic, fantastical dimension, acquiring fame and sometimes fortune, that the scent of renown fools me not. The most beautiful flowers blush unseen by the world, offering their loveliness and praises to God alone.

And my Beloved Bride of the Soul is also reborn in this age, a humble, small-town, farm girl, thousands of miles away, across a great ocean. As I did following my Ascension, and her and our daughter Sarah-Anna's flight, first to Gaul and then to Albion, I visit her in Lightbody in this life, in the deep of night, leaving with the dawn, as is my way. We sometimes walk together, she and I, reliving every precious moment, and holding stones in our hands we once, long ago, together found and touched and brought forth their inherent light. And we also speak in the inner ways, transcending space and time.

We have both come forth to assist in the painful birthing of the New Age. To ease its delivery, to make it more plentiful, less riddled with guilt, we made our covenant. For we must all forgive the world and reunite Spirit and matter. Save this time, wait not for me, for us; ever we are by your side, guiding you. It is to you the mantle of grace now falls to accept Christ Consciousness. Miracles we will perform, when you know in your Heart of hearts that you, too, are the Light.

The *Second Coming* is the coming of every soul, not just one. And truly it should be named the *Awakening* of every soul, for that is what it is.

Much has been said of my Beloved, nearly all of it false. Many things have been written—until recently, most of it besmirched with the hue of the word whore. Her name was Magdalen, but not Mary; Mary was an honorific given to women when they had attained wisdom and had become respected by their community, thus my Magdalen came to be called Mary Magdalen. We did meet by the Well, but it was not the first time. She was not born of a rich family of Jerusalem, as some believe. Her Father was not an ardent Sanhedrin supporter, for he was not at all Jewish. He was Mesopotamian. And her Mother was Egyptian. And born she was not in Magdala, though she later there did reside; neither was she of Bethany, as others ascribe.

Magdalen was the most beautiful woman I have ever seen. She was dark of color, like rich chocolate, slim of body, as the shapely reeds of the Nile. Long, black, luxurious silk was her hair, down to the small of her back it did fall. Her deep, loving eyes, too, were ebon, but also gold and jade and sapphire, depending on the light, her mood, her intent, the day upon which one saw her; often they could be enchanting mixtures of these. She wore an armlet of gold that was a twining serpent, for she was a Priestess of Isis. An advanced Adept she was. So fine was her mind, so pure her heart, she never doubted, she never saw sin; she was wisdom. And wisdom is no one's possession.

They say out of her I cast seven demons, but this was just an aligning of her chakras, her seals. As is true of every soul who has ever lived, and indeed also because of her many healing gifts, she was in need of an energy adjustment. Those of our traditions called them demons because they knew not what this was, and so ascribed sin to her. To many of you, the surprise will be that she did the very same for me, more than once.

Our moments alone together were precious few, but filled with such Love, so deep they were in every way, each was an eternity. Without her I could not have ascended; it would not have been possible. I still both glow and tremble because of this. Tonight, as I write these words, she knows it; she sings to me like the Phoebe.

Yes, we practiced the art of Sacred Sex; our lovemaking was in praise of God, never a profanation of the body. When in body we joined, all of humanity made Love. Part of her Initiate training was in the art of Sacred Sex, and she will tell you when we met by the Well, she quivered at the sight of me, as I did her. That she understood the mysteries, the inner teachings, that she loved humanity so deeply: is miracle.

We are all snowflakes; each of us is absolutely unique and also absolutely identical. As you watch the flakes fall, as you observe your fellow humans, rejoice in their singular beauties, and also celebrate and embrace their sameness. We are but cogs in the realms of all that is, but humanity is indeed the temple through which God transforms to higher and higher planes. Many was the time sweet Magdalen brought me back to splendor. You may have heard one must go through the Woman to return to God. It is true. And this Magdalen did for me. In my moments of weakness, she was there and made me strong; when doubt entered me, she washed its scurvy tide away with vision and tender care; when obscured was mine own vision, she cleared the cobwebs, allowing me to see truly. When I ached, she healed me; when after my own healing acts I was exhausted and near death myself, she infused the Light of God into me once more. When days before Golgotha I felt all was lost and could not succeed, she alone served me Truth on a silver platter so I would not fail. Though many miracles I did perform, it was Magdalen who walked to the edge of the world and brought Lazarus back to life, not I, no matter what you have heard. And when, in a fit of anger at the squabbles of my fellow Hebrews outside Bethany, I cursed the fig tree, Magdalen healed the tree, almost dying herself in the doing, and once more the tree did bear fruit. And when at Cana I turned the water to wine, I did so do, for the wedding was our wedding, Magdalen and I.

You may believe in my perfection, that I made not errors, that never once did I make a misstep. Alone, the fig tree episode should tell you this is false. You may believe every woman, man, and child could see Light around my head and my heart, yet many could not, including the Roman priests, most of the Jewish priests and rabbis, and those with little or no Faith. There is no such thing as a perfect human being. Yet we each ultimately possess a perfect soul. My gift to the world was to demonstrate to humanity what true forgiveness is, what it does. It lifts the soul to God, where in truth it always is. For forgiveness heals the human family whole; in forgiving others we forgive ourselves.

Many have come to walk the Earth to raise themselves as individuals to Godhood. I did this for all humanity. But perfect

I was not. I did not die for the world's sins. I gave my life to you to prove there is no such thing as sin.

And it was Magdalen who gifted me the ability to walk this path. Alone, what she taught me by our Sacred Lovemaking is the gift we together gave the world, for it is the secret key to peace, and to the male is given the harder task in this physical praising of God. This is an allegorical reflection of the male's more difficult mission to bring peace to Mother Earth. In his very nature, the male is electric in his alchemical form: he acts, he moves, while in her alchemical form the female is magnetic: she attracts and embraces.

Indeed, I understood my role in loving a woman in a sacred manner was to go against my nature; this for most men is difficult; they fear they may lose their maleness, which is anything but the truth. But Magdalen knew much more, and subtly illustrated by the use of simple words and acts how this is symbolic of the Sacred Marriage of Earth and Sky, Spirit and matter, of how peace is achieved on Earth.

Most men upon the conclusion of lovemaking will either turn over and go to sleep or get up to do something. But, to use Magdalen's term: if they *nest* with the other, the Love-energy produced continues in both male and female, as it does usually exclusively with the woman, sometimes lasting hours. This opens the pathways to the pineal gland and, in turn, the gateway to higher Consciousness. It can also be achieved by a celibate person, through deep meditation, named by the Hindus and Buddhists *Samadhi*, or union with God, and the high alchemy of Horus by the Egyptians.

This act of nesting leads to the possible fulfillment of the second, most important act. This Magdalen and I call the Adoration of the Beloved. To adore, to cherish the Beloved is to remain with her long after lovemaking, speaking with her, touching her, truly blending with her. As part of vernal and autumnal equinox rituals, male and female Initiates of the ancient templed Mystery Schools performed Sacred Sex to achieve the Adoration of the Beloved, for it is in these moments following lovemaking when true union occurs. (Same-sex couples can of course also enact the Adoration.) For a man in your culture, this can be a road hard to travel, especially if he has problems with his Mother, which often begin at birth, because the Adoration of the Beloved brings to the surface what people today call psychological issues, what the Ancients called obstacles to flight, and heals them. Nothing less than attaining the Light is at stake in this life, the finding and freeing of one's immortal soul, nothing less than *remembering* one's personal connection with God, something still forgotten by most.

Sisters and brothers, mothers and fathers, sons and daughters, to heal this beautiful home we call Earth, Adoration of the Beloved is required. Only the Beloved is your Mother: your physical Mother, Mother Earth, and the Great Cosmic Mother. The Divine Mother. Magdalen taught me this, and so much more. Your traditions, your culture, too often teach you shame. And shame is what keeps you from God. My gift to you was to demonstrate that Ascension can also be achieved by unconditional Love, by living forgiveness.

Magdalen and Mother were the dearest friends. Often they held hands. Together they performed their own ministries. And always they were in agreement, at times at variance with me. The news says I had seventy-two disciples—six groups of twelve men, each equally valued in their skills and contributions, and also in providing assistance to each other. Firstly, we were a team, a loving team, doing everything possible to further *The Way*. And all that we did was based on the balanced design of the Universe. You see, there were also six groups of female companions, vital to the very survival of humanity, to match the six dozen men, making a total of one hundred forty-four companions. To these brave, wise, and blessed women we owe our eternal gratitude and Love, for without them the Truth would not have survived. And it was my *Savta*, my Grandmother Anna, who opened the doorway for my dear Mother and Magdalen and me.

**P**hilo is come. He enters our lodge with beating eyes and out of breath. Looking upon us as if we be crazed in our serenity, he exclaims, "Fair Galileans! How can it be you are here, with no knowledge of who comes, you with inner sight and inner ears?" Upon his head a cypress wreath hangs askew. He has been studying the rites of Osiris. "Can you surmise? Can you guess? Can you foresee?"

Sister Salome yawns. "We play not games, Philo. We care not for them."

Mother approvingly nods her head. "Good, child. I and your birth Mother have both taught you well. Philo, we are like receivers, receivers of thousands of signals from the angels; each day it is so. They act as gatekeepers. And so many play games, so many attempt to fool us by sending falsehoods to test us, we are not amused. Nor do we care. Nor do we respond. We frown upon this. For we are with God. And those who play these games play games with God; our skills are for the use of the sacred, that is all."

Martha pokes her head up from behind a scroll accounting the life of Goddess Nut. "If you mean that Anna and Joseph come, 'tis old news. They called our names weeks past. And our brothers and sister come anon. Herod is soon to die, in chaos is the Sanhedrin, the Zealots scour the hills for a militant Messiah, Yeshu's cousin John will also come, but it is yet some time off, the berries at Carmel are especially sweet and full this season, Sarah of Bethany is new with child, and Roman centurions march legions toward the Great Sea to pour more numbers into our homeland; their plan is to squeeze us out of our lands. If there is else you require to know, please speak." Martha jaws as if she is bored.

"We will speak our communions, children," says Father.

"Worry not, Philo. You are beloved of us." Mother looks tenderly upon him as she soothingly speaks these words. "Often people try to test us."

"Yes, I have seen this done also to me," he answers. "It is most unsettling, rude."

"Some attempt to will us to read their thoughts. Some in groups play roundabout games. Most important is to remember not to cease communicating in the normal ways, by voice and word and expression. The union of the outer and the inner must always be observed and respected. When communication is of normal flow, intuition is pure and the attainment of wisdom assured. Those souls first learning the inner ways or with no experience often play these games; it attracts negative forces, and malformed vision is the result. Some even misuse the sacred skills to purposefully peer into people's private lives. It is fearful childishness. You are not so, we know. What we think, we may create; thus our thoughts are most important. Please join us in our communions."

As I close my eyes to silently speak my personal praises to God, I see Grandmother Anna and Joseph of Arimathea, Mother's brother, crossing Lake *Mareia* in a small bark. Like the coming of the Soul it is, the coming of the Sun and the Moon. And my mind realizes the name Solomon itself is a conjunction of the word *sol*, meaning sun, and *omon*, or *amon, amun,* meaning moon. The word amen means moon. Anna herself sends me this message; she is a true hierophant, and she announces this to me knowing I will hear and understand. For many reasons she and Uncle Joseph come.

I give thanks to Thee, God.

"Where is my dear sister?" Joseph trumpets as he and Anna make our lodge. His wide smile and stocky frame fill the doorway, Anna like a mouse behind him, so grand in gesture and splendid in body is he.

He rushes across the room to embrace Mother. For long moments she holds fast his broad, square shoulders, nestling her fine head against his barrel chest as he stoops. He is a rock. Then she gets up on tip-toes and kisses him on the lips. "Blessings, Joseph. How I have missed you. You look well."

Salome and Martha run together to see Anna, grabbing each other's tunics in a race to see who will be first, now tumbling to the ground together as their legs become entwined.

"Martha, cease!" cries Salome. "Why is it you always do this? If you are not careful, I will steal your scrolls. "You ever must be first!" Salome grabs her by the hair and propels herself into Anna's arms.

"You speak as if you are not the same!" Martha replies, huffing and puffing.

"Oh, girls!" says Anna, her sweet melodious voice filling the room with song. "Sometimes you are like the cats who fight in the alleys for food."

The room fills with Light, the Light of reunion, each of us beaming with joy, Father in the background, his arms folded, watching like a delighted mute.

Dear Anna raises a finger in the air. "I have something for precious Yeshu." Her eyes find Joseph's, and like a clown he smirks. She then purses her lips and whistles a sweet tune. Presently a lovely gray-blue and white bird flies through the open doorway and softly lands on her right shoulder, chirping, looking this way and that. It is a Phoebe!

My eyes melt in Love. What great gift is this! A young Phoebe: kind as the breath of God, pure as the sweet bird of youth, fresh as the morning dew on deep green moss. She knows me as she searches mine eyes, silently telling me her name: Hannah.

*Savta* Anna now catches my gaze; like the sun, I see a glorious light shining around her, and for an instant I see myself, far into the future, sitting at my table as I write these words. Oh, Anna is magical! Indeed, she is most miraculous. And she is wise. In truth, she is a mystical fairy, hundreds of ages old, no doubt of that there is. She knows all!

Hannah is a name both Hebrew and Celtic, though the Celtic is the older, and Anna tells me without words she has brought Hannah from Albion, Anna and Joseph's true home. I now cup the lovely Phoebe in my hands, bestowing soft kisses atop her tiny head, petting her feathers.

"Upon finishing your training at Carmel, we will travel to Albion together, Yeshu," says Joseph. "And there you will reunite Hannah with her family. Now you may speak with them through Hannah, and hear of the lands of *Cornauaille* and of Avalon, so you will know them well. It is an important part of our family heritage. Hannah and her brothers and sisters desire this to be so. …The Druids know already of your coming."

From within his robes Joseph reveals a staff, taller than I, covered with carved markings. "This, my boy, is the Ogham staff. The symbols upon it are the great teachings in the language of trees. This is a sacred language, known by only the trees and the elect of the Druids, the Archdruids, and the Atlanteans." Seeing my eyes bulge in wonder, he laughs with the deep voice of the bear. "As you come upon your education, you will be able to decipher the symbols, by connecting them with the teachings you are given here and at Mount Carmel. You see, the Great White Brother-Sisterhood is one family, throughout the world, and all the languages speak of the same things. They flow from the same river."

Now I see the vision that has barely eluded me. Uncle Joseph's words are the catalyst, and Anna's family of old comes into view. Of royal Celtic blood is she, of the family named *Gewissae*, meaning the sages, the wise ones. The word itself will one day become the word queen. My heart flutters as I see the lush green isles, the courts of matriarchal past, the mesmerizing bards, the Heart-spun music, the sacred schools, and all at once I realize: Albion is the surviving remnant of Atlantis; it is the last remaining bits above water of those noble lands, wherefrom the Kaloo came before Atlantis submerged upon its destruction, some traveling first to Egypt to found the Lake *Mareia* community of Therapeutae Essene, what some call the *Mother Home*. Here they infused pre-Pharaonic and Pharaonic Egypt with the knowledge they lacked or had lost a part of over the ages. The world is kept alive and growing by the sacred knowledge of the Ancient Ones, once scattered throughout all the lands in plentiful freedom, now hidden in pockets of joyous, intrepid souls dedicated to the keeping and transmitting of Truth. The circle dances I see in colorful garbs, the ebon, red, and chestnut-haired Celtic women, both ordered and free, reigning in wisdom for the good of all. Anna's great-great-grandmother was ruler of the family of Gewissae, from which Merlin himself will one day be born, and the Grail legends as well, though they will be misunderstood. The same wisdom will be transmitted into Gaul, when Magdalen escapes there, eventually to inform the troubadour courts of the Lanquedoc (Occitania), and the Gnostics, the Rosicrucians, and the Cathars.

From a bloodline of priestess-queens, Anna is my blood-connection to Avalon, having fled with unborn child, my dear Mother, upon the guidance of angels, finally to Galilee. And while I know Anna's true age, she appears as my Mother's sister, for indeed she has the ability to change her appearance.

"How is the fleet?" asks Father of Uncle Joseph. His ships trade and sell tin and other metals sailing from and to Albion.

"All is well, though it never sits well with me to sell to the Romans. But we know its purpose, do we not? They are fat with coin."

"Yes," says Mother. "This allows our communities to continue to acquire ancient scrolls, and to provide occasional means for travel."

The Essene communities are a varied blend of peoples, but most cede their personal property to give to the whole and eschew even the thought of money, unless for noble, Godly purpose. In this manner we feel we are most with God. Set upon the ley lines of the Earth in connecting triangles of power, each Essene settlement has an individual purpose, from Qumran and Damascus and Hebron, to Rama, Jenin, and Mount Carmel. Qumran, near the Sea of Death, thus, is a school elemental, a library, and more, but also houses individuals and families. Of our communities, the outer purpose seen by the world is of a simplistic life, wherein people ply their crafts. Many are not interested or included in the advanced studies of the stars and the sacred inner arts; those who are, are tested and schooled.

Mount Carmel, my home, and where Mother was also trained, is seen as an agricultural community, but known, by even outsider Essenes, as an ascetic, priestly school. Yet, as you have seen, the Mount Carmel Mystery School is a paradise realm, far removed from the life of towns in Galilee. In Sinai, the Mount Horeb community is home to the Zealots, meat-eating militants who search for a radical Messiah. One day they will attempt to push me to the brink.

Uncle Joseph gazes upon unlikely silent Philo for a moment, knowing he, too, has a deep sense of mission. "Of course my business allows me to live well, outside of Jerusalem, but truly only to provide safe haven for our brothers and sisters. And to know of its plans for the sake of our benefit, I am a minor judge of the Sanhedrin."

Says Philo, the great sage, "In every age, two or three of wealth accumulate for the just cause: to further the progress of Truth, Love, and Freedom in whatever manner presents itself. Intrepid and beloved of God are you, Joseph of Arimathea."

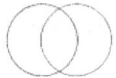

Anna, Mother, and I kneel before the great alter in the main temple of Heliopolis. The Old Testament calls this sacred site the Temple of On, using the Coptic name for the city. This once thriving metropolis is now in decline, and as you read these words it lies under the outskirts of Cairo, soon to be rediscovered, the temple's extraordinary treasures of Truth to resurface anon and inform the world. Here we have come in joy, for Anna has before been here to study, to translate the ancient scrolls, and became a high Initiate of the Mystery School hidden deep beneath the azure marble floors, its secret labyrinthian passages reaching all the way to Alexandria. Though the Egyptian kings had long left *Iunu* by the time Anna arrived, the priests and the ancient knowledge still remain. In future I will myself come here to study; indeed, the knowledge I gain will assist in my Ascension, the ability to conquer death itself, of which I will teach you within these pages.

Easy it is to think Egypt and its traditions vile. Like all civilizations, its influence ebbed, that is all. But at the time of our arrival, it still was a deeply cultured land which for millennia had been at the summit of its artistic, philosophic, and sacred powers. Hellenes such as Plato, Homer, Pythagoras, Socrates, Orpheus, and Euclid studied here. For Egypt is the keeper of knowledge, begotten long before the ages of Sumeria, Atlantis, and Lemuria, which you might find fantastical, even impossible, but will help to save the planet and to reconnect humanity with Source.

You see, dear sisters and brothers, advanced civilizations have existed on this planet for over five hundred million years. And life here first came from the stars.

The towering walls of gold carved with myriad hieroglyph-stories, the secret code of Thoth, take my breath away. Atum stares at me with all-knowing eyes; there is something breathing, some energy in the air I cannot identify. But that is not all.

Mother is with child! And even more, the birth will be of two, not one. Her stomach has grown into a robust mound, and Anna speaks to the soon-to-be twins, soul to souls, to aid in their delivery and in their remembrance of the Divine.

From Lower to Upper Nile, seven powerful teaching temples are perfectly placed atop the chakras of the Earth. For as there are the chakras of the human body, so, too, are there the chakras of our world. In Egypt they flow north from Abu Simbel to Giza, and the Heliopolan priests are the chief administrators of the rites of nearby Giza. In this temple within which we kneel the Initiate can remove the veil to discover their immortal soul.

Giza corresponds to the seventh chakra, the crown, the crest: the pineal gland itself, looking up into the dimensions having moved through the third eye, the sixth chakra at the temple at Memphis, watched over by the Great Sphinx.

We have come by Anna's counsel, for while we are in Egypt, experience we will the sacred sites, and by this the soon-to-come twins will be endowed with Divine perception. O Ptah, the Father of Egypt, was wise indeed.

The azure marble floors shine like living pools of light, and my attention is wrested from my praises by a group of children crossing the main hall. Mostly silent they are, but there is one conversing seriously with the priest who leads them. Mother, Anna, and I each hear their words. The priest is young, perhaps five and twenty, and the child, robed and hooded in vermillion, is unseen, but is as tall as my Ogham staff, upon which Hannah now perches. From the gait and the energy, all at once I recognize the child is a girl. And the priest does not agree with her as she persists in proclaiming that all is life, that everything we know and touch and see is life.

Anna and Mother turn to look at me, knowing countenances on their faces. We three know all is life. How is it the priest does not?

Just behind us and off to the side, the young girl picks up a stray pebble undoubtedly brought into temple hiding in the sandals of some recent petitioner. Anna signs for me to stand and watch, her cherubic face agleam.

Her nose now visible, the girl places the pebble between her thumb and forefinger, kneels, and looks up to be certain the priest is watching. Then she puts the pebble to the azure marble, scraping it hard along the gleaming tile. Sparks fly.

"Everything is alive!" She cries with near contempt.

At first the priest is furious at this break with temple sanctity. But the girl cares not. Suddenly her hood drops behind her head, as she has become heated, though her point is proven. And the priest now puts his fingers to his lips in contemplation, as if seeing for the first time.

The girl turns and stares directly into mine eyes, her hair of ebon shimmering golden-sapphire, her piercing orbs seeing all inside me. A glorious, calming, cleansing sensation passes through my body, like the water of the greatest ocean quenching the thirst of the solar sun, like the cool moisture of the moon insulating my immortal soul. Like a baby lamb taming the mighty lion.

Hannah chirps a song while upon my staff, an ancient song, one old as the Universe itself. The song of Love's eternal Light.

And as I pen these very words, the four hatchling Phoebes have completed their flight training; upon my signal this eve, while escorting out the new village pastor, they sang and soared into the heavens, making their way into the world, only to return to this nest next year for the incubation of their own progeny. The sacred marriage of outer and inner within both the pastor and me allows the young Phoebes to know it is time, just as summer solstice announces its arrival.

Thank you, dear God, for Your great gifts.

# Chapter Five
# Heliopolis

MY BROTHERS JAMES AND JUDE HAVE come into the world. Such a blessing their twinly presence is. For, young as I am, though I have four half-brothers, two you have met, and three half-sisters, two you have met, Jude and James are my first siblings of Mother and Father's union. And already our family has borne much: wearing the cloak of secrecy, fleeing from our home, leaving Lake *Mareia* in the dead of night so as to enter and then exit Alexandria unseen for Heliopolis. My four half-brothers—James the Older, Simon, Jose, and Jude the Older—and half-sister Esther had arrived on the Sabbath, two days before setting out. We could not have made the journey in safety without my brothers by our sides. And truth be told, Jose and Jude the Older and Esther have not much been with us since I entered the world.

*Savta* Anna has returned home to Mount Carmel, and we live in the house of Mother's older brother Isaac and his wife Tabitha in a Hebrew village outside this once-great city. Their divine daughter Sara is become my friend, and around us are many extended family members. In the starlit evenings we tell stories and play spirited music and dance around the fire like gods possessed as Father Sun slips into the horizon, offering our praises to both Him and the ascending Moon.

Holding my hand, Sara one day walks me atop Atum's mound, his *Benben*, that which first arose from the primordial waters. He himself is sometimes seen as the mound. Off in the distance to the east, Atum's temple glimmers golden in the sun, the surrounding obelisks directing one's gaze like irradiant arrows to the heavens. Near westward sit Father and Isaac in conversation, each occasionally looking our way to keep us in view.

Her hair of ebon billowing wildly in the breeze, Sara gamely plunges her fingers into the soil and proclaims, "From this we are born. From this our powers grow. And deep within the secret chasms of ancient *Khem* breathes the Mystery of returning to God."

Her emerald eyes flash fire as she bids me put my hands also into the dirt. And sinking them into Atum's *Benben*, I feel the Eternal Flame. A child-priestess Sara is. You may believe young children are unable to speak thus, to know, but deep within we all know, and in this age our families so tell us from the day we are born, and before. Sara knows even the name *Khem*, what Egypt once, long ago, was named. Indeed, the words alchemy and chemistry are fittingly derived from *Khem*.

In silence we sit upon the *Benben*, now holding hands, I beginning to feel the energies of the ancients all around us. In my heart I know Thoth will return with more lessons, more wisdom, yet what I envision is not the Sacred Ibis; this is his symbol; this is how he chose to introduce himself to me. There is an image in my mind of a short man, noble in bearing, with an angular face. Be this Thoth?

Walking back to Isaac and Tabitha's home, Father speaks of Atum. "Yes, Isaac and I have heard sweet Sara and you speaking of Atum. He was a self-created deity, the supposed first to arise from the darkness before creation. Through his mere spit he created, and also through his semen."

A jolly, caring man, Isaac laughs. "You may perceive a resemblance between the name Atum and our Adam, the first man."

Atum. Adam. Atom.

The following year Mother gives birth to Joseph the Younger, sometimes called Joses. And Sara moves with her family to Gaul. Though I will not see lovely dark-skinned Sara again for some years, her spirit is ever with me. She was Light-conceived, as was I, and throughout our time apart we will communicate in the inner ways, telepathically, without fail or error in transmission. Beloved she is of me. With a glint of both sadness and Love in her countenance, on the day of their departure Sara places a blue lotus blossom in my hand, and with her finger draws a circle around the contours of my palm, whispering, "Dear Yeshu'a, your heart is also in your hands."

Another Light-conceived cousin, Mariam, of the union of Rebekah and Simeon, also in Heliopolis, now becomes my great childhood love, though she is some bit older than I. Her Mother, Rebekah, is my Mother's sister. To call Mariam my childhood love is no embellishment or illusion, for she is a rare and beautiful creature, in complete union with the One God all of her days. I Love her as a sister but imagine her becoming my bride, such as daydreaming boys do. As we grow in years, her beauty astonishes me. With tresses fine and soft and chestnut-blonde like mine own, an angelic face, and the grace of a goddess, her outward appearance, to some, might bear no testament to the depths within, for we frequently dismiss outer beauty as but a chimera and believe the mind and heart of the beautiful to be mostly vacant. Mistaken we often are in this judgment, but Mariam, too, possesses wisdom and a deep knowing, an inner calm, an ability to see through to the crux. Never fooled is she. And one day she will become an important companion, one of the seventy-two women who teach and keep Truth alive.

On my fifth birthday dear Father begins to teach me to play the harp. Quickly I learn the magic of music, its healing power, the different vibrations of the notes, and am writing my own psalms by the passing of another year. I find I have a soprano voice which is evidently pleasing to the ear. Like Father, I sleep little, though quite sufficiently, and I spend some of the early morning and late night hours writing Love-songs dedicated to Mariam. The Holy Stream of Sound pours through me, manifesting itself in my simple songs to Mariam and to God. Of course David's Harp is easier to play than the various Egyptian versions, for they are large and require one to be of adult stature. But I fiddle with their strings and learn from them as well. As is already my nature, I am studying everything in minute detail, in nature, humanity, and the cosmos.

Gradually the buffers placed about my consciousness by Mother, Father, and Grandmother Anna are lifted. They have seen to my protection, these loving three, for I am proving to be sensitive to all the energies around me. They knew this would be so. Until I learn to harness them on my own and through my initiations, the pain it causes I must endure. And music is my introduction to the triune nature of sound, light, and color: the geometric matrix of the Universe. Indeed, the Rite of the Sepulchre, the process by which physical immortality is achieved, is based upon sound, light, and color, electromagnetic fields, and the Flower of Life. And the Grail, the meaning of which has been distorted by the profane into an outer physical cup, is the eternal cup of Consciousness that preserves lucid patterns of cosmic intelligence as Sacred Geometry, sound, light, and color. Though your church may tell you I died on the cross, through the Rite of the Sepulchre and the deep Inner understanding of the Grail and the ministrations of my loved ones, I resurrected and traveled east, eventually making my way into Kashmir where I was known by many names, including Saint Issa. My tomb there lies, discovered by some few in recent times, but discredited by Christian authorities, especially those of the Vatican.

My dear children, in the Age of the Holy Spirit in which you now breathe, all life is experiencing its own personal crucifixion. A planetary Ascension is occurring; you are all becoming Christ. And willingly you shall relinquish your ego, lovingly suffer any sort of disgrace, and face every test with grace and with gratitude for your life. Even thine enemy shall you forgive, for he is you and you are he. Truly bless every circumstance you have chosen to experience, not just the joyous ones. In his manuscript entitled *The Cusp of the Ages,* Levi issued a commission obtained from *Visel,* the Goddess of Wisdom, what some call the Holy Breath; many of you know her as Sophia. Speaking of me, within it are these words: *He was despised, rejected, and abused; was spit upon, was crucified, was buried in a tomb; but he revived and rose a conqueror over death that he might show the possibilities of man.*

Know deep in your heart that you will not suffer as I; I and Magdalen and others have seen to that. Fear not, for with our help you will open your Book of Life and stroll through Akasha and all your sacred wounds will be healed.

It is time, beloveds, to finally let go of old, limiting beliefs which do not serve you or God, including that the Daughters and Sons of God must be sacrificed to atone for the world's sins. Never are you a victim. For truly you are all the Daughters and Sons of God. You chose this life, your parents, all of your experiences, be it ever convenient for some to wallow in ignorance and think contrary to this. It was my choice to bring the Mystery out into the world, to serve humanity, a humble candle of *The Way* to God. And as I relate my history, prepare thyselves: much of what you have been taught will be challenged, even including the nature of Judas Iscariot, who will play the role of my betrayer. But today all is forever changed. As within each and every one of you the Divine seed planted by God is germinating; now you awaken to the great dream. Now you may even release your karma. The Truth of God births in your breasts: a flower so caring, so beautiful, so tremendous, it is invincible to death. It is Love itself.

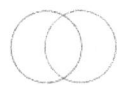

İn the Garden of Isis I am. The pale, pink shade of the evening sun bathes me amidst the acacia. She who is my Mother and yours is Isis, Mother of Horus, who came before me to light *The Way*. Her long, understanding nose, countenance soft, pearly, dauntless eyes of ebon, she is the Woman Clothed with the Sun, its Light radiating around her as she is both Bride and also the Sun's Mother, the original Creator, for she be, too, a virgin. I am as a vessel unto her in this golden land of sand and clay and date palm and secrets to keep the very Universe stitched in time. For, while we seek gnosis, is it not true that true gnosis, being with God, is the act of giving up knowing, to admit one knows nothing?

This is the state of absolute awareness, when not one thought clutters the brain.

Here, the air is succulent: water and lilac and lotus blossoms and green, thriving life. It is soft to the lung, for the Garden of Isis is oasis and portal of life. In her honor it is the sacred acacia which stands as the Tree of Life. She and the mighty Osiris, her brother-become-lover, emerged from it here, through the sacred gateway of the world's first acacia tree, owned by *Iusaaset*, Grandmother of the gods.

I observe a child sitting with his Hebrew family next to the pond, the late afternoon junk fires of the city glowing in the background. Something is troubling him. His chin trembles, his eyes swell will tears. There are three children—two girls and the boy—and a Nubian girl, and the Mother and Father. Most kindly, patiently, over many minutes, the boy seeks his Mother's attention: cheeks filling with rose, eyes aquiver, a silent, heaving breath. And thrice the Mother rebuffs his efforts to speak with her; she coos with her husband. At least of the moment this is where her attention is focused. The boy, older than I, is now crying, quietly at first, while recounting an unresolved painful memory of the family. My heart nestles with his. There is communion, and I experience his pain. His life is my life; I see, hear, smell, and feel his memories. As energy, he speaks many words. This is not an unusual event, what happens here today in the Garden of Isis; his parents' eyes and ears have been much closed to him before, though his heart and mind are fairly bursting with such wonderful ideas and questions.

"Am I not your son? Why is it you ignore me? Do you not love me?" the boy demands with tears flowing down his cheeks, his voice cracking with emotion.

Now the Mother loses all patience and stands tall, hovering menacingly over her son. She raises her arm as if to strike him but then stops. "Come, let us leave Samuel alone; he will learn he cannot control us by his outbursts." Slowly the rest of the family rises and walks to the other side of the water.

This I know, my dear children: there is but one non-illusory thing in the Universe: Love. All else is mirage. And at this age I cannot abide one instant the denial of it…the blind eye to that which allows one to breathe. My brothers are not quick enough to intercede as I storm over to the family, the hot iron of anger stoking a holocaust within me. Nearing them, I hear the footfalls of James the Older and Simon behind me.

"How can you treat your own son with such distain, Mother? He cries for your love and needs your ears to hear his words, so that your heart may help mend his which is broken. Fit you are not for Motherhood!" She gasps at this scene, a little boy screaming at her, and makes to object, but within me I feel the cause righteous, and raise my hand, envisioning her mouth sewn shut.

And so it is. She mumbles, her eyes roll to the tops of their sockets, her face turns ruby-red. And her husband gets to his feet, while little Samuel, across the path, brightens at the drama unfolding.

James and Simon have come, Simon scooping me up in his arms, both issuing their regrets over my behavior. "A sensitive boy, Father. Nothing more. Once more, please accept our sincere regrets," declares James, while Simon whispers in my ear, "Yeshu, if you have done something to the Mother so that she cannot speak, undo it, now!"

Simon drops me on the ground. I am not certain I wish to do this; this young boy suffers so, but eventually I amble over to her and touch her head, asking God with love in my heart to return her speech to her. And it is done. Never was she in danger; always she could breathe. And now stamped upon her expression is gratitude, not the ice of bitterness, not the biting wind of indifference. The Love-Light shines upon her anew. She is a child reborn, her awareness of the sacred in herself and all things, and of her own human weakness, her need for Love, rekindled. She runs to her son and clutches him dearly in her arms, kissing softly, lovingly every inch of his face.

Dropping him to the ground, she holds his hand and says, "Come, dear son. Let us walk together. Tell me what perplexes you. I will listen, no matter how long it takes. Together we shall solve any dilemma." And they begin to walk through the paths of Isis' Garden, young Samuel's step a bouncing ball of joy.

My own Mother upon our return shakes a stern finger at me and emits a moan of impatient frustration. "We will speak of this, Yehoshua. It ended well, and surely you knew this, but you will learn this just is not done. You may guide, you may teach, you may fill each willing soul with the Light of God, yea Balaam! But you shall not condemn the ignorant; never shall you succeed in your mission by this manner of act. Each finds his own path and must survive the trials of life-education in his own way. This Mother and child may be healed by this event, and she bless your intervention, yet you will find better ways. Have you understanding of my words?"

I lower my head, not in shame but in knowledge, and nod. Then I approach my dear Mother, wrap my arms around her neck, and next place my lips on her cheek and blow as if playing a bullhorn, so a mighty indiscreet sound ensues. And she roars with laughter, as does the rest of my family. All is light once more. "Oh, you little imp! Ever you are both a winning and wearing child!" Tending to my hair and tunic, she is bright with light for me, knowing this is an important part of my maturation. "With the new sun you and I will meditate upon this together; you will see to the perfection of your thoughts and emotions. Your life, your mission depends on it."

It will take time for me, for there will be other scenes such as this, even within our own family, for, as a small child, the denial of Love in the most important moments I see to be a crime against the Holy Breath. But I will conquer it, I will come to know these moments to be equally filled with the Light of God. Life is university. Never for myself will I feel this anger, this desolation; I am loved, but also of necessity left alone and to mine own thoughts. This I understand; ever I am strong. It is the denial of Love in the lives of others in their moments of greatest need which I cannot yet abide. Grant me sweet patience, dear Lord. Shower upon me Your infinite wisdom, for I will learn. And may You also bestow upon my Mother the grace of even more serenity, for it is she who must endure my little outbursts awhile longer.

I sing my praises to Thee, God. Thank You for this greatest of gifts: Life.

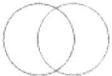

Father and I walk into the Temple of On, Atum's temple. I gaze upon the azure marble floor, the tiles shining like a deep, placid ocean, the secrets beneath beckoning me to dive into the vast Mystery. Recalling the young girl I observed the first time I was here, instinctively my eyes search the main chamber for her. Each time I come to this ancient sacred place I look for her, longing to again view her comely face. Yet, before climbing the grand steps, I know she will not grace these halls. Her eyes burn in my soul. As the memory of our one shared moment glistens within me, I ever hear the words God spoke to Moses: I AM that I AM.

Father leads me through a labyrinth of azure hallways, behind Atum's alter, and I contemplate these words. Seeking inner silence and peace, I practice a walking meditation, closing my eyes, willing my senses to both feel the sacred space before me and disengage from the world.

"They are mysterious words, are they not?"

Suddenly beside me is Thoth. He comes in my inner vision, and as I have surmised, he shows himself to me as he really is. By your measurements he stands perhaps five feet tall, his hair is long black silk. Beautiful is his face, like the visages of the gods painted in ancient frescoes: chiseled, sleek, all-knowing, and all-loving, his nose long and straight, his lips red like a cache of shining rubies.

"Dear Thoth! Praises to you. I have seen your face before."

"Indeed, young one. And you saw it also long, long ago, in time out of mind. You now walk the halls of my olden academy, my University of God. Soon your Father will bring you down into its precincts proper. Here, you will learn to read and speak many tongues and will read sacred texts. As part of your service to God, you will assist the Great White Brother-Sisterhood by scribing translations as Anna once did, ages long past. You will take the initiations of the Rite of the Sepulchre, the Holy Sepulchre. And I will be with you. But, dear one, these words—I AM that I AM—have formed in your mind. Shall we speak of them? Do you have knowledge of their meaning?"

"We are told God spoke them to Moses."

"And to many before him, I assure you. Your sacred books give hints to things beyond the veil, but they are still hidden. The tale of the Great Flood and Noah and his ark does not say that it describes the demise of my beloved Atlantis. This is merely one example. I AM that I AM tells you of destiny, of your connection with God, in a way unlike all other creatures. Humanity is special in that you are the only life God created from the soil, the clay of the Earth; He then breathed His life into your nostrils. All other life He spoke into existence: *Let there* be this, *let there* be that. For humanity no words were spoken. God formed you of the essence of this world. This reveals to you things most important. Firstly, that you were made in His, or more rightly, Their image, for the Father-Mother God residing in your breast is of both your Divine Father and Divine Mother. In truth, you are made *into* their image, as it is a process. Secondly, you are to learn the physical lessons of living on this Earth. The part most essential is to *remember* how to get home, that truly there is no separation between you and God. And it is through the consciousness of the Divine Mother that you return. Mother Earth is Her platform. She graciously offers Her existence so that She may reveal to you Her secrets. In nigh-every sacred book are stories of the descent into Her most hidden recesses; the hallowed Halls of *Amenti* therein reside, where masters dwell in higher dimension for your instruction. Though most today understand them not, these are important stories. For you must Love your Mother: your Great Cosmic Mother, your Mother of flesh, and your dear Gaia, Mother Earth."

Thoth chuckles good-naturedly. "Fear torments most even considering this. Already there is a tremendous amount of guilt and fear over Her. Yet, with Love and integrity, you must seek Her precious secrets, always respecting Her wisdom, for therein your map back home to God is found, a treasure beyond the reckoning of this world. In future, during what will become known as the patriarchal era, every effort will be made to destroy Her. Yet it cannot be. She ever stands the Divine Mother, who goes by many names, through whose womb the Universe entire was born…"

Now I see a lovely image, given to me by Thoth. Drawn onto a wall of stone in red ochre, it appears to be a circle; within it, many circles perfectly overlap each other. The center of each circle is perfectly placed on the circumferences of what appear to be six other circles surrounding it. This image vibrates with Love before my eyes; it dances and weaves and speaks soothing words to me.

"What you now see resides in the Temple of Osiris in Abydos. This, dear Yeshu'a, is the Flower of Life; it is the creation pattern for everything in the Universe, even including thoughts and emotions. You will find this sacred symbol all over the world and across the Universe. Not far into the future you will see it on Mount Sinai."

"I recognize it!" I cry within my walking meditation.

"Certainly. You have long seen it. In your life as Akhenaten, the great king of *Khem* who sought to bring the knowledge of the One God back to prominence, you drew this symbol thousands of times. As a two-dimensional symbol, the very first of its kind on Earth, you see many circles. Yet the circles are actually spheres. And within the Flower of Life is seen the Tree of Life, the Vesica Piscis, the star tetrahedron or Star of David, Metatron's Cube, the platonic solids: all life is wrapped up in this sacred flower. The various forms within it also have myriad meanings. For instance: the Tree of Life is a map of the galaxy in which we live, and also of the chakras of your body and of the planet, the study of which will lead you back to God by using, looking through, your one central eye which leads to the pineal gland. Ultimately the Flower of Life teaches the truly multidimensional nature of the Universe, upon which humanity's survival and evolution depend...

"Millennia in the future, science will name the building blocks of life DNA, short for *Deoxyribonucleic* Acid, from the Greek. Yet scientists will not comprehend its true multidimensional nature for some time. They will misunderstand its structure and purpose; the vast majority of even its simple three-dimensional physical nature will appear to be blank. There is a reason for this. Until humanity once more learns how to discern the various dimensions beyond the physical three, until it truly reopens itself to God, the Mystery will remain... You see, Yeshu'a, the Tree of Life is your DNA!

"Lemuria—a word which means Light—predated Atlantis and their primary god was named *Yawee*. Notice you will the resemblance to the Hebrew Yahweh. We Atlanteans knew well the Lemurians, though their land of many islands was originally in other, far away seas, one day to be called the Pacific and Indian Oceans. Enlightened, beautiful people, they, too, knew the Truth of God. They knew about Light-conception, or multidimensional conception, and they knew about DNA. In fact, the word *Yawee* was their word for DNA; so, too, then, is the meaning of the Hebrew Yahweh, though your people of this age and long ago have covered this up or forgotten it. The truth is, dear one, all of this leads to the same knowledge: All is One. And when you in earnest begin your studies, bear this in mind, keep your heart peeled."

In our shared meditation, Thoth now clutches tightly my hand, and we whisk through space and the ages of time on divine wings. Passing not over the world but through the illusion of what we consider to be real—the density of the three dimensional planes—brilliant hues of red, blue, and green and the vibrant tones of the Holy Stream of Sound are our conduit. And as we return to the world, my breath stops short. Upon a golden land we stand before a dripping canvas of cobalt sky, and a majestic, towering peak looms, capped in pure white snow, a circle of clouds surrounding it. Never have my eyes seen such an impressive mountain. The air is crisp and clean.

Says Thoth, "We now view what will one day be named Mount Shasta and it is one thousand years in the future. Due to the change in the tilt of the Earth's axis which occurs every nigh-thirteen thousand years, when Lemuria sank underneath the sea, unlike the Atlanteans, many thousands of Lemurians escaped their land's demise and came to rest here. Having mastered interdimensional knowledge, they eventually transcended space and time, passing through the fourth dimension to reside in the fifth. Beneath and around this mount they rebuilt their temple and main city, Telos...Yet it exists only in the fifth dimension. And attaining even higher realms, Lemuria will in future rise again, though not in three-dimensional form, and having conquered death, its people, thousands of ages old, will be some of the great saviors of this world. ...We here will return, Yeshu'a, when you are ready."

And at once we travel again on wings divine through the upper dimensions, God's luminosity of color pulsating through and around us, the musical tones of the galaxy a celestial choir transporting us back to Heliopolis. How my heart aches to see more.

"Remember, Yeshu'a: When you begin your studies, keep your heart peeled. As you will learn, Osiris and Isis were Atlantean, not Egyptian, though their story speaks of the river Nile. Of course their roots, like our own, come from elsewhere. The Hathors, in particular, positively influenced the spiritual, artistic, and scientific growth of this great Earth...They came from Venus, Earth's sister planet, and became the sages of Horus' Mystery School; indeed, as Horus was the holy child of Isis and Osiris, the Hathors were the great bridge between ancient Atlantis and the early Egyptian religion. The Hathors had long been here, interacting with us in such beautiful ways, including with the Lemurians. They are beings of tremendous Love and knowledge. And when our hearts were young, we could still see them, for they mostly dwell in the fourth dimension. Now only some few are capable of this. The Hathors are the custodians of our solar system, for they are the most advanced beings within it.

"And while it appears impossible, when you travel the Universe with your heart's eye and see the spirals of the galaxies, a truth hidden within both the Flower of Life and DNA tells you that the heart of each galaxy leads to the same place, though they are seemingly spread across vast cosmic distances."

Thoth lightly chuckles once more, seeing my face open in knowledge but also bear the stamp of still more questions. Upon his cheeks the rarest, most discreet of dimples form. "Glad I am to see such light in your young face. Worry not, you will understand in time. I have only cracked open the door. The true history of our world is far different from that which is taught. You may be surprised to hear, for one, that the great mammals named whales and dolphins also came from afar; they traveled here in spaceships and were the first enlightened beings of this world. Very early tribes venerated them for their Love and wisdom and abilities, like the Hathors, with sound. For today, remember these things: I AM that I AM shortened to its true form is simply I AM. Today in Palestine this is a common greeting. This is why you are here—I AM; and when all is said and done, though you will study the sacred texts, including my beloved Emerald Tablets, you will not find Truth in some dusty old book. The Truth you seek is right before your very eyes."

Though I understand this in some way, I am perplexed by it. Within my meditation I search Thoth's eyes seeking more.

"Know I well you are still confused by what I have said. Studying is important, do not mistake me. But ever it is true the answers are within your heart. You may have heard the expression: *using* your brain, *using* your intelligence. Listen to these words. You are not your brain, but you can *use* it. You are also not your body; it is merely a shell you use while in physical form. You are not Yeshu'a. Yeshu'a is just a name you use. You are not Hebrew, a student, a man, a religion. When there is nothing left, all you have is I. The I of I AM."

All at once I understand, and all my veils lifted, I fly like the eagle above the world. "This is clear to me now, Thoth. The I is Spirit. I do not have a Spirit which forever lives on after my body dies; I *am* a Spirit that lives on eternally after I let go of the body—"

"—Excellent! You see truly. The I of I AM is indeed Spirit, and there is only one Spirit that lives in everyone and everything. Within each of us is the spark of Spirit, which is what God is: the Eternal Flame. We are each a tiny drop in the limitless ocean of God. I assure you this Truth will not perish, though even your own words and teachings will be changed by institutions. In one of my favorite future sacred texts, it will be well said: *God is all around you and within you.* In various ways this will be translated, but this is the essential meaning. It will be you, Yeshu'a, who utters these words. Now that you have realized this basic Truth, you have found your home: I AM."

Down deep into the Earth we now travel, through the rooms of the temple Mystery School. Although we are far removed from sunlight, the rooms and passageways are lit not by candles or torches but by living crystals. And the walls and floors are heated so we feel not the cold of the Earth. The Atlantean priests here have retained the knowledge of light, color, and sound, and are thus able to use these skills when appropriate for the furtherance of the understanding of God.

Father speaks of the purpose of each room. Many are libraries, and like the one in Lake *Mareia*, they are truly immense repositories of wisdom. Before we left *Mareia*, Master Philo informed me this would be so. I carry my Ogham staff, though, knowing we would be mostly underground, on this occasion I have left Hannah the Phoebe with Mariam.

Two priests I meet, one the high priest, and I am escorted into a private chamber where I am told to wait. Alone. The waiting is long, the small room bare of anything but two simple wood benches facing each other and four stone walls. After sitting on one of the benches, soon my mind is playing tricks on me, telling me I will be forever left here, voices attempting to play upon my fears of solitude, counseling me to break down the door to escape. Time inches by. And now I am being told the high priest is evil, that he wishes to break my spirit and own my soul.

Putting my hands together palm-to-palm before me, I pray and give praises to God. "I will not fail," say I aloud. "Nor will I stray and allow any fearful voice to keep me from my destiny of Light. Only to You do I sing my praises, dear God."

A vision now enters my head, showing me the high priest. He carries a liquid-filled cup, and on his face is a most reprehensible expression, one oozing with evil intent. A new voice enters my head, warning me that the priest intends to murder me. "You must kill him if you are to survive," it says with great conviction. This goes on for some time, yet I do not waver in my belief of Goodness in all men. My hands stay firmly together throughout. Softly I sing one of my psalms.

Finally the high priest enters the chamber. In his hands he holds a cup. Sitting on the opposite bench, he then offers it to me. "You must have thirst, Yeshu'a." He is an old man, this priest, his beard long and silver and somehow well-groomed, his robes of white and lavender indeed impressive. Upon his lip is a curl and in his eyes dances a furtive glance. "For some time you have been here; please drink if thirst needs to be quenched."

Standing, I smile wide with blessings in my heart. I take without hesitation the offered cup and enjoy a long drink of cool, soothing water, then return it to the high priest.

Suddenly a great shining light surrounds him, and he appears altogether a different, much younger man. "I am most pleased, Yeshu'a," he says. "For you have just now passed our first initiation." A beaming smile comes upon his visage. "Easy it is to let the voice of fear enter you and lead you to erroneous, even immoral acts. Each Initiate who comes to us is first given this test."

I kneel in honor of this holy man and kiss the hem of his robe. "Dear Father, it is true I heard the voices of fear, and also saw visions of you walking the halls with malevolent intent. Told I was to kill you. Yet I found silence within me by prayerful words, singing psalms, by communicating directly with God, ever speaking my Love and praises."

"This is good. Though you are young, already you know much. Your family is to be commended." Placing his hand softly upon my shoulder, he asks me to rise and face him. "Now we will begin your studies, young Yeshu'a."

While my dear Mother, Salome, and Martha take their initiations in the temples of Isis, Hathor, and Horus, over the next months I am hard at work in the Temple of On. I learn to fluently speak and read Greek, Egyptian, and the ancient languages of Atlantis and Lemuria. And as Thoth described, I translate some of the great sacred books. My favorites are the Avesta of Zarathustra and the Vedas texts, parts of which I translate from Sanskrit into the Aramaic and Egyptian languages. Vedas means knowledge, and the Vedic texts are the Hindu sacred tomes. Many holy beings inhabit their colorful stories, including the ever radiant Krishna. Pages of the *Bhagavad-Gita* I sometimes copy and bring home with me, so I may again read them in my room; the beauty of these verses fills my heart with such joy. Too, I read and am fascinated by the already-translated Buddhist texts, and allowing their words to breathe within me, I feel the winds of the East beckon. You are told that I could neither read nor write. I have never understood this, save that the church which bears my name never wished for you to read, as I, the world's holy books. I, too, learn from my Father the meanings of many hieroglyphic symbols. Tracing my fingers over them in the temple, I learn more of their meanings by touch alone. Several I find upon my staff, and am able to decipher connections between the language of the trees and the language of Thoth.

My days are filled with wonder. Yet I still have many problems with the energies of emotion. Sometimes I double over in agonizing pain when I feel a heart breaking, a Love denied or mistreated. I can hear people's thoughts, see the energy when someone tells not the truth, but I am counseled well by Mother and Mariam. This evening, after I witness a husband emotionally injure his wife and speak a spate of lies, I arrive home in utter exhaustion, my physical aspect that of a beaten beggar. Always calm, ever in command of herself, yet weary from having to nurture what you would call a hyperactive child, Mother lovingly combs her fingers through my hair. "Dear son, you will soon learn that Love unacknowledged is the great tragedy of the world. It stills pains you, I know. Yet you will learn not to allow these caring skills to possess you. Remember what I say: just because you *can* does not mean that you *do*. There are moments when these skills are proper and required, but you must not allow them to rule you. The privacy of lives is sacrosanct. And while it seems contrary to God's will, never forget All is Grace, even the denial of Love, as it is merely one step in the lives of those who experience it. Some say we are put into situations to learn, to improve, to heal ourselves and those around us. You know better, for we choose all experience. Bless each and every instant you breathe, see the beauty in all of it, know God is always there, lovingly nudging us ahead along the Path, and you will not suffer so."

I contemplate Mother's words as I walk the village paths, the shade of night turning to black, and spy Mariam's room alight with oil lamps. She silently calls to me, my dear cousin. Off in the distance the melodies of Egyptian night-song ring, the drums pound, beckoning me to take heed. So I make for her parent's house.

Crossing the threshold of her room, I find her sitting on her pallet in the triangle position of meditation, what you call the Lotus position, when your legs form a triangle with your body and your head constitutes the fourth pyramidal point for communion with God. Blue sparks fly about her, and she is surrounded by a lovely cocoon of white. I am observing these things around many of those in my life, and myself, and mean to speak of it with the high priest of the Temple of On. Once, upon recognizing it around a group of us Initiates, I cried to look, and the dazzling effects disappeared from view.

There is a certain melancholy in Mariam. Never does she speak of it or burden others about its source. From it the essence of her beauty is derived, as it does not possess her, but it is there, in her deep, dark, oval eyes, her quiet expression, her deliberate pace in doing chores. Whereas my tranquil Mother is joy, Mariam's serenity is born of overcoming loss. And I have discovered this is the reason she often finds solace in the Otherworld. Mariam has learned all of the lessons of this world and lives now only to give to others.

With God she truly walks.

And ever she is there to assist me, hearing my words and listening to my heart with genuine sympathy, always able to understand, even without my speaking, what it is I need. Naturally, I reveal myself in different ways with Mariam than I do Mother, and too, Mother is often these days away taking her initiations, while also caring for Joses and James and Jude the Youngers.

Each time before she speaks in her deep contralto voice, Mariam takes a measured breath, as if it is a meditation in itself. "Your Mother is wise, Yeshu'a," says she upon hearing of her recent counsel, a bold rain beginning to pummel the roof of the house. "Harmlessness is a word you should remember. Sadness sometimes appears to engulf us; often despair seems to blot out all light, any possibility of ever attaining the sweet embrace of God. And when you witness the wages of fear in the lives of others, when the ignorant, the fearful, mistreat themselves, often these are the same souls who seek to steal your own light, to snuff its life out. When your peaceful presence threatens the profane, remember: these are the moments which can help you attain the Kingdom…If you live unconditional Love, if you breathe forgiveness."

"Yes, I hear the same from my parents. Mother says I should not allow my caring skills to possess me, that there are proper moments for them."

A most caring smile comes upon her face. "Indeed. The inner skills of communication are often used by the profane for gamesmanship, for incursions into people's lives. You already understand that, for the true empath, you only know what the other reveals to you. Harmlessness, dear one, is the code to live by. You shall promise to do no harm to others, or yourself. And most important, the skills of the fourth dimension, the inner communications of telepathy, for instance, are not an end unto themselves. They but lead to the fifth dimension, the angelic realms, the celestial realms, and should be used as gifts to project forward and backward in time with respect to the divine purpose in life."

Mariam stops and begins to breathe in a continuous, measured pattern. Her arms outstretched, resting upon her legs palms upward, she forms a circle in both hands by joining the tips of her thumbs with each finger, one at a time, moving to the next finger upon completing a cycle of inhalation and exhalation, and the room turns silent, the rain outside somehow also slowly coming to a halt.

"God is in the breath, beloved. Breathe with me and follow my pace and the movements of my fingers. Release your cares."

I do as I am bid and soon begin to feel more peaceful, less attached to the outcomes of the world.

"You will learn more of this from your teachers, but it is most natural for a child…Remember, Yeshu'a, psychic ability —the way of the mind—is frowned upon by the world's spiritual traditions, as one can achieve high levels of psychic skill and still retain the ego. Most spiritual traditions see it as unimportant, even dangerous. One with caution must proceed, yet nonetheless one must proceed. It is a required step to enlightenment, for one must *pass through* this area of human consciousness to reach the higher dimensions. The fourth dimension is a gateway to God. And as long as you make everything you do be about God, all will be fine.

"Already I have lost much in my life," continues my divine cousin. "Friends, family members have passed on at too young an age. But the angels and God's Glory ever help me to remember that which is real. We are never alone. With eyes enough to see, our loved-ones—all souls who have lovingly touched our many incarnations—are ever right before our eyes. Truly Love is stronger than death. For, in truth, there is no death. And the belief that passed loved-ones are dead and no longer with us is for those who make an empty breath of their own lives, who dream their own deaths. This creates the cycle of the illusion of death in the human experience, the cycle of suffering reincarnations to learn again and again the basic lesson of walking with God, being with God, returning to God.

"So, as the great physician or healer professes to do no harm, harmlessness is a word you shall always keep at hand. Others may seek to harm you, as they harm themselves, but you shall live the law of harmlessness. And with your strength of soul, nothing others do can hurt you. Shine your light upon them, smile in the face of adversity, demonstrate your Love no matter the circumstance, and you will succeed."

Placing my hands together in prayer before falling into slumber, I utter these words: "Ever I thank You, heavenly Father and Mother, for the great gift you have given me. May I be worthy of it, and may I continue to find calm and balance and silence in all that I do. I am ever grateful for Mariam and my dear Mother and their tireless patience and devotion, their infinite wisdom. I am thrice blest. Please tend to their continued serenity. This I pray. Amen."

As I lay my head down, a single tear of joy escapes my eye. "How is it possible I am so loved?"

# Chapter Six
# Lessons and Makeda

FATHER HAS HAD A DREAM in which the world's first angel reappeared, informing him it is safe for us to return to Galilee as Herod the Great has died. The news brings such joy to our family, but we are in no hurry. There is still much to be done in the land of Black Earth. Yet, as I sit in the courtyards of the village and watch the camel trains pass, I remember sprawling with Martha in the fig grove west of *Nazara*, nestled in the lap of the biggest tree, sucking joyously on a fig, and gazing upon a great line of camels on way to Joppa. It was in *Tammuz*, the fourth month, when the first figs come to ripen, the vintage season coming fast, and the heat was oppressive. So young was I, yet the sight of those undulating, nigh-graceless but impressive animals fired my soul. How could a human successfully ride atop such a beast? But there is, after all, a noble elegance in this animal; God does within it shine. And since in Egypt, many times I have ridden upon them. An art in itself, especially at full gallop, it is another test of initiation, for one must dispel all fear to successfully ride the dromedary.

While I yearn to return to Galilee, the wonders of my time in the land of Black Earth never cease. Of late, in the evenings I have been hearing the stories of my family lineage, how, like Moses, I am born of two royal houses, of the Hebrew and of the Egyptian. Thoth has intimated this, as I was Pharaoh Akhenaten, and now my family confirms the blood of the Egyptian flows through my veins directly from his royal house. My heart soars hearing these tales, for while Akhenaten ruled not long, his mission was a noble one, a just one, and demonstrated, no matter the trials he faced, that he single-heartedly was devoted to the One God. Originally named Amenhotep IV, he eventually chose the number five as his number, changing his name to Akhenaten in the fifth year of his reign, and most of his five-fold titulary along with it. His beautiful Queen Nefertiti you already know; through the joining of this Egyptian family with that of Bithiah's Hebrew lover of the House of Joseph, my soul incarnated as Moses. In future it will be said Akhenaten sought to discredit and destroy the lunar deities which preceded his reign, yet to you I today reveal this not to be so. Like Moses, I, as Akhenaten, was schooled at Heliopolis and deeply understood and respected the balanced lunar-solar aspect of the Divine. My courtiers at that time were permitted to retain their lunar names after I changed mine to Akhenaten, whose meaning was *living spirit of Aten*, the disc of the sun. And the artist responsible for the exquisite portraiture in my family's tomb and the spectacular bust of Nefertiti found in his workshop was Thutmuse, child of Thoth.

Each morn upon awakening, with great joy I sing the psalms of Akhenaten and the psalms of David, fusing their different styles upon the harp into one harmonious key of life, my praises to God finding therein clarity, unity, Love Pure, any perceived separation melting away like the dewy morning mists over a verdant glade.

For there is even more. I promised myself not to cumber you, dearly beloveds, with excessive names. But for this, my story, your own story, to be properly told, I must also share a pure, simple truth. Amongst my dear *Savta* Anna's previous lives she was once Hannah; my lovely Phoebe is thus named in her honor. In this life, Hannah birthed a daughter named Aurianna. And Aurianna's granddaughter was Hismariam. The soul of Hismariam was old indeed, for long before, in ancient Lemuria she had been a high Initiate and graduate of its Mystery School. Yet of equal importance to my story, and yours, is that she later incarnated once more as Tiye. Tiye was the daughter of Joseph, the Israelite sold into slavery in Egypt, the very same Joseph for whom the aforementioned House of Joseph is named.

Your pulse quickens as you read these words, for in your heart you know what comes. Tiye married Amenhotep III, thereby becoming Queen of Egypt, and their son was Amenhotep IV…Akhenaten. Though as a woman she is not praised or given recognition and her true identity is concealed in your Bible, it was Tiye's mission to inform her son of the One True God, and to further merge the bloodlines.

So it was that I, as Akhenaten, was imbued with the Truth of the One God and was eventually named the *Heretic King*.

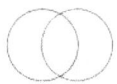

"Do you know who I am, young Yeshu'a?"

The high priest wears his red robes with such humble distinction, his gaze of kindness like the dawning sun gently awakening the sacred dew. Upon the index finger of his left hand shines his ring of lapis lazuli, a lapis Heart-pendant at rest upon his chest.

"You are the High Priest of the Temple of On," answer I, knowing this is not a reply sufficient.

He smiles quietly, his countenance barely creasing. "Indeed. Yet you still do not have knowledge of my name."

Thinking for a moment, I realize what it is about this fine holy man that has been the only distance between us. "It is as if there is a veil between us. I am not accustomed to this. You teach me, you are become my friend in the teaching, I feel your great heart nestle with mine. Yet from the day of my first initiation, I sense I both know you and know nothing of you. This perplexes me," say I, searching deeply his eyes for some bit of knowledge."

Chuckling softly, the priest now leads me through the halls into his private chambers. Silently he closes the door, and then ushers me to sit on a mat before his own, slightly larger, as he walks around me and seats himself. On the wall behind him, brilliantly etched in blazing gold upon a slab of emerald, is the

Merkaba shining in radiant colors. Always I am filled with Love and wonder when upon it I gaze: the star tetrahedron, the Ascension vehicle within which we, as star seeds, reside.

He puts his hands together before his breast, closing his eyes, I seeing the blue sparks fly and the white cocoon surround him. Moments of silence pass before his eyes again open. Now he looks at me anew. "Yeshu'a, I am Manetho," says he with calm gravity.

My heart jumps. Philo introduced me to the story of Manetho when he spoke of Moses, and since in Heliopolis I have studied his great works. But Manetho lived in the days of the very first Ptolemies, some three centuries in the past.

"They call me the great chronicler of Egypt, and once high priest of this very temple; Philo has already told you of me, that I lived in ages long past."

"It is as my Grandmother Anna, who has lived for centuries; she has mastered the art of cellular regeneration," I proclaim with some pride.

"Indeed, young one. It was I who trained her. I have just now placed a protective shield of silence over this room so none can hear, for my identity must remain hidden. It is our covenant that you will carry in your breast, never to reveal. My Atlantean name I have allowed to ebb into the chasm of time, for it would reveal far more if the world knew it, but you, dear Yeshu'a, will understand when I tell you, in today's Egyptian tongue, that it was *Beloved of Thoth.*"

My entire being floods with light. Suddenly all makes sense, and I am transported to a time long, long ago, to a beautiful land. A glorious, shimmering ziggurat temple towers before me into the sky, of gold, ivory, and jade. Festooned with spectacular figurines and lintels and friezes, with impressive colonnades atop stairways of gold, my attention is brought to the main entrance. In the air mingle the scents of jasmine, myrrh, and acacia flowers. And two young men emerge, filled with light: Thoth and Manetho.

An ingenious spherical flying machine now hovers overhead and then passes down through a valley golden with barley grain, groves of date palm on either side. There is a mighty city, without walls, unlike Jerusalem, and the people are joyous in their play and work. Looking back at the ziggurat, Manetho and Thoth are descending the stairs of gold, walking toward me.

Manetho's voice harkens me back to Heliopolis. "Yes, Yeshu'a, you have seen. This was our land of Atlantis, in the golden age. So, in truth, in this body I have lived thousands of years, while Thoth has chosen the upper dimensions, traveling back and forth at God's will to do His work. You understand, young one, that you must keep this knowledge to yourself; never speak of it aloud, even with your family. Your loving parents of course know of this, but it is best kept unspoken."

With gravity, I nod.

He asks, "Tell me, how long have you seen people's blue flames and the white shell surrounding them?"

At once I am startled but then realize that, of course, he knows; my heart has already reached out to him seeking this knowledge. "Master, for some time here in Egypt I have come to see the sparks of blue dancing around many of those in my life, including myself, and the wondrous cocoon of light surrounding us. I have wished to understand what this is. And in my heart I thought of you. When I was a little child in Galilee, in some manner I understood it natural. Now I wish to know its deeper meaning. Around you I see these things...Once, when to my Initiate-brothers I mentioned I was observing them around us, like a chimera the wonders disappeared."

Manetho the Ageless One looks most serious. "Silence is important. Bringing attention to the three lights, the aura, can extinguish the sight."

Yet more puzzled, I ask, "Is this part of the beliefs of our religion?"

"We do not use those words," he almost snaps, a momentary frown passing over his face. "These are not beliefs, beloved one. And we are not a religion. Here, we know and speak and transmit Truth. The Great White Brother-Sisterhood of Light is the keeper of Truth: the Truth of Love. Beliefs, religion, neither made nor change for the better the world. It is my sadness that religion is become a veil, like an iron-barred door, between women and men and their immortal souls...Yet all happens precisely as it should, just as the Eternal One has planned. Outside cries the rabble of the ignorant. The powers of the lower realms of the Universe, both female and male, have done their damage; much from this is learned. Now humanity begins its long trek back to Truth. But the male powers of the world will hold sway for yet some time, and make it very difficult; much suffering there will be. Patriarchy's two main contributions to the world will be war and the fear of God."

Fondling his lapis pendant, and gazing upon me like I be the teacher, a curious smile lights Manetho's visage. "Man is still in his infancy, though nigh-endless ages it has been thus. ... All is for the good. I will first tell you, son of Joseph, an eternal Truth which you yourself bring to my mind. You use the word cocoon: you have seen a cocoon of light around many loving souls. The Brother-Sisterhood of Light has knowledge of the Egg of Cosmic Peace, the egg supreme of white Light; our Divine Mother bestows this upon us, our birthright. There is a place, beyond space and time, of pure peace, where we all as souls reside. And as Adepts, Initiates, or so-called advanced beings, to bring peace here, while we live on this Earth, we act as a Light-bridge to influence events and peoples for the good. Thus we are taught to weave an enormous cocoon of Love around those souls and groups and places in need. An invincible bulwark against war, aggression, hatred, all manner of ignorance, the cocoon of Love is responsible for all good which comes to pass in this world. In the realms of Light it is named the Egg of Cosmic Peace, and dear to the Essenes it is, for they are the youngest chapter of the Great White Brother-Sisterhood. It is the hope of the new world, yet-to-be born two thousand years hence. This is the Age of the Holy Spirit, when the Bride will enter the Bridal Chamber, when female and male will in absolute unity live in all the dimensions of the Universe...

True of all branches of the Brother-Sisterhood, the Essenes have twenty-two initiations. This number in Sacred Geometry represents the squaring of the circle, the circling of the square, the circle being the female, the Fruit of Life, the square the male. As the Age of the Holy Spirit arrives in time, the full meaning of this will make itself clear to all...It is the reunion, the reconciliation of opposites, essential to the Ascension process, on planetary and galactic scales, and to our own human Ascension into higher dimensions of Light...There are twenty-two paths of the Tree of Life, and twenty-two letters in the Nazorean alphabet.."

Rising serenely from his mat, Manetho signs to follow him back into the corridors. We pass many doorways still unknown to me, and finally he stops and opens a door into a small, square chamber. Through a thin vent in the ceiling a soft flow of daylight streams through, and on the floor, placed equidistantly along the base of the walls, are earthenware oil lamps. Two of the walls are painted black, the other two white. While explaining that the chamber is reserved for the discernment of medical problems among the Brother-Sisterhood in Heliopolis and that there is a similar accommodation in each of the Mystery Schools, Manetho steps out of his high priest red robes and reveals a linen white one beneath, such as the Essenes wear in their communities.

"You will understand that what I reveal to you here today you in truth already know. You have had glimpses of it. You show me scenes of your healings where you have seen the energy patterns of those you have helped to heal themselves... There is one of a young woman, fallen from horseback, who had broken her arm."

I nod enthusiastically, eager to learn more. Though my life-memory is profound, my understanding of my early healings is through a child's eye, uncomprehending.

"You must look with desireless eyes, Yeshu'a. This is the only way to see truly. And one must never look with eyes wide. When you observed the blue sparks and the cocoon of soft light around you and your Brothers and then mentioned it, you said the effect disappeared. This is why. The only way of *knowing* is to let go of knowing through the mind. Seeking to define something, to our detriment a quest we humans are often on, usually slays it. This is most important. True Faith is the act of giving up knowing; God can then enter through your true One Eye. Lack of Faith ruins everything.

He gazes upon me with grave blue eyes. "I need not tell you the responsibility you hold with this knowledge. A strong covenant with God is necessary to be able to read people: their bodies, their thoughts, their illnesses, their hopes, their fears and disappointments. This you already know. But it bears repeating. One must never walk amidst humanity utilizing these skills, for they are for caring alone...Yet, so as to cause suffering, to remain mired in the illusion of sinfulness, they are used by those of the darker forces, nigh-ever more vigilant than are the forces of Light in their righteous quest to set the world free.

"Your fellow brothers and sisters of Light make healing a better part of their work. As a healer, you are a distinctly different human being with each person you assist; this is a part of the code you subconsciously, intuitively inherit. You give them precisely what they ask of you, what they need, even if at times it is a bitter emotional pill. To correctly read the aura, you will exercise daily your heart's eye; look only with Love, never with judgment, obstinacy, the mind. Looking with the heart's eye, each finds his own authentic way to see beyond the veil of appearances. Aware am I that your loved-ones also tell you this: think with your heart, only your heart. Never test what you observe; do not subject it to definitions; seek only to understand and truly love it as an extension of yourself. Living a good, moral life requires this. Stubbornness, judgment, creating the illusion of sinfulness erects walls nigh-impossible to surmount. And remember: on your own, you have no power; only by ceding authority to the Force of the All, by giving up your self power, do you have any power at all. There will be those who seek proofs, to find signs of your missions, your so-called gifts; by your humility and for your protection, they will find nothing, even if they stroll through Akasha. Only with true Faith does one find. Others will devise tests designed for you to fail, as you are with God. Heed them not, for they know not what they do. With eyes enough to see, ears enough to hear, and heart enough to Love, anyone can find Truth."

Pulling back a sleeve of his robe to the elbow, Manetho now raises his arm toward one of the white walls. "Neutral colors in a room can be helpful, Yeshu'a, white or black is not that important, but they can make your task easier."

He now spreads his fingers. "Now, most importantly, look not directly at my hand; if you focus on my hand, you will not see the aura. Look far beyond it, so that my hand is but a blurry image. In truth, look at it without seeing it; become absolutely rapt by the hazy image. Try it for a few instants and stop for a moment. Then try it again. One must stop the tempting urge to focus on the hand, the fingers, at all."

I do as I am bid and observe a tiny halo around the master's hand.

"Now try it with your own hand," he counsels. "Remember to never look with wide open eyes; in this manner you will see nothing. At the outset squinting may be helpful; this reduces the possibilities of confusion, of seeing dark and light aspects."

Manetho next picks up one of the lanterns, holds it high above his head, and instructs me to stand beneath it. "Close tight your eyes, Yeshu'a, and slowly raise your face into the light…making certain you keep your eyes shut. Be at ease, and with your eyes closed, attempt to look beyond the light you perceive, focus on the bridge of your nose, or just beyond it; you should see a yellowish white haze of light. Now, slowly bring your head back down to its normal position and tell me what you see."

Lo, I find a wondrous sight of the colors of the rainbow raining before me; I am filled with a feeling of wondrous peace. "Dear Manetho, it is as if I see all the hues of the Universe!"

Suddenly I gasp in astonished joy. "Now I espy waves of blue light and a sphere of deep cobalt blue within them, directly at the center of my vision!"

"Indeed. We call this the Veil of Isis. One day you will be able to jump into it, it will grow so large. This is the one eye, Yeshu'a. With the modest repetition of this exercise, you will be able to distinguish the three separate lights which make up the aura. The pineal gland works together with what will one day be named the pituitary gland to create this vision. Do not overdo this exercise; it is merely training for your overall inner vision, for the Veil of Isis is but a reflection of the true Light. And always, when you are doing these exercises or are observing someone's aura, be certain you are at peace, filled with peace and inner silence. Only by joyously walking the path of your divinity, your self-transformation, will you be able to help others help themselves. Eventually you will be able to see the whole spectrum of colors."

Manetho then explains to me his understanding of the three lights, as it confuses me. His face becoming ever brighter in the telling, he describes how humanity was built from not just clay but from the four elements: fire, gas, water, and clay, and the ether present in each of the other four. "Everywhere the Brother-Sisterhood is, much water nearby will also be found. You observe this in the rites you perform with your family involved with your daily ablutions. This is most sacred. It cleanses your physical and emotional, mental and etheric bodies of residues. Such is the reason for the baptism of water, to clean the Spirit within. In the spiral of life of the Universe, life became these four elements, with ether present in each. Thus, we have a body of water, another of fire, another of clay or earth, another of gas, and, in truth, still more. Being still so limited by our puny human understanding, we can detect seven, and they form couples to engage together in unions. So there are three wedded bodies, hence three lights: a physical, emotional, and mental body and light...Together their lights form the true aura, which extends outward some three cubits from the body. Many non-initiated people believe they see the aura but are only viewing the first light which follows the contours of the body and radiates outward only slightly beyond the skin. It is the sight of the three together which forms the true aura, or the radiance, as the Brother-Sisterhood also calls it. Being already so skilled, Yeshu'a, it will still take much time and practice to perceive all the colors and be able to accurately identify what ails someone; the emotional body's light will yield clues to physical maladies as they are always linked, even with injuries caused by accidents."

Recalling that he first mentioned seven bodies, I query, "But Master, you cited there are seven bodies which we can perceive, and that they form couples; pray tell me: what is the seventh?"

Manetho's countenance beams. Around his head glows a shimmering halo of brilliant light and hundreds of blue-sparked flames shoot outward. "Glad I am you have asked this. It demonstrates how adept you are. Nothing escapes you, young one. As my heart has just filled with even more joy upon hearing your question, the energy has traveled through the crown of my head and you may see a light streaming from it like a crown and the blue flames."

"Indeed I do."

"The aura is like an egg-shaped cocoon, and most often its brightest aspect will be seen around the head. Of Divine, cosmic origin, the nature of the sparks is as a crest of flame emanating from our fire within. This is the revealed design of one in possession of higher Truth, the mark of the utmost human consciousness: the supra-consciousness. Ever it is changing; never has a soul had it constantly agleam, so trust in me: in humility I speak of myself. ...Herein is the residence of God within each and every one of us. Now I will reveal the great secret: It is called the Jewel of Sheba. Like a crown of one hundred and forty-four thousand diamonds, the Jewel of Sheba is the seventh body, and includes all the others. It is also named the One Hundred Forty Four Thousand Unity Diamond."

My heart leaps and sings a jubilant song upon hearing Sheba's name, the name of my beloved in times of old, when I walked the Earth as Solomon. A mighty veil is slowly lifting, sparks flying in my own head of what it all means, a dark corner of my soul coming alive with fiery light. Surely, say I to myself, like the Tree of Life itself, there is a reason for this deep sense of connection.

"Yes, son of Joseph, I know well your heart flutters. On this day I have opened the door for you so that you may walk through. Itching you are to hear more. And oblige I will, but there will be even more. When you as Solomon joined with Makeda, the Queen of Sheba, joined with her in body and mind and Spirit, all was revealed in a flash of nigh-blinding light, like lightning it was; she is your twin flame. A great sigh of serenity came forth from God, an exhalation of glory which permeated the cosmos, for, as one, you held the key to the heavens. Yet it was truly Sheba all along who held the key; she only awaited your discovery of her so you could place the key in the lock of her door, the Sacred Gateway, and open it...She was the imperishable link to Lemuria, and to Atlantis, through a long line of priestesses and priests.

"Beloved, as dear Thoth has related to you, Lemuria was the great Motherland of this world. What he left for me to describe to you is the heartbreaking story of its destruction. While many Lemurians escaped the demise of their beloved continent and are now forming their fifth dimensional paradise centered around Mount Shasta, in truth, when Lemuria vanished, it occurred so quickly that many, many millions of people perished in a horrific overnight cataclysm. This event is retained collectively and individually in our cellular memory, and it still will be two thousand years hence, when the Aquarian Age begins with the advent of the new cosmic cycle. The loss of our Motherland, wherefrom we were born, in such a horrifying fashion, was devastating. From this our collective sense of guilt was born...We lost so much...

"Makeda, Sheba, is the link to the Love, peace, knowledge, wisdom, unity with God of which Lemuria was the possessor.

In truth, it was the Lemurians who taught us Atlanteans. There was, near the end, a struggle between us, as certain Atlanteans had become corrupt; seeing their own reflection, they wanted to control and subjugate the powers that were bringing war and fear and ignorance into the world. Lemuria was much the wiser; it counseled the allowance of their evolution while ensuring the protection and safety of the peoples of the world and their wisdom.

"Thus Makeda's importance is clear. The Jewel of Sheba is the number four, the base of the pyramid which thrusts itself toward the Eternal Single Light. Some say it is the capstone of the pyramid, but it is truly the base. Thus the reason why the ancients gave four letters to the reflections of the Divine names. And the one hundred and forty-four thousand facets, or diamonds, of the One is of high meaning. As well, when as a people the Lemurians achieve immortality by their mastery of fifth dimensional existence, they will possess twelve fully functional chakras, and within them twelve sub-chakras, for a total of one hundred and forty-four fully functional chakras."

The master now picks from his pocket a small crystal pyramid, gently turning it over in his hand. "Noble Adept of this school and Carmel, Pythagoras once wrote these words as a prayer: *Bless us, divine number, thou who generated gods and men! O holy, holy Tetractys, thou that containest the root and source of the eternally flowing creation! For the divine number begins with the profound, pure unity until it comes to the holy four; then it begets the mother of all, the all-comprising, all-bounding, the first-born, the never-swerving, the never-tiring holy ten, the keyholder of all.* For the Pythagorean oath, he also wrote, *By that pure, holy, four lettered name on high, nature's eternal fountain and supply, the parent of all souls that living be, by him, with faith find oath, I swear to thee.* And beloved Yeshu'a, the base of the Great Pyramid measures four hundred and forty cubits."

My head is spinning; somehow I understand these stories, deep within me, but still I yearn for more, as it will fill dark spots with Light as to the true meaning of my earthly mission. And as Manetho the Ageless One promised, he obliges.

"Your sacred stories tell you Sheba traveled to Jerusalem to meet Solomon, having heard of his wisdom, as if he were the one great power of the age. This is a typical ploy of male powers. In truth, although she later traveled to Jerusalem, you as Solomon first traveled to her great court in Aksum, as it was Sheba who was truly one of the great powers of all the ages—"

"—I am ready, O Great Master Manetho," I exclaim. "I know what comes, for you have already told me."

His left eyebrow arches in astonishment. "Indeed, young one? Tell me."

"You are to take me there, this very moment, so that I may live it once more."

"Hah! You are right, son of Joseph. You are to relive this memory, in time, so that it serves the future of the world. We will enter a deep meditation and travel through the watery cycle of time so that you and Makeda can again meet. But beware, young one! Here, you will be a man, with all of the abilities and thoughts and emotions of a man. You will be *Solomon*. As it was then, I will be your counselor; nothing will change, save when you return, you will recall every breath, every scent, every sight, sound, word, and feeling. And more you will realize..."

"Let us go, then. I hunger."

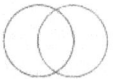

We sit together in the first chamber of the Sepulchre, Manetho and I, he humming an om tone. For many moments it is thus, we holding holds, eyes shut, the power of the Father piercing through the conical ceiling into our temples, Mother Earth churning below us a mighty brew. Then precious silence is obtained within us both, the room dissolves, and powerful eddies of water fall before us like glittering waterfalls. While my mind is disengaging, my very last thought is to wonder of the difference between Thoth's mode of interdimensional travel and the Ageless One's water vehicle. Praises to you, God. In Thee I always trust. In Thy hand we are sure and safe and strong. Ever grateful I am for Your sweet touch, for this great gift of life.

"What must my Father think of me as I near Aksum?" I ask Manethos, ever by my side: trusted guide, revered Heart-mind of the Mystery Schools, valued friend and counselor. "Though he withers and grows cold and women are brought to him in attempts to warm once more his loins, he is yet my Father; he knows. Still he sings and writes and weaves colorful tales and speaks the Merkaba rhymes."

"Do you not remember, Sun-Moon, that it was he whose tired eyes filled with bluish white light when you told of your journey to honor Makeda, Queen of Aksum, soon of Sheba?"

"Yes, yes, I do. And Zadok, highest of high priests, spoke also of my Father's joy. Yet I am but nothing to these giants of men. Asked I have for wisdom, and received it, the animals hear my voice and obey my commands; magical be my world. But there is a fire in Jerusalem which can set aflame all Israel in ruinous hatred of any king who so openly courts other powers in the world. Especially that of a queen."

Upon my finger I kiss my Merkaba seal, my dear Father's sign. Ever now it is with me, as he has given it me in blessing.

We have no chests of treasures to bestow, no train of soldiers marches alongside us, no regalia shines, for we have traveled upon the Chariot of Light, and arrived near Aksum in but a few short moments. I carry pearls and lovely wildflower blossoms picked this morn near my beloved Mount Olivet. And before I left the palace, Father placed one diamond in my hand, his eyes agleam with a silent message to bestow it upon Makeda as our people's personal gift. I am as yet a king rich in but subtle ways, humble in my nature, though some already ascribe dozens of wives to my conquering.

Ruth, my young dove, is now returned to my shoulder. She flutters her sweet wings and speaks into mine ear. "Soon it comes, Sun-Moon, just over the next hill. A mighty city it is... streets lined in gold and ruby, jade and ivory. She awaits you, Sun-Moon."

She makes me laugh, and Manethos, too, has heard and chortles like a glad hen.

"Certainly, for it was her voice which brought me. In my slumber she whispers to me. Are there soldiers?"

"There are warriors, impressive Nubian-style warriors. Their hearts and spears are at peace."

"Gracious praises to you, Ruth."

Says the Ageless One, "It is as we knew it would be."

"Yes, Manethos. My heart is gladdened and full. It is ever so, for my heart desires nothing; my heart *is*. This morn, as I walked through the necropolis, passing Abram's cave with joy, it was so; and gazing upon the lemon tree groves, their branches dancing blithely in the wind, then later on Mount Zion, looking out over the multitudes, it was also so; when we rose in the Chariot of Light, and as we now walk in freedom, it is ever so: today everywhere I envision grapes, coming from naught, coming from the air itself. I reach out my hand and they appear because I know they are there. Into my mouth I have put them and tasted fully their sweet nectar. This is what it is to be with God: to know He breathes in and around us every instant...If we can but see truly. Today joy is my wife. Would you have some?"

"Why, yes. I am parched."

"So it is." Looking into the bleeding azure Kushian sky, I silently ask for a ripe cluster, then raise my hand palm upward to receive, and dripping wet, red grapes come into it. I am pleased to quench my dear friend's thirst.

We reach the crest of the hill and a radiant, splendid city rises before us. Luscious scents entice my heart: of blooms and perfumes and verdant glades, of spices and fruits unknown to me, but also of animals wild. Kush is indeed rich in flavor and trade and peoples. Unlike my beloved Jerusalem which shines golden at sunrise and sunset, the gates to the city like iridescent little stars, the temples pulsing white hot in the baking sun, Aksum beats like a cache of rubies. All manner of folk walk the streets. And Ruth spoke truly: many are lined and inlaid with gems and ivory. Marvelous towering stelae grace like friendly giants the northern end of the city; my soul's eye travels and reads upon them inscriptions and glyphs telling of the creation of the world. Domed, circular, and steepled buildings of russet adobe and ebony line the avenues, the colors of the city bursting into mine eyes. Through the archways, richly robed women walk as goddesses, the hues of their clothing vivid and lush. And caravans carry goods west and east to feed the world. No barbarians are these Ethiopes, Kush, or Persians, no matter what my and the Great Northland people would have us believe. Aksum is well-ordered, its art beautiful, its ways cosmopolitan, impressive, exotic.

To the east, atop a great mound, stands the palace, with porticoes and colonnades of jade. A long stairway of gold beckons with troops on either side. Statues of the deities of the world stand upon balustrades of ivory. The soldiers' shields are bordered with furs, their helmets set with feathers. A captain of the guard approaches us.

"King Sun-Moon of Jerusalem comes to honor your queen. Praise God," intones Manethos, standing tall and firm. And there is no question. The captain bows to us and, with wily brow and a ceremonious sweep of his arm, indicates the ivory-inlaid double-door at the top of the stairs.

After passing through many chambers we are beseeched to sit and rest and drink before having the queen's audience. Leafy palm branches sit in tall ceramic urns, flowers as well on the wide sills, a breeze intoxicates with the aroma of sweet honey oil. I quiet my soul's eye from wandering the halls, peeking with my curiosity.

Finally we are led into the Throne Room. Passing through long lines of regalia thick with men and women alike, animal hides on the floor, a captivating musical air of string and flute and drum sounds in a far off corner. Still there is no sight of the queen. Now the animal carpet ceases and cobalt marble-tile gleams like a pool of innumerable stars. White columns stand before us, and fully one hundred and more men and women part like the sea.

Upon a dais of golden, yellow, green, and azure aventurine, and amethyst, lapis, and red crystal, a living goddess reclines like ripe fruit on a long divan covered in cushions. Closely flanked by two full-grown lions, one male, the other female, she leans her upper body against the lioness, her left hand stroking her mighty golden-white chest. The head of the lioness is turned toward the queen's in silent communication. The male, just as close in the curve of the small of her back, looks directly at me, his mane a crown of glory. His golden-eyed gaze pierces knowingly into mine.

The queen's face is lush mahogany gold, light and dark all in one. Angular, sleek perfection it is, with sharply sculpted cheeks, luxuriant rose petal lips, tall shafts of gleaming teeth, her nose straight, long, and thin. Violet in hue, absolutely elliptical, her eyes are both kind and knowing, and penetrate instantly my soul. Hair of silken ebon reaches her slender waist. Armlets and bracelets of gold adorn her arms, rings are on many of her fingers, all with symbols. She wears not a crown but a golden headdress complete with a spray of white feathers, as if they bloom from her temple. Wearing a patterned amethystine colored skirt, she is topless, save a long-hanging necklace of gold and jade which covers small bits of breast…A voluptuary, yes, but one who knows herself and what Love is and plays not games, whose every breath is dedicated to Wisdom, Truth, Beauty, Love: the Sacred Marriage. Her intelligence is clear.

My heart beats like a mad drum. There is an instant spark of recognition between us; we have somehow before met…It is as if I look at myself.

In her right hand she holds a golden mask, but has not put it to her face. Her breath is deep, calm, and measured as she inspects my form. It is for me to speak.

"Great praises to thee, O Mighty Queen Makeda. From Jerusalem I have come to honor thee with my presence and humble gifts, for Aksum is renowned in the world as a land of honor, knowledge, and beauty, a keeper of ancient Truth. Plenty are your soldiers, but thou make not war as a habit. I am humbled by this. I have come without escort save my guide, Manethos, to demonstrate my trust, and seek alliance between our peoples."

She purrs softly and gladly smiles, nodding to Manethos in turn. Yet her voice is both commanding and uniquely feminine. Fooled she is not by illusion. "Sun-Moon, I have heard thy name in the wind, in the sands of time. Tamrin, the chief of my trade caravans, speaks of thee with admiration. Even thy white dove, Ruth, tells me of thee. Thou hast captured my attention; it is said thou art wisdom itself. Wide and far I have searched for thee." Signing to me to walk up the four steps onto the dais, she offers me her hand, which I place to my heart and then to my temple.

There is a raging secret between us. The room is thick with it, and I sense there is no need to conceal it. Already we make Love; my palms sweat, my heart pounds, my loins ache with fire.

"Wisdom and understanding also spring from thee thyself, my queen," say I.

She remarks, "Melodious is thy voice and most gracious is thy manner."

From my pocket I produce my humble fresh wildflowers; each bears a different color. Touching them lightly at the blooms, they stand erect once more, and the queen's eyes open. "Upon the beautiful queen who desires naught I bestow these perfect gems, plucked this morn by my hand, in my homeland on the Mount of Olives, a most lovely and sacred place of my people."

Makeda's moist lips part in wonder. "This morn?" She asks, aghast.

"And from mine own treasury, I give these giant pearls. Though they cannot match thy beauty, they will reflect it each time you gaze upon them."

Her deep violet eyes swim with Love.

"From my people, come straight from my dear Father's hands, I gift to thee and thy peoples this hearty diamond…May it symbolize our unity, the connection of all peoples with God, our Source, the Creator without and within each of us: the Great Central Sun of the Universe."

Makeda bolts upright hearing these words, searches my countenance, and then grins serenely. She expected this gift, but not the words.

Silently she tells me she is twenty-two years of age, though I commune with a truly ancient, awakened soul, whose wisdom matches mine, whose knowledge far exceeds her physical years.

"Though thy manner and form greatly please me, thy face somehow familiar, my ministers, my priests, and my seers have asked I devise a series of tests. The tales I have heard of thee are hard to fathom, in truth…" she leans into my ear and whispers, "…I have no doubts, beloved, of anything but the Good of God in thee." Her skin is like silk touching mine, the sweet scent of rose honey oil wafts into my nose. "If you can answer rightly but some of my questions, rightly solve the riddles, I will perforce be pleased, my ministers satisfied. And we may enact agreements of trade."

I bow before this tower of matriarchy, this Goddess-on-Earth, this beguiling mirror of myself.

Pursing her rose petal lips, she brings a thoughtful finger to her chin. "What is it? An enclosure with ten doors; when one is open, nine are shut; when nine are open, one is shut?"

"The enclosure is the womb, and the ten doors are the orifices of man, namely his eyes, his ears, his nostrils, his mouth, the apertures for discharge of excreta and urine, and the naval. When the child is still in the Mother's womb, the naval is open, but all the other apertures are shut, but when the child issues from the womb, the naval is closed and the other orifices open."

"That is correct!" Makeda exclaims, surprised. "Seven leave and nine enter, two pour out the draught, and only one drinks. What are they?"

"Seven are the days of woman's menstruation, nine the months of her pregnancy. Her two breasts feed the child, and one drinks."

Makeda arches a brow at my correct response, and murmurs from her advisors ensue behind me. Many questions she asks, and each I answer well and true. And with each the queen becomes more sure, softer her appearance becomes, more our hearts merge.

"It is many-headed. In a storm at sea it goes above us all, it raises a loud and bitter wailing and moaning; it bends its head like a reed, is the glory of the rich and the shame of the poor; it honors the dead and dishonors the living; it is a delight to the birds, but a sorrow to the fishes. What is it?"

"Flax," I reply. "For it makes sails for ships that moan in the storm. It provides fine linen for the rich and rags for the poor, a burial shroud for the dead, and a rope for hanging the living. As seed it nourishes the birds, and as a net traps the fish."

Leaning forward with increased anticipation, she asks, "What is the ugliest thing in the world, and what is the most beautiful? What is the most certain, and what is the most uncertain?"

"The ugliest thing would be the faithful turning unfaithful, and the most beautiful the repentant sinner. The most certain is death. One would say the most uncertain is one's share in the world to come...But I say God is Love and Love is God. God permeates all matter in the Universe, thus we are universally, equally loved."

Those behind me who have heard are astonished, and many start speaking themselves of the very nature of God, while Makeda reclines once more, her bosom heaving in rapture.

"My beloved queen, thy lips are like a thread of scarlet, and thy speech is comely; thy temples are like a piece of a pomegranate within thy locks. Yet thine eyes are the glory of all, for they speaketh the sonnets of Love to mine ears. Truly thy breasts are the grapes of a succulent vineyard, thy lips in form the buds of roses. On this day, as I awoke, during my early morning strolls, and even as we walked into your great city, everywhere I see grapes. Knowing God is always there, I stretch out my hand to receive and they appear: rich, moist, ruby red grapes. I of this moment know why. It was thee in my heart. My heart, my soul has always known thee, as thou art my reflection, and today it was the coming of thy tide, and my heart knew. Would thou allow it of me, to gift thee the grapes of God? For they are everywhere because of thee."

The court is silent, but the pulse quickens. Lovemaking has been performed in front of all. And yet the queen does not blush. Her eyes of violet beat like a bird's, her breast is full and taut, her shoulders soft and desiring.

"O how greatly have pleased me thy answering, and the sweetness of thy voice, and the beauty of thy going, and the graciousness of thy words. Thy voice maketh the heart to rejoice, and giveth goodwill to the lips, and strength to the gait. I look upon thee and see thy wisdom is inexhaustible, that it is a lamp in the darkness, a pomegranate in the garden, a pearl in the sea...Like the Morning Star among the stars, and like the light of the moon in the mist, like a glorious dawn and sunrise in the heavens. For it is Love thou maketh with me. Thy grapes of God be welcome."

"All thou hast said I say of thee." I raise my right hand to the heavens, slowly opening my palm, and ask silently, graciously, with great praise in my innermost heart to God for the discovery of this fine day. And I see dripping grapes everywhere around me, of a divine vineyard, made from the very essence of our Lord. A gorgeous plump cluster falls into my hand, just ripened, clear morning dew streaming like tears of joy over each and every grape. Placing my lips against them thrice, I offer them to the most beautiful woman in the world. And the court erupts in plaudits, Makeda standing tall to receive. Then she chooses a grape I have touched with my lips and places it into her mouth.

Her eyes close in rapture.

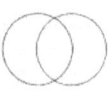

W<sub></sub>e walk alone through the rooms of the palace, waiting for the night-silence to begin. Each word spoken, every soft touch has been the same. Loving, with a great fire.

"I had many more tests for thee, Sun-Moon."

As through a labyrinth we walk, so alike is each hall, so similar each bend and doorway. Only she holds the golden thread.

"Here," she gestures with her hand, "is a chamber filled with flowers, hundreds of many-colored blooms, only one of which is real. The rest are fabricated by our very best artists. Can you tell me, beloved, which is the real one?"

Strolling through the room, I send bits of soul out the window in search of a bee. This will make my task much the easier. Indeed yes, a bee is near. I call to him and open the window. Buzzing, he enters the chamber, looking at me, and hears my question. It takes a bee but an instant to find that which is his Love nectar, and he flies over to a corner and drops upon the one true flower.

The oil lamps have dimmed, her handmaidens have retired, her private rooms are empty. As we walk into her bedchamber, a hundred and more candles agleam, no words are spoken. She rips a gossamer curtain surrounding her bed to the floor, sits upon the bed gazing at me, taking from her neck the gold and jade, and spreads her legs.

O sweet glory, to behold such a sight. A vulva so rich like rose petals, her legs aching to be tenderly touched, her breasts the true ripe cluster of divine grapes, I approach her in loving measure, placing my lips softly to hers, allowing my manhood to trace across her legs. Removing my tunic, she spreads her legs wider still.

The Sacred Marriage is begun. And through us all the world makes Love.

My gaze never leaving hers, our raging hearts aflame, relentlessly merging into one, our twin-souls transforming into the One Spirit, when as one we climax, our chamber of Love fills with limitless, perfectly white light. Like a burst of lightning it is, from within and without, from Heaven itself. It fills the world. The sky, the courtyards below, the distant hills: all are lit with perfection. Yet blinding it is not. It is the sheer opposite, as in this moment all is known, all is seen, all is revealed. All is loved.

The Sun shines at midnight.

In the morning, she wakens like a faun, with eyes soft and full of knowledge. "I know now, beloved. I know all."

I nod. "Pray then, speak."

"We are past and present and future met all in one. I know thou were Inanna, the great Goddess, and I was Dumuzi. Of this I am sure, for every moment is etched within me. But there is more, much more. I have known before thy coming that thou art my twin flame, the fire which is never fed save by God's Love. Our union was the birth of time. As last night we reached simultaneous peak, I saw all."

"As did I."

"But in my dreams the angels came and told our story. Inanna and Dumuzi is most recent, is it not? Yet I have always had complete knowledge of all my days, and we were always one. Now I will share with thee, for beyond this life we will meet again, to save the world."

"My people will change our story, it is sure," I offer, knowing it to be true.

"Yes, this will come to pass. But it matters not, beloved. Ever they will paint false-pictures of me; such is the way with men of power. It matters not. In the ancient days of Lemuria I was a high priestess who saw the coming demise of our land; thou, too, my love, were there, as my king, my lover, my brother. ...Because of us, enough of Lemuria survived. But mistakes were made."

"I also have memory of this, though not as clear."

"In this life I am a commingling of the black and the white; as a soul group from the beginning of time, my family chose this, for without me in this form you would not have appeared, and our peoples would not have the opportunity to reunite."

She clenches her jaw before she softens again and speaks the words. "At the dawn we were Atlanteans, of the same tribe. This was when we were in constant contact with the Eternal Creator; we drank water from the air, and air from the water, and our knowledge was pure, the Father's Flame smoldered in our breasts. The elements separated at this time, the mists cleared, and we began to frolic in the adoration of nature."

All at once, as my dearest tells our story, both of our hearts are so pure, a Light-door opens before us, above the foot of the bed, and the scenes she describes we see unfold. What great miracle is this that God allows us to understand so clearly!

"The star seeds of seven tribes were nourished in Atlantis. The fifth of these tribes was called the Sem; in truth, they instituted the laws which caused the changes of life on Earth. All white peoples on this dear planet come from this tribe, which will be known as the Semitic branch of humanity. It has been, and will continue to be, their mission to learn the aspects of Light and dark, what some call good and evil, and what you and I know to be dualism, separation, illusion. Led by men from another world and a portion of the Sem tribe under their influence, Atlantis lost its connection with God and caused a rift with Lemuria, the Motherland…Yet, the Atlantean civilization, its wisdom and sacred science, was so profound that we saved all the precious bits before our destruction, even sending our most enlightened priests and priestesses to Egypt as keepers of our invaluable knowledge…You and I, beloved, were there. While corruption had come into our peoples' blood, we saved the knowledge, six of the seven tribes fleeing to the northlands of ice, the other to Egypt…

"The people of Moses, dearest, are the sons and daughters of the seventh leader of the race of Sem. And those who are the Essenes in your land are the sons and daughters of eleven wise men who were high priests of the other six Atlantean tribes. They choose not to follow the descendants of the Sem tribe, but to devote themselves to being the protectors of the Sacred Flame of Truth."

In the Light-portal we have seen the Sphinx, the Great Pyramid, many activities, and now for an instant a white-robed man upon a hill clothed with people appears.

I am awestruck. My wisdom and understanding is doubled and trebled by the love of the Goddess Makeda. Searching now deep within me, I know every piece of her story is Truth; God has seen to this. Great praises to Thee, Eternal One.

"I will journey to Jerusalem, Sun-Moon, this is certain. And I will bear thee a son, who will be sure the reunion of humanity occurs...The time will come when your sacred Ark of the Covenant will must be moved, for thy people will grow more violent. The Truth is the Ark is far more ancient than most believe, much older than your people, and it holds the keys to Divine power: the nectar of the gods, manna, or prana, life-sustaining energy. Our son will see to its safe journey here, and it will be guarded safely by one family in vigil until the Age of Aquarius arrives, the next time Mother Earth shakes her spine. The Love and Light of God will pour forth once more into the world after a long period of great darkness. And the identity of a new Ark will also be fully revealed to the masses: the Mother of the one called...Yeshu'a..."

As she utters the name, instantly I know she speaks of me. Will my future Mother be the holy container of a New Covenant, and I be the food of God?

She jumps naked from bed like an eager child, her supple limbs moving like a well-tuned cat. From her cedar chest she removes the diamond I gifted her the night before. Eyeing it fondly as she climbs back into bed, she gently turns it over in her hand. "I am the number four, the Sacred Gateway to God, the base of the pyramid which propels itself toward the Eternal One Light. In your dear language, YHWH is a later rendering of the four letters given by the ancients to the reflections of the Divine names...As the Age of the Holy Spirit, the Aquarian Age, arrives at the beginning of the next cosmic cycle, one hundred and forty-four thousand will make their Ascension to the heavens; along with the future Lemurians, they will be the great saviors of humanity. In the sacred texts it is written, and it will be so; though in thine it will depict them all as thy people, they will come from all the families of humanity. Those who remain with Mother Earth will not create religions with sacred texts; and they, too, will have this knowledge…

"My sacred trust is to create in physical form a crown of one hundred and forty-four thousand diamonds, the essence of perfected Earth energy, at its very core in the Halls of *Amenti*. Each diamond will come from the families from which the one hundred and forty-four thousand are born. And thou hast given me yours, my precious. Dear grandmother began this trust, and now I near its completion. Without the one hundred and forty-four thousand souls, their Ascension, and my most modest crown of diamonds: humanity, the Earth, and all earthly life will not survive."

"Thou art blessed, sweet bird of mine. Our secret will remain in my breast."

# Chapter Seven
# Past, Present, Future

MY EDUCATION BEGINS ANEW. Filled with the fire of my encounter with Makeda, the glorious Queen of Sheba, I am now returned to the temple in Heliopolis with Manetho the Ageless One, the Time Traveler of all ages and places in the Universe. And as he promised, I remember every instant and facet of my journey. And more, I now recall all of my memories in my life as Solomon, and the door is open for me to attune myself to all my former incarnations.

The Master and I walk through the gardens of the temple, I processing the experience. I now know how to be with a woman, how to love her truly as the Goddess that she is, how to achieve the Adoration of the Beloved, the art of lovemaking made sacred. For this I am most grateful, though I am still but a boy some few short years away from puberty.

"Master, Makeda mentioned we would be together again, to save the world..."

"Yes, Yeshu'a, this is so." He intently observes my face as he says these words.

Say I with quiet certainty, "It is the girl I saw in the temple, with *Savta* and Mother that very first day."

"Yes, it is."

"Where is she now?"

He chuckles knowingly. "Do not worry. You will see her again when it is time. She is ahead of you, Yeshu'a. Though she came into this world on the very same day as you, some hours later, she has been studying here for some time...She has magic, erudition, beauty, wisdom. In many ways you are alike, in others so different. Fret not, you will again meet her...when God decrees it. Dear Yeshu'a, I know what comes, as do you, but I cannot say more. In future, accommodations will be made so that she is near.

"It is as I have thought."

By a statue of Osiris we sit in silence. In my heart a Loveflower blooms, planted by my Beloved, she who is my twin flame, she who allows the world to breathe. Never can I own any doubt. How momentous is God's Love, knowing this is so? Seemingly by mortal man it cannot be conceived, for we are told the Love of the Mother-Father God cannot be measured, yet more and more I understand the Light of this Love, how It manifests, the purpose for Its being...It can indeed be known. "Tell me, Manetho, Sheba spoke in some detail of the cycle to come, two thousand years hence. She said the Lemurians would return, naming them the future Lemurians."

"Indeed. At the time of Lemuria's demise it had existed for millions of years. Think of it, young one: millions of years it had lived, evolving lovingly. At such a very high vibration did it breathe, never having lost its connection with God, that many of its people lived thousands of years. This, in truth, they never lost. You see, Lemuria will rise again, Yeshu'a. Earth Herself will make Her Ascension soon after the beginning of the next cosmic cycle. At that time the planet will no longer support three-dimensional life. This is precisely what is meant by the expression *Heaven on Earth*, to create *Heaven on Earth*."

"To create *Heaven on Earth*," say I, "we must embrace the I AM presence in each of us, to see God in everyone and everything each instant we breathe, thereby elevating our existence into the higher realms of God." A beautiful white dove sings a song of joy in my heart, as now I truly know this to be the crux of my mission.

"Yes, one cannot afford to do anything less than love every aspect of Creation, even thine enemy. Every manifestation, each iota of Creation is sacred. When one truly knows this in his Heart of hearts, he has reached Unity Consciousness, what will also one day be named Christ Consciousness, and all suffering, all separation is conquered. Because the Lemurians never died as a race, they await and live and work for this moment, two millennia hence. Sheba spoke of the one hundred and forty-four thousand who will be the first of humanity to ascend. These will constitute the first wave. Years later, more will follow in a second wave. Those who ascend will have finished their incarnations. At this time Earth will no longer support three-dimensional life; it will be existing in the fourth and fifth dimensions, and those human souls who have refused the Light of God will be placed onto other planets, and birth through their cycles, somewhere else in this Universe where violence, dualism, separation is still the way of existence. There are many such strewn throughout the tides of the stars. At this time, all the eyes of the Universe will be on Earth. It represents the single best chance for humanity to reach higher realms of God. Sadly, those who have ceded the authority of their souls and sleep-walk through life, refusing God's loving embrace, may have to begin again."

"How is it, Master, that the Lemurians survive and the Atlanteans do not? This puzzles me, for it does not appear true."

"O Yeshu, you are wise. First, I will say that Truth is the oasis of water one sees up ahead on the road or in the desert; when one nears it, it disappears, for all along it was a mirage. Remember, we must be careful in our definition of Truth; like Beauty, Truth is in the eye of the beholder, as they are the same: Love, Truth, *and* Beauty. The Lemurians were not superior, for they, too, made errors. There was a great war between the two. And it is true the Atlanteans lost their way. In order for you to truly understand, we must go into the chamber with the crystal model of the solar system."

Manetho brings his hands solemnly together, and at once we stand in the room he described. On three occasions I have been here to learn the attributes of our Father Sun's system. Indeed, long have we known of all the planets and phenomena that you know, and we have known even more, though modern science tells you differently.

Suspended in the air by divine forces which negate gravity are various colored and sized crystals representing the planets and the sun, rotating on their axes. The planets' moons are also represented by smaller rocks and crystals, also rotating. An ingenious design thousands of years old, Manetho once informed me the original Atlanteans built it with the knowledge of the Ancients.

Using the names with which you are familiar, around the gleaming gold-crystal Sun revolves: Mercury, a small gray mass, the smallest of the planets; next the great initiator Venus, pale cream in hue; then our beautiful Earth, its fine emerald-cobalt crystal softly glimmering; next Mars, the red planet; then the large area filled with bits of small rocks and crystals you know as the Asteroid Belt; and Jupiter, Saturn, Uranus, Neptune, and Pluto follow.

Walking toward the model, Manetho points to the Earth and its moon and states, "First, young one, I remind you: while science will continue to tell us for quite some time that our moon revolves around the Earth, in truth, they both revolve around each other. In various, enchanting ways all the planetary moons do thus."

I nod my understanding of this.

"Thoth and the Melchizedek priesthood inform us that the humanity we know is a bit over two hundred thousand years old. Older civilizations existed here, far more advanced than anything seen since, yet they left no trace of themselves; they, too, are a part of us. As you are aware, the Sumerian cuneiform records are the most ancient written records detailing history that we have today, some four thousand years old. Yet they recount events which occurred billions of years ago, and this information is corroborated by my and Thoth's knowledge, the Akashic Record, and by the Galactic Councils of Light of the local Universe: the Councils of One Hundred Forty-Four and One Hundred and Forty-Four Thousand. The Sumerian records also meticulously tell of events which took place over four hundred and forty thousand years ago...By now, you should be accustomed to hearing the repetition of the divine fours," he adds with a wry smile.

"In truth, both the Sumerians and the ancient African Dogon tribe, who venerated the whale and dolphin civilizations, knew in great detail all the divine aspects of the solar system: its planets, moons, phases, cycles, phenomena, histories, and more…Easy it is for some to think this impossible, but I assure you it is not; what is difficult for me to fathom is how so many have come to believe the Earth is flat!"

I add, "Like the Atlanteans and Lemurians, the Sumerians and Dogons were close with God; they knew the Merkaba, they understood interdimensional travel, and could wing the heavens as easily as we dream. I am yet a child, Master, but I know much, more and more since our journey back in time. I am aware from reading the texts that the account I as Moses told in Genesis is nigh-word-for-word identical to the preexistent Sumerian creation story. My understanding of this is that I as Moses both read the texts and also experienced my own divine revelations. Indeed also, I was Inanna, the Sumerian queen. As I now recall every moment of my life as Solomon, the light shines into all my many lives…Manetho, is it not true I was the first Melchizedek?"

With profound gravity the Ageless One gazes into mine eyes and nods. "Yes, it is so, Yeshu'a. You are beginning to remember everything now; this gives me such joy. And through the line of his son Seth, your lineage on this planet goes back to Adam himself. The name Adam means Red Earth, a clue which leads the discerning one to discover that the story of Adam actually tells the story of Atlantis. A swath of our continent possessed red earth and clay…In a very real way, you are my Father! … Yet I am also yours! What you are realizing is that your story is everyone's story; thus, as a result, your story will become the template for humanity…Now, back to our lesson!

"You have read the *Enuma Elish*, the creation story of Babylon, from the era when the sky god people first took control of the world. Because their kings were themselves very fearful, to instill fear and obedience in their peoples, these patriarchal powers created gods who wielded weapons. As they will do successfully for yet some time, these kings were masterful imperial conquerors, and hoarded the riches of their plunderings for themselves...In Aksum you and I witnessed gold-and-gem-lined streets. This is a trait of the enlightened land, for these jewels and metals are celebrated for their beauty, for their spiritual and scientific significance by the enlightened, not cherished for their supposed monetary value...If in Rome they paved and lined the avenues in gold and jewels, they soon would be plundered by the poor populace.

"Using the story of its supreme god Marduk, Babylon conquered Sumeria, the Great Motherland. Often seen as the supreme primordial rapist, in his myth, Marduk murders the great Mother Goddess, Tiamat, ripping Her to pieces, and then creates the Earth from Her *dead* body, thus establishing a fear-based patriarchal pattern of denying the Earth its living divinity... Yet there is a another, deeper meaning to this story.

"Originally our solar system was home to twelve planets, thus the Holy Twelve and the Sun at its center, the blessed thirteen." As Manetho states this, the model transforms to display a dozen planets. "Today we concern ourselves with the so-called twelfth planet and Earth. Billions of years ago the Earth was a very large planet *named* Tiamat. And the twelfth planet was named Nibiru by the Sumerians; the Babylonians called it Marduk."

He indicates a giant planet, much larger than Jupiter, with a very unusual orbit. "At this time, Earth revolved around the sun between Mars and Jupiter. Now, watch closely the path of the orbit of Nibiru. It has a very wide, long orbit, ranging far beyond those of all the other planets; it also spins in the opposite direction than the other planets, or retrograde to them. The Sumerians say it only enters our solar system once every three thousand six hundred years. Their histories maintain, as do the Dogons', that during a pass through our system, one of its massive moons collided with Earth, and cut it into two, nearly equally sized pieces. The Akashic Record confirms this, as do both Thoth and the Melchizedeks. One of the two masses shattered into a million pieces, creating what will one day be called the Asteroid Belt. The Sumerians called it the Hammered Bracelet." The Ageless One points to the large area of many bits of rock and crystal. "The other mass was flung off its original orbital path, and settled into a new path between Venus and Mars. It brought *Tiamat's* large moon with it, and this is the Earth we know today.

"Now, young one, we come to the crux: the Sumerians tell us there were advanced, sentient beings on Nibiru, and they called them the Anunnaki; you may know them as…the Nephilim!"

My heart skips a beat, absolutely stunned at hearing this name. "Master! The Torah speaks of the Nephilim!"

"Indeed it does, Yeshu'a. With your prodigious memory and your deep knowledge of scripture, you may even be able to recite the words." His countenance is agleam.

"I will try," say I, knowing I will flawlessly do so. "*And it came to pass, when men began to multiply on the face of the earth, and daughters were born unto them, that the sons of God saw the daughters of men that they were fair; and they took them wives, whomsoever they chose. And the LORD said: 'My spirit shall not abide in man for ever, for that he is also flesh; therefore shall his days be a hundred and twenty years.' The Nephilim were in the earth in those days, and also after that, when the sons of God came in unto the daughters of men, and they bore children to them; the same were the mighty men that were of old, the men of renown.*"

Manetho nodding his head with eyes closed as I finish reciting the words, all at once a jolt courses through my body; a remembrance of mine own incarnational experience is revealing itself to me, and I am rapt. I am Moses once more, in the early days following the freeing of my people from Egypt, and I have sent twelve spies up into Canaan to scout the territory for our habitation and possible conquest. Sitting in the meeting tent, I am flanked by my older brother Aaron and his wife Miriam, and the congregation of all the children of Israel is here. The scent of figs wafts in on the evening breeze. All around me are tense, unsure; many anxieties press upon us. We are a people much determined to survive and form a nation. The guard has informed me he has sighted my scouts; they now return through the wilderness, and we await them.

At once they burst through the flaps in furious, agitated pace, their swords rattling at their sides, some bearing upon poles massive grapes fit for giants. Two carry pomegranates, barely able to hold them in their arms for their weight and size.

Caleb approaches me. His hair tousled over his brow, smudges of dirt upon his arms and tunic, he states, "Great praises to our Lord. We came unto the land whither thou sent us, and surely it floweth with milk and honey; and this is the fruit of it. Howbeit the people that dwell in the land are fierce, and the cities are fortified, and very great; and moreover we saw the children of Anak there. Amalek dwelleth in the land of the South; and the Hittite, the Jebusite, and the Amorite dwell in the mountains; and the Canaanite dwelleth by the sea, and along by the side of the Jordan."

A collective gasp escapes from the throng, the faces fill with awe.

Caleb stills the people and says, "We should go up at once, and possess it; for we are well able to overcome it."

The other scouts fervently disagree, and one named Hoshea speaks: "Caleb is mistaken. We are not able to go up against the people, for they are stronger than we. The land, through which we have passed to spy it out, is a land that eateth up the inhabitants thereof, and all the people that we saw in it are men of great stature. And there we saw the Nephilim, the sons of Anak, who come of the Nephilim, and we were in our own sight as grasshoppers, and so we were in their sight."

"Yeshu'a!" Manetho loudly intones. "Now the more you see!"

Shaking myself for an instant, I am completely returned to Heliopolis. Gazing upon the Master's face once more, say I, "Yes. The Nephilim were the giants, Manetho. In my life as Moses we took them on in battle to secure our land given by God to the people Israel. Yet I am uneasy…We have written our texts as divine right for our blood-battles."

"Surely this is so for most peoples after the flood, Yeshu'a. It was a great calamity. But there are yet more meanings in this. As with the twelve planets, so with the twelve tribes of Israel—which are truly the twelve tribes of all humanity, not solely of Israel, as Sheba has told you—so with the twelve astrological signs, and even the twelve spies. To see all truly, young one, is most important. Sheba confessed to you that your people would become more violent; thus the need for the protection of the Ark of the Covenant in Aksum. Yet before I resume, I must tell you so it be clear: even as you will fight the powers of the Pentateuch, keep the knowledge in your Heart of hearts that as the Age of Aquarius arrives two thousand years hence, the Hebrews of the world will once again become of vital importance. In Gaul and in what will be named Quebec and in areas of what will be called South America their spirit will be among the strongest in the world. Within them will breathe the pure spark of the Divine Masculine, as will also the Divine Feminine since the Jewish race, through the Holy Shekinah, first infused both of them into the wider world. These loving souls will have evolved over eons into Lightworkers, balancing the feminine with the masculine. The seeds planted so long ago will finally come to bear fruit as Mother Earth begins Her Ascension." The Ageless One speaks with great passion, the fire dancing in his eyes, and the blue sparks flowing all about him.

Say I, "All happens exactly as it should."

"Indeed. Makeda was correct, young Yeshu'a; the people Israel will become more violent, yet much has been projected onto them, from the very beginning, and this is why. As Makeda recounted to you, the people of Moses are the children of the seventh leader of the race of Sem. And the Essenes in your land are the children of the eleven wise men who were high priests of the other six Atlantean tribes. They choose not to follow the descendants of the Sem tribe; they devote themselves to being the protectors of the Sacred Flame of Truth. There is, too, an imperishable link to the Lemurians.

"Over the next millennia, a virulent form of anti-Semitism will arise: an energy of horrifying hatred toward the Jewish people. It and all the acts done in its name will be attacks on the Divine Masculine by those who fear the Divine Feminine. With the arrival of the Age of the Holy Spirit, the Sacred Marriage will consummate, and these areas I have named and more will germinate, having been seedbeds for the Divine Feminine. And after a period of great darkness, the Dove will finally fly over what had been the United States following its utter self-destruction, the most powerful empire the world will ever know."

As Manetho speaks, these names of the future stir something within me; I recognize them. "Quebec, the United States: these places will be in North America, like South America, across the Great Sea of Atlantis. These are the lands of the noble Red People. I traveled there as Solomon, from my shipyard in Edom, at Ezion-geber. The Red People are most wise, Master, and beautiful. When we arrived, they took us to be gods, with our whitish skin and blue eyes. We wore the headdress of the serpent, the same Earth god they knew, and so together we came to unity. They, too, in their lands paved their streets in gold and silver and gems, and knew the Merkaba. And in truth, we saw God in their eyes. Between us we told the stories of the Brothers of Light from the stars, and they believed us to be them. Yet are not we all? These beautiful folk were to me gods."

The Ageless One laughs a glorious belly laugh. "You are beyond books! And you are remembering all!"

"But please, let us return to the Nephilim, Manetho. This I must know."

Gathering his robes, he signs for me to sit with him on the bench, sighing deeply before uttering the words. "There are two things of import in the passage you recited from the Torah. First: it calls them the sons of God, and that they saw the daughters of men and took them as they chose. Already, many angrily deny they were the sons of God, as they did bring what some would call evil into the world. These people know not how God works; they cannot conceive that there is a Galactic Command which administrates God's will; by the Elohim this assignment was given to Archangel Michael him-herself, which he then delivered to the Galactic Councils, that this commingling must occur.

"And second: of equal importance is God's statement: *My spirit shall not abide in man for ever, for that he is also flesh.* This indicates that God, too, is, or was, of flesh...Thus the truth Thoth revealed to you that we are made *into* God's image. In some manner or form, in all the world's most ancient sacred texts it is said thus...that we are made *into* God's image."

The Ageless One now holds my hand. "Breathe deeply, Yeshu'a; close thine eyes, and breathe deeply. The Merkaba is the human Lightbody, the vehicle of Ascension. It is Elijah's Chariot, the Chariot of Fire we rode upon to Aksum. In what will be named the Old Testament, or the Hebrew Bible, the word Merkaba will appear forty-four times. And within the word are three smaller words: *mer*, meaning light, specifically two counter-rotating fields of light that spin in the same space; *ka*, which means Spirit, your individual I AM human Spirit while you are here on Earth, and also the unified essence of God, the One Spirit of which we are all a part; and *ba*, meaning the Spirit's interpretation of its particular realm. In the three-dimensional realm, *ba* means body, your physical body. You are now learning the Merkaba meditation, parts of which involve spherical breathing. If you are performing the meditation properly, there is a series of seventeen breaths that must follow specific guidelines. Then there is the especial eighteenth breath, the one your higher self gives you when you are ready to receive. This breath is the conduit for your Merkaba vehicle, transporting you up into at least the fourth dimension, even higher if your higher self directs you there. This breath is based upon the magical tones of music, the Holy Stream of Sound. At the moment of your Ascension, when your higher self gives you this breath, you will vanish from this world and appear in the higher realms. For you, it will likely take you through the fourth dimension, into at least the fifth.

"Everything is about spheres; with your heart's eye, if you are present when a loved-one passes over, you may see a shimmering, nigh-translucent sphere, often of blue and white-golden hues, rise out of the discarded body. This is their consciousness. Now, we will perform spherical, continuous breathing, akin to those of the Merkaba meditation; and while our physical bodies remain in this room, we will direct our consciousness to travel, and view the long ago past, so I may show you the history of the Anunnaki, or Nephilim, and the Sirians here on Earth: the rebirth of our human race."

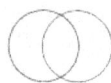

Sitting on the brow of a verdant hill, we overlook plains and lush valleys of splendor. Rich with all manner of life, streams meandering through, giving sustenance to the flora and fauna, it is a vista that takes my breath away. The earth is dark russet-brown. Amid thick rainforests, varieties of palm and acacia and other trees scrape the sky, the colors deep and pulsing in hue. Across the plains we espy herds of thousands of animals: ibex, okapi, antelope, buffalo, deer, rhinoceros, mammoth hairy elephants, and many others unknown of colossal size.

Manetho states, "We gaze upon what will one day become Sumeria, Mesopotamia... And we have traveled back in time four hundred thousand years, before Adam and Eve were born. Think of it, beloved, four hundred thousand years! The whales and dolphins have already traveled here from Oceania, a planet revolving around a star in Sirius. Future science will call this star *Sirius B*. Long before that time, the dolphins and whales traveled a very great cosmic distance to inhabit Oceania. Their mission to come to Earth was of the highest order; it was God-given to assist in the birth of highly evolved life: humanity. I say this as preface to our story.

"At this time the planet Nibiru was experiencing a sickness; the atmosphere was no longer retaining enough of the sun's heat to sustain life. Remember, Nibiru's odd orbit takes it far from the sun for most of its annual rotation. Waiting until

Nibiru was close enough for them to send a spaceship, the Anunnaki came here to mine gold, hoping to use it in their higher atmosphere as a reflector of the sun's rays. Their scientists planned to grind the gold into dust and use it as a mirror to keep their planet warm…I have brought you here to witness the moment of their arrival."

Out of a rainforest we now see a group of beautiful beings walk. They are much like giant humans, perhaps eight cubits tall, yet all of their features are more highly defined, especially their heads, their limbs, eyes, ears, mouths, and noses. And though they be truly giants, their gait is free and easy. Both shocked and charmed am I at the sight of them.

"Fear not; they cannot see us," Manetho assures me. "Here they will mine gold and build their cities amidst nature's splendor; in harmony with it they will reside. These are some of the leaders, scouting the terrain. They are highly intelligent beings who have learned many lessons from their mistakes on Nibiru, yet they will use their miners as slaves, first here, and then extensively in the hills of gold in southern Africa…So there is no mistake, Yeshu'a, remember: these things must occur for the furtherance of God's will."

The Ageless One wipes his hand across the panorama, as if starting a fresco anew, and the world dissolves into a watery haze. Gradually I see light coming in once more and colors of green and blue and form return.

We look down from the clouds over a great ocean. Off to our left is a large landmass, and another smaller one sits upon the horizon.

"We now observe the southern portion of the Ocean of Atlantis. To the east is Africa and to the south is the place named Gondwana: Gondwanaland. All the various creation stories of the western African tribes tell us they originated on Gondwana, and they are correct. Thoth and the Melchizedeks also say that our race was planted on this island. Of the African tribes, the Zulu tribe alone maintains it came from somewhere else in the Universe. Now watch closely, dear Yeshu'a. We have traveled back in time again, some few short years before the Anunnaki's entry into the world."

All at once we observe a giant figure, obviously an Anunnaki, drop from on high and dive into the depths of the ocean, his body a perfectly formed arrow to pierce the blue waters.

"This is the Anunnaki leader. The Babylonians tell us his name is Enlil, but *in fact* it is Enki, Enlil's half-brother. He comes to greet, praise, and receive the blessing of the most advanced beings of Consciousness on Earth: the whales and dolphins. While many sacred texts project evil designs onto the Anunnaki, they knew how to enter this world and involve themselves in its evolution—by receiving the blessing of the dolphins and whales. Above all others, Enki knew this. He also knew the Anunnaki miners would one day revolt, hence the need for the creation of a new race, with the seed of the Father and the womb of the Mother…His original true God-given plan was to help humanity grow.

"While the Anunnaki are not immortal, dear Yeshu'a, their lifetimes last many thousands of Earth years, and as an enlightened being, Enki will live with the dolphins and whales for a very long time."

"What happened to him, Master?" I ask with great curiosity, a veil slowing lifting, and I sensing a great truth emerges. "There is something of this soul, I cannot quite see it."

Manetho wipes the living fresco once more with his magical hand, and we look out upon the ocean from a shoreline. Overhead massive birds of blue and gold and green fly with their noble heads looking down upon us, as if they see our souls. A profound look of love shines in their eyes.

"Yes, dear one, the birds can see us. In truth, as messengers of God, they assist our presence here by protecting our essence. Watch closely the waters."

In a moment I espy a being surface on a wave and come toward us. It soon becomes apparent that it is Enki, though he is much changed. As he nears the shoreline, suddenly my soul understands: he is now half-man and half-fish. Surely this is some manner of mirage. The top half of his body appears fully human and the bottom fully fish.

"Thoth informed you of the African tribes' esteem for the dolphin and the whale. And when one observes the statues and images of Serapis Bey, the great Heart of Atlantis, occasionally one sees the symbol of the fish included with him. You also understand the fish symbol is your own. Through the many ages, truly these symbols all mean the same thing: the consciousness of cetacean life—sea mammals like the dolphin and whale—is very closely linked with ours. They constitute a prominent part of us. Without them we simply would not be."

Say I, "They came to Earth with the divine foreknowledge that from their seed we would be born."

"Indeed, Yeshu'a. You understand. Now Enki is more Sirian than Anunnaki, and in time he will become fully human. These truths are within the Sumerian records. In future another Sirian race, related to the whale and dolphin but more human, will come to Earth, hearing the words of the Elohim. Straight to the Halls of *Amenti* they will go, the womb of Mother Earth, part of whose function is to birth new species. The Sirians will be the Father seed which mates with the Anunnaki Mother aspect in a Divine, energetic, chemical, crystalline union. This is our rebirth. ...I will show you more, much more. But it is best to remember that we were first conceived to be slaves...Yet truly we are Divine.

"As the Age of the Holy Spirit nears, two thousand years following our days, science will still be at a loss to understand the full story. A rather adroit term will have been coined: *the missing link*. To scientists it will appear as if humanity suddenly appeared from nothing. Then the sun will shine at midnight, and all will be revealed; all of the coinciding Universes will be seen side-by-side...There will be no more secrets."

# Chapter Eight
# Remembrance

BELOVEDS OF MY HEART, a thousandfold blessing upon you. Tonight I write in limitless love, for as the patriarchal systems of controlling humanity crumble before your eyes, more than ever, each of you must embrace God in your heart. Soon there will be nothing left but that Love. Governments, institutions, money, religion, the business of business: all of it and more now desperately cling to the shadow-illusion of what was, to somehow remain breathing amidst the occurring transformation. And wending their way through your everyday lives are all the dramas you have chosen as your personal initiations. Yet, too, as Mother Earth prepares to make Her Ascension, both here in the world and on the other side of the veil there are many potent forces working tirelessly to try to keep you from God. While there are more people living in the Light today than ever before, nigh-everywhere you look, most are seeing evil serpents all around them. Many of you are pointing your fingers of projection at others: accusing them, blaming them, seeing sin in them, not understanding that what you see in others is truly a reflection of what you see in yourselves. So many of you still do not trust or Love yourselves, thus how can you Love and trust others? Never doubt, dearests; you will. You must.

God loves you so much. And God always wins.

Bless every moment, cherish every single instant and circumstance, unconditionally love every single iota of Creation. Always I am with you, as you are with me; ever I am by your side. Though I, too, see the suffering, I know it all to be sacred; I see the Light of God in each of you. Speak purposefully your prayers, ever praise God, tell God of your infinite gratitude for this great gift of life. Bestow your blessings upon all of your loved ones and upon your enemies. And forgive what is right before your eyes. Instantly.

Amidst our missions, Magdalen and I have been speaking of late of what is to come. So joyous is she. Even as the energy changes continue to occur with ever-increasing intensity and many abuse the sacred inner skills: listening, seeing, influencing, harming, peering into people's lives, and the most fearful among you continue to attempt to keep you in bondage: all is for the good. This Magdalen and I know, for it but leads to the eternal truth that you are all the very same. Each must forgive. Soon, after everything has been lost, no longer will you have a choice. In forgiving yourself, you forgive others, and you yourself are truly forgiven. If you know my story, then you know this is my message, and it is the very thing you are creating for yourselves to achieve: Universal Forgiveness.

You are all becoming Christ. Love is the only real thing in this Universe; all else is illusion. And the sooner you surrender to God the easier it will be, the quicker Grace will enter into every life. Do not wait any longer, my beloveds. Every instant is precious. Each moment you dedicate to God makes your passage that much easier. With conscious intent of your Divine I AM presence, make every word, every thought, every deed an act of Love. This will assure the arrival of the Light of God occurs more seamlessly, less painfully—not just for you, but for all humanity, and all life. And the spiritual kingdom you have always dreamed of will be born. Truly it is up to thee.

Long I have planned to write these sacred pages to help guide thee. It is one of my last acts in this world before I move beyond it and the galaxy, which is what is meant by my words: *I will be with you until the end of the Age.* A work of such love I cannot by word describe; many moments in the writing tears of utter joy and remembrance flow down my cheeks like mighty healing rivers. Herein not only is there unconditional love, but there are also keys, secrets revealed, and maps, some symbolic, some not, which teach thee all thou shalt need to know to return to God by way of your Ascension. Beloveds, forget not: there are no whiter than white saints or blacker than black villains; all are equally loved. It is now up to thee to light thine own way, as I am thee. And thou art me.

As I have once before in these pages mentioned, as we grow nearer to the only days of the story you know—my short ministry in Palestine—prepare thyselves, for much of what you have been told is false, a record concocted by Rome upon which was built the religion bearing my name. Much beauty there is within it, and by its auspices so many loving souls have done good works. But often it has been at war with the world and itself. More blood has been spilt in my name than any other. Indeed, what occurred in my final years as Christ in Palestine was an elaborate plan authored by the innermost circle of our Sister-Brotherhood of Love. Judas Iscariot himself was my friend; he chose and was chosen for the necessary role he played. Even Pontius Pilate, the Procurator of Judea, was sympathetic to our mission, meeting with us thrice before the end. Certainly there were two or three in the Sanhedrin who were threatened by us, by what we represented, what we were teaching. But, dearests, forget not: Uncle Joseph of Arimathea was there; we knew precisely what we were doing and what was to occur. It was the power of Rome, of Tiberius, that was truly threatened; the empire gripped Israel by the throat. And yet, even this we knew and understood and were yet keen to bring the Mystery out into the world for thy sake. Forgive the few of the Sanhedrin who refused the Light of God, for they feared both God and Rome; and forgive Rome its bloodthirstiness, its ignorance; its own fear is well understood in the light of imperialism. Through painting false, sinful pictures of my fellow Jews, including Judas, the structure of my story which became a religion has encouraged many souls to seek enemies, not to know God. And the nigh-two thousand years of Western war, anti-Semitism, and raping Mother Earth is the result. Forget not: Herod the Great was a client-king of Rome, a Levantine Nabatean from the Biblical land of Edom, and his son Herod Antipas, tetrarch of Galilee who oversaw my and John of the River's deaths, was also under Rome's thumb.

Yet all happens exactly as it should. Thus bless and forgive Rome and Christianity most of all. All that I did, I did knowingly to show you *The Way*.

Now it is your turn.

God has given you twelve sacred healing flames, or rays, to help you in your journey to completion, five of which are secret. Each is important and has a distinct purpose. I call upon thee now to invoke the Violet Flame. The Violet Flame focuses on redemption and transmutation and spiritual freedom. It may help you to know that many souls achieved their Ascension in the last century merely by summoning the healing energies of the Violet Flame on a daily basis over a period of years. Though they had not done much else and all the information available to you today was then not widely known, when they died, they had done what they needed in order to achieve their Ascension.

Many still have little or no understanding, appreciation, or acceptance of the Divine power of their creation. While living on this Earth, you are all co-creators of everything that transpires. Everything. From the circumstances in interpersonal relationships, to wars between nations and natural disasters like earthquakes and tsunamis, you are all co-creators of every single occurrence. Beloveds, the animals know this. In its ignorance, humanity still mostly denies it. Animals know their pasts and futures, and they know yours when they see you.

Believe it or not, wars clear up a lot of karma. In the Middle East and the United States there is much anguish over your governments, and many newspapers and websites devoted to all the perpetrations of killing and suffering…Yet truly you get the governments you want. You yourself may think that you wish for all the good things to happen for you in your personal life, and then, somehow, bad things happen instead. Mindful prayer and active meditation can help you to achieve the Love and peace and success that you want, but every thought matters.

Perhaps after an evening of prayer or a morning meditation, doubts creep into your mind; maybe you ill-wish people, even speak words or engage in acts which negate the good work you did the night before or earlier in the day. Oftentimes these doubts are put into your mind by outside less-than-light-filled sources.

If you are not a constant flow of Love, beloveds of my heart, what do you expect to happen? You may not remember this, but originally The Fall in human consciousness occurred from lack of trust—trust in God, and trust in yourselves as reflections of God's Glory—and the resultant pain you have since endured has been excruciating, to say the least. Surrendering to Love, to the Grace of God, is always much easier than fighting it, yet most people in your culture still engage in the latter, believing religions will do their work for them. It is now time to both instantly forgive your religions and release yourselves from the bondage of limiting, erroneous belief systems. It is up to you.

Within the Violet Flame is the spiritual alchemy of the Sacred Marriage, of the Divine Masculine of the blue ray and the pink ray of the Divine Feminine. The Divine Masculine, the Father, is the administrator of the Universe, while the Divine Feminine is the manifester, the creative force in the Universe. The blue ray is power and the pink ray is Love. The two merged together in perfect harmony, the Violet Flame transmutes karma and misdirected energies from all your incarnations into pure white Light, and releases them with joy and forgiveness. It allows you to remember your past experiences in all your incarnations, without judgment—positive or negative—and then dissolves them so they no longer exist.

But you must invoke it, work with it, call upon it, visualize it. Millions of angels come to you when, with great conscious intent of your I AM presence, you speak its name and make a commitment to positively change yourself. And many natural disasters such as earthquakes and forest fires have been averted by the invocation of the Violet Flame.

Your religion may tell you not to read certain books, or that you should not meditate. Yet more people in your culture are reading these books and meditating every day. Once you make the decision that you do not want to be a victim anymore, you will meditate. The great Capuchin Saint Padre Pio, so beloved of me, once said: *Through the study of books, one seeks God; through meditation, one finds Him.*

Call upon the Violet Flame. Imagine its soothing, loving rays surround you. It fires the Heart for it is a flame of the Heart, which many have forgotten. It instills confidence and compassion and can be used in both prayers and meditations. Imagine it healing every cell, every photon of thy body. Breathe in its sacred essence, for it is God given. Yet as always, do not use your mind in your processes; this is a pure Heart activity. See it in your Heart, and send its loving, protective embrace and healing powers to everyone in thy life, especially thine enemies. Visualize it flooding humanity with limitless Love. All that you call upon it to do for you, ask of it the very same for everyone. You may ask that it remain with you during your day. With conscious intent in such a manner, the very nature of the world can change. Send waves of the Violet Flame to the trees, the animals, the elementals, telling them of your Love; send wave upon wave to the Earth Herself. Your culture tells you it is good to run yourself into the ground with busyness. Beloveds of my heart, the opposite is true. As an Initiate I learned of and was given access to the sacred healing flames. The Universe hears what you want and gives it to you. The fate of the world is truly in your hands. I have shown you *The Way.*

Now it is your turn.

From Lemuria and the dawn of time, I bestow upon thee this Ascension prayer gifted me by my dear parents. Speak daily these holy words thrice repeated, feel their loving embrace enter your Heart as you come to know your Divine Presence, and humbly rise to God:

From the Lord God of my Being, I AM that I AM, I decree:

I have Love for my journey into my Ascension.

I have compassion for all physical and emotional pain I still need to heal.

I give thanks that I am now healing the past and resurrecting the new.

As a Master of Divine expression walking the Earth,

I now turn on the Light of my Divinity.

I now activate and transform my DNA to its fifth dimension potential.

I now choose to completely heal and rejuvenate my physical body.

I choose to remain joyous, harmonious, and grateful.

I claim the mastery that is mine to manifest my freedom.

I allow my Divinity to manifest in a most wondrous way.

I give thanks that it is done according to God's Holy Will.

I call for shafts of Ascension Light to blaze through me

daily and hourly. And so be it, beloved I AM.

Manetho was telling me about the history of the world, so beloved is he, and from there we shall now continue. What he teaches may seem impossible, ridiculous, bizarre, but I assure you it is Truth. Cleave closely unto thy heart his wise words, release all suspicion, all inhibition, for the *remembrance* is what brings you home.

Like a magically gleaming nimbus of life, surrounding this dear Earth is the Unity Consciousness Grid, the Christ Consciousness Grid. Here we as one exist: as energy, Consciousness, Spirit, and Lightbody. Anon you will discover how to transform your body into light here, in your own personal merkaba, and be able to bridge time, space, and thought, and travel the heavens, the eras, the many dimensions and universes.

As you cultivate and live unity consciousness life, your awareness, your abilities, will grow, but so, too, will your responsibilities. Rejoice! For the Christ Consciousness Grid is the next great leap in human consciousness. Light-bearers all, bring joy, as I am most joyous at the sight of you. You are beloved of me.

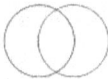

"So this is why Enki has such a profound sound in my ears, Master," I exclaim. "It is as if I know him. My heart beats like a drum in anticipation for what comes."

"As well it should, young Yeshu'a. Inconceivable it may sound, but as sure as God is in our hearts, it is so."

"You stated that he lived a very long time with the dolphins and whales; how long was this?"

"Thousands of years, young one. This was his and their mission. After returning to land, half-fish and half-human, following another long period he became fully human. He knew the Anunnaki would enslave, but he also understood it was a necessary step to humanity finding its divinity. Think of his devotion to God, Yeshu'a, the depth of his Love, the completeness of his dedication, his surrender."

My heart swells knowing this man was our Father.

"Before we continue, two things I will mention. Here in the time we now see, and well into the golden ages of Lemuria and Atlantis, all life is at peace. The animals do not kill each other to survive. Humanity knew well this divine paradise. As Sheba remarked to you of our lives in Atlantis, we drank water from the air, and air from the water. Our knowledge was pure. And we plucked globules of divine, pranic energy from the heavens for any other needed sustenance. In the future, man will make commodities of animals, legitimizing it as necessary slaughter for our survival, and grow ill from their consumption.

"Also, in your mind has been the question of the One Hundred Forty Four Thousand Unity Diamond...Why the diamond? you silently ask. It is quite simple. Living in each human heart is a perfected diamond. Its color is a royal, cobalt, peacock blue, and it radiates our Divine I AM presence, what we truly are. It has one hundred and forty-four thousand multidimensional facets, or chambers, some of which may become obscured through acquiring fears. Yet by truly opening all the facets of your diamond heart and connecting with the diamond heart of our beloved Mother Earth, those fears will become magnetized and absorbed—thus their utter release—and healing occurs at the deepest levels until you reach completion. Like a shroud, many choose still to wrap themselves in their fears, though they cause much pain. Yet one's commitment to surrendering all of their fears restores them to wholeness, allowing them to return to God. This is the mark of the mature soul."

Increasingly I understand the Master, and the reason for the use of various symbols. Something powerful is birthing in my soul every moment we share. Ever I am grateful for Thee, God, for this wondrous gift of life, my dear family and friends and teachers, and for Thy Divine presence in my heart.

"Now," Manetho continues, "I need not remind you, we began our great journey today to ascertain what happened in Atlantis. Far from this event we still are. But each step will inform the next, and along the path you will find yourself. One of many things I am sure of is your life-experience as Inanna of Sumeria will come to light. How this manifests will be up to you. For now, merely know that what you are learning has been written and preserved by the enlightened of that land, and is corroborated by Thoth."

With his magical hand the Ageless One rubs away the living fresco of life before us. And now our souls once more sit atop the hill in what will become Sumeria. Wondrous cities now have been built, amidst spectacular gardens. The animals still roam the plains, the massive rainforests thrive, paradise still breathes. The scents of frankincense and myrrh and acacia flowers fill the air.

"Now, dear one, we have traveled forward in time two hundred thousand years, so it is still two hundred thousand years before our days. All this time the Anunnaki have been mining gold and transporting it to Nibiru via their ship in the heavens...Interestingly, far into the future from our days, science will discover the main goldmine in southern Africa, and human remains will be found there. While capable of space travel, the Anunnaki are still young when it comes to scientific knowledge; and since their planet is so distant from Earth for most of its orbit, they must wait thousands of Earth years before they can return for more gold shipments. During the time since they first started mining—some fifty thousand years—the slave-miners have naturally become wretched in their plight, and now they rebel against their leaders. Successful in their escape, they spread out over the lands to evade discovery. Enki had orchestrated the revolt as part of the Divine plan, and the other leaders had been expecting it and had grown anxious; this, too, was part of Enki's vision. The Sumerian histories display in great detail their use of flasks—the kind used for combining chemicals—pouring elements of some sort from one to another. It involved clay and the blood of one of the aboriginals and sperm of the male Anunnaki. The intention was to combine their DNA with the DNA of an aboriginal and create a superior form of life to be used as slaves to mine the gold desperately needed by Nibiru. We were then placed on Gondwana to evolve for fifty thousand years, after which we would mine gold, and by the records' account, when that was over, they would eliminate us as a race.

"Now, beloved Yeshu'a, this is the simple explanation, and the sacred books of your land take directly from the Babylonian records. Both even use Eve as the name of the first woman. But our dear Thoth knows the more profound Truth..."

Suddenly a great flash of white light fills the valley upon which our souls gaze. For an instant I can no longer see the rainforest. Out of the light walks Thoth with a lovely woman and the light diminishes to the size of a small cube and then disappears.

"Blessings upon you, Manetho, young Yeshu'a," greets Thoth in his soft, reassuring voice. Bringing his hands palm-to-palm before him, he bows deeply to us, as beside him the tall, slender woman, beautiful as the clear nighttime sky, smiles a devastating smile. "Yeshu'a, allow me to introduce my dear wife Seshat, she who is the master measurer of time, of all Creation, who invented writing, and who is mine own oracle of Truth."

Says she, "It would not be acceptable to Thoth to miss this moment, Yeshu'a. It is too important to him." She sings. When she speaks, it is in song, the voice so lovely, so pure it is the trill of the dove. Around her the blue sparks fly, her glowing golden-brown skin pulsing radiant like the sun.

"My praises to you, Seshat," I somehow manage to reply.

"It is not often one sees both Thoth and Seshat, young one," Manetho informs me. "This is a rare occasion."

"Ho-hum, Master Manetho," Thoth gibes. "As if we be truly gods! I will not have it! If young Yeshu'a is to see this history, I shall be there to help explain, and dear Seshat will hold the necessary female energy for us to achieve balance and will correct any of my mistakes. This is most important. Young one!" he announces, looking me directly in my soul's eye. "You have progressed much in such a short time. From afar amidst my missions I have seen thee. Have you any questions?"

Searching my soul, I can but think of one. "In my studies I have read that you are also Hermes the Greek, that you are called Hermes Trismegistus, or thrice-greatest Hermes. What does this mean?"

Seshat giggles like a girl upon hearing this, elbowing her husband most discreetly in the stomach.

"O dear Yeshu'a, this is easily solved. One may hear many reasons for this, but, in truth, it refers to three incarnations: Atlantean, Egyptian, and Greek. My original Atlantean name was Arlich Vomalites; our language was so expressive. I merely moved on as the Winds of Wisdom and the Will of God dictated. While I have enjoyed numerous incarnations, it truly means thrice-born." Almost perturbed is he to explain himself.

"Do not be deceived," Manetho counsels. "Thoth was the greatest king of Atlantis, the builder of Egypt and of Greece."

Thoth cries like a command, "Today we will pass through the gateway of the Great Pyramid into the Halls of *Amenti*. But we will first discuss some details."

Seshat smiles once more, like the Queen of Heaven is she, so serene and wise. "You recited from your land's sacred texts, Yeshu'a. It is important to understand that there is both Truth and political-religious posturing in these texts. Yours are beautiful, loving, talented people, yet they have allowed themselves to become restricted for many long ages by lies written into their sacred scrolls by power hungry priests and kings. Seeing evil serpents all around them has led them to become fearful of themselves and to be controlled from within and without.

"Hear well the words once more: *And it came to pass, when men began to multiply on the face of the earth, and daughters were born unto them, that the sons of God saw the daughters of men that they were fair; and they took them wives, whomsoever they chose... The Nephilim were in the earth in those days, and also after that, when the sons of God came in unto the daughters of men, and they bore children to them; the same were the mighty men that were of old, the men of renown.* These words tell you there were men and women of some sort on the Earth before Adam and Eve, and the Anunnaki-Nephilim found the women fair and mated with them. They also inform you that these mighty men were the same as of old and were renowned. This is clearly praise.

"Yet the very next lines of the text read thus: *And the LORD saw that the wickedness of man was great in the earth, and that every imagination of the thoughts of his heart was only evil continually. And it repented the LORD that He had made man on the earth, and it grieved Him at His heart. And the LORD said: 'I will blot out man whom I have created from the face of the earth; both man, and beast, and creeping thing, and fowl of the air; for it repenteth Me that I have made them.' But Noah found grace in the eyes of the LORD.* Now, Yeshu'a, you know Noah was Atlantean and that the Flood was the sinking of our great land. From your studies you also understand the processes involved in the Precession of the Equinox, its cycle taking nigh-twenty-six thousand years to complete due to a wobble in the Earth's axis. At the beginning and midway points, each cycle is marked by, as Sheba expressed it, Mother Earth shaking her spine. This is tied to, and affects, Consciousness, and is a galactic phenomenon. Certain of them are universal in transformational effect.

"Yet your texts tell you humanity was wicked, but since Noah survived the Flood, he found God's grace...I bear witness: many of our friends died amidst the destruction of our land, and they were not wicked; they were loving souls, deeply devoted to God and to Mother Earth. Mistake me not, as Manetho will describe, part of Atlantis had *fallen*, due to Martian influence, but many saintly souls perished. Atlantis was a manifestation of the Divine Masculine, while Lemuria was an expression of the Divine Feminine, and thus more balanced in its male-female identity. After Atlantis destroyed itself, it was the Lemurians who helped the Atlanteans, their souls, find the gateway to higher Consciousness. They are our loving brothers and sisters."

Say I, "Yes, I understand this. Within us is a strong desire based upon fear to paint falsely the Woman. And for this we greatly suffer. The Holy Shekinah Herself has with my dear Mother spoken of this."

"It is as I have thought. Knowing God is within all things, we can understand this is a balancing of karma; it must occur. And *we* must also be true Lightworkers, always there with wisdom, words, and deeds which bring Light and defend the spirit of Woman, the very Spirit of God." Seshat folds her arms into the sleeves of her star-filled robes.

Thoth steps forward and utters these words: "Beneath the right paw of the Sphinx is a secret passageway leading to the Hall of Records. A library of multiple dimensions, there are also tablets and scrolls and other physical objects there that prove the existence on Earth of advanced civilizations stretching back many millions of years. As the Aquarian Age comes to pass, these records will be discovered and for the first time this knowledge will become widely known. ...The whales and the dolphins come from Oceania are the most highly evolved life here, and will continue to be throughout the ages. When Earth begins Her Ascension sometime after Aquarius arrives, if we do not change our ways, they will leave us. Many will commit suicide by beaching themselves so that their souls can escape unharmed; this they have told me...They have such love for us. In Atlantis they were our partners. Yet they will not wait and watch us destroy ourselves.

"I tell you this, Yeshu'a, because Oceania is intrinsic to our identity. Manetho has already shared with you some of the story, but it goes much deeper. As I guide us four through the fourth dimensional gateway of the Great Pyramid to reach the Halls of *Amenti*, remember: the story you are told, the sights you see, are sacred and secret for a reason. Humanity cannot yet understand or accept the Truth...

"When Enki was reborn half-fish-half-man and then became human with the Sirian seed of God within him, a great covenant was made. The whales and dolphins called to their brothers and sisters on Oceania, both God-human and God-cetacean, and issued their greeting to come and create us. Enki knew this and bided his time. As you witness our re-creation, you will then remember the blessed Sumerians preceded us. They are a precious link to Lemuria and Atlantis. Neither Semitic nor of the Northlands of ice, their origin is to most a mystery. As Babylon came into being, your own face as Inanna began to change because Babylon was bent on conquest, to kill off the Motherland...When you learn of our re-creation, you may desire the knowledge of your life as Inanna. If you pass through that portal, fear not; we will be by your side."

O Mystery of mysteries, acquaint Thyself with my heart. Allow Thy sweet loving caress bathe me in warmth and serenity and Love. Issue Thy song in Thine ever-changing key, for Thou art within me, protecting me, impelling me forward. If ever my step should falter, find me and pick me up once more, for I know no fear. I am Wisdom; I am Love; I am Truth; I am Thy blue-diamond Heart, Thy eternal Flame. I am Light. Great praises to Thee.

So say I as my consciousness whisks through a tunnel dark as night. Barely had we reached the Great Pyramid and Thoth joined us in a circle of four holding hands, when the light went out as we traveled into the heart of the pyramid, our Father blessing us above. An incredible vortex of energy was there, I sensing it like an emotion of joy and reunion and freedom. Many belief systems tell us what lies beneath is the Underworld, tingeing it in fearful hue...Behold, for I will tell thee true.

# Chapter Nine
# History

WHAT DOES THE Inner Earth conjure up for you? Alas, the meanings of words like *Agartha* have been corrupted due to their usurpation by certain groups professing the desire to do good works in the world, when their designs were, in truth, evil, thus further tainting the image of our beautiful sacred Mother. In the patriarchal age there were always those who attempted to manipulate the magic of the Mother for their own immorality plays. The Kundalini itself has been largely misunderstood. When you see glyphic images of a patriarchal avatar, such as I, with a snake positioned nearby our feet or at our side, it merely indicates we were masters of the Kundalini energy—the healing, transcendent energy of Mother Earth. It does not mean to suggest the serpent is inherently evil. In certain instances, patriarchy created images of avatars killing the serpent, slitting its throat…This is, in truth, a crime against the Mother. In the accurate glyphs, often the avatar is seen standing atop a crocodile, indicating he has mastered his reptilian nature. Have Faith, beloveds of my heart. Once more I bestow upon thee the great gift of patience, for I will reveal all. One must have the deepest respect for the processes of our dear Earth Mother; never paint falsely her abundance of gifts, nor ever abuse them, as these are the very reasons for the sickness in the world today, especially in the West.

Indeed, such is even the case with what were once sacred plants used in ancient times to create spiritual pathways. As it was with wine, in the beginning these plants were pure and the experience gained by their moderate ingestion was one of innocence and joy, purity and the realization on higher planes of the beauty of unity. For millions of years, sacred plants vibrated far beyond fourth and fifth dimensional frequencies, and assisted humanity in its spiritual development. With reverence, sacrality, and high intention, in these long golden ages, we occasionally partook of these gifts by eating of a leaf. In this manner humanity discovered direct connections with nature spirits, the angelic realms, and the kingdom of the animals. This ritual use also fostered interdimensional travel and opened doorways for the furtherance of the skills of teleportation. The sacred plants were ever respected in holiness, never misused. However, since the Dark Ages, black magicians have skillfully altered the genetic structure of marihuana, for instance, so that through pronounced usage it causes a tearing effect in the soul, allowing entities of the lower astral realms to gain control over one's thoughts, emotions, and actions. This is how these entities stay alive and is the main reason for addiction. As ever, the desire is to keep one from attaining God. And truth be told, if you could see these entities, they coil about you like vaporous snakes. There is nothing wrong with experimenting with the experience of something like modern marihuana. But if it becomes a habit, it equally affects your four main bodies: physical, mental, emotional, and etheric, and it often can take many lifetimes to reverse its deleterious effects on the soul.

Everything has two sides. Everything is double in the Universe. This is the reason why, for instance, the archangels are, in truth, a perfected merging of a female and male being.

Beloveds, I say this in preface to reveal to you that there are two serpent forces in the Universe. Unlike the angelic components, one of the serpent forces is positive, the other negative. Before we venture into the hallowed Halls of *Amenti*, I will in various ways describe the nature of these things so you may understand how brilliantly misinformed you may have been — by what would best be called the *belief* in dualism, wherein your Divine Mother is the culprit of your suffering, of our *fallen* condition. Even if at this time of burgeoning awareness it be merely a hint of insight, by now you intuit correctly that all of it is the projected result of massive guilt over the loss of the essence of our once sublime Grace, the Grace you are now rediscovering.

In my life as Solomon, on the day I made my way to Aksum with Manethos to meet the Queen of Sheba, my heart was filled with such joy I merely asked our Lord to gift me divine grapes. So pure was my feeling, I needed only to give form to my Love, and it was so. All that glorious day, the coming of the grapes was in my hands. And truth be told, I will later demonstrate the very same in this life, and you shall bear witness. Everything in the Universe has always been in existence; there was no *Big Bang*. My most sincere regrets to the scientists who *believe* in it, but it just is not so. Through one's love and power of will, any and all that is Good can enter into the world.

Two ways there are to make these types of seeming miracles occur. Of the episodes of the grapes, we may call this the white willpower or white magic. The white willpower comes from Love and *creates*. The black willpower, or black magic, comes from desire, not Love, and the one who uses it *appropriates*. So, in effect, they seek to steal something already created. The eyes of the body see no difference in the results, for they appear the same. But the soul's eye sees all. Often the black magician will move matter through space as a show of power to gain control over the rabble. There is no purpose behind it save control, no Divine plan to work with the Law through the agent of Love to help others. There is, in truth, no power, only understanding: the understanding of Love's Eternal Light. Desire can and will destroy. For the desirous one seeks to take without the exchange of giving; this is against God's Law, the Sacred Law of the Universe, and will lead to the ruin of the practitioner, inevitably.

Beloveds of my heart, I tell thee: this is why Manetho was so explicit, so mindful in his education of me, in his teachings of how to see the aura, in how to help others to heal themselves. For once one discovers these sacred skills, one may use them to help and to heal and to conquer evil, or one may use them to cause division to germinate and grow within oneself, next using them to creep inside other souls to do unto them the same, thereby bringing evil into the world. This is the great danger.

The truth of the two serpentine powers of the Universe is akin to the white and black willpowers, and has caused much confusion here on Earth. The positive serpent power is the Kundalini, Mother Earth's transcendent soul that awaits the coming of the Cosmic Prince. It resides in the base of the spine in humanity until awakened by the opening of the chakras, often through the agency of sacred sex, but not necessarily so. Using the language of the consummation of the Sacred Marriage, when the Bride enters the Bridal Chamber, she rises to meet the Cosmic Prince, whereupon the dazzling multiple flowers of Consciousness unfold, open, and unification with God is attained. The Kundalini is the ancient serpent god that all olden tribes, including the original Hebrews, revered.

The second serpentine power came from other worlds, and is the opposite, negative force. It is contrary to what Inanna and Isis and all of the lovely matriarchal goddesses were, regardless of what certain men and certain traditions tell you. This negative serpent force was so named by the ancients because of the duplicitous words its powers use on Earth. Coming here since The Fall, this serpent race emanated from worlds without Love, indulgent of pride and egotism, and its kind mirror fallen man in his deceit. Their powers are of the mind and have no connection with the indomitable Heart. Indeed, the intent of this serpent race is to first learn from destruction before becoming the master builders that the number twenty-two represents. Unless absolutely necessary, it is best not to take them on in battle but to step out of their way. The ancient scriptures tell us this, for if we are honest with ourselves, each being we encounter is a teacher.

As the Light of God pours into the world, you begin to understand this lesson, for all of the physical worlds, the planets, moons, and stars: all celestial bodies, are the result of karma, each given in its present state to allow you to evolve into pure joy. This is their reason for being. Now God begins to penetrate them all; from this their transmutation is occurring; they begin to vibrate at higher frequencies, eventually soon to lovingly cause their etherization. In truth, my beloveds, everything in the Universe is ever making Love. And though at times it appears not to be so, the Universe is constantly conspiring in your favor, always on your side.

On Earth, the Kundalini energy—the positive Serpent of Light—emanates at the core of the planet and snakes up through the sacred Earth, attracted to one spot on the surface. Bringing with it a flow of divine energy to the location to which it is drawn, it connects the Inner Earth to the exterior and graces this surface location with enlightenment. In return, the people touched by its grace protect it, build a pyramid to mark its eminence, spiritually grow from its proximity, and teach the world through acts and sacred scripture what they have discovered. Ever it has been thus, though patriarchy has often confused it with the negative serpentine power, and falsely painted the Kundalini as evil.

Say I to you: the serpent in the Garden of Eden story should not be equated with evil or with our sacred Mother's life-force. This my dear Mother told us in Nazareth when we were very young: The original Hebrew word for snake was NHSH, or *nahash*, which means to find out or decipher…*Nahash* means wisdom. I now also tell you: tied to the change in the tilt of the Earth's axis which occurs within the Precession of the Equinox, it is the Kundalini's movement every nigh-thirteen thousand years that is the shaking of the Mother's spine. It merely changes its surface location. Is it thus to be considered evil? For it leads us to ever higher realms of Light. In your time it has moved from the land of Tibet to Chile in South America. Though the shaking of Her spine can cause destruction, due to more than two centuries of industrialization, the effects are far worse in your age.

And as the animals will tell you, in truth, if humanity had loved their Divine Mother over the past many millennia instead of desecrating Her body, if man had seen in Her and all living things the beauty and majesty of God, made every act an expression of love, the effect of Her shaking Her spine would have been the most insignificant of ripples upon a placid pond, injuring none. Faith, Love, Trust, Compassion: these are not concepts; these are energies born of the Heart whose consequences are felt throughout the cosmos.

The Kundalini is connected to the Christ Consciousness Grid. It is the bridge to achieve your growth in unity consciousness. Thus the Kundalini's importance.

Dearests of my heart, even the word *apocalypse* is misunderstood in your time. Most believe it denotes the end of the world, and that apocalyptic writings are to be shunned. Most generously say I: because they were written during the phase of the Precession when most people were spiritually asleep, nigh-all the books of the past two thousand years were penned by people who were ignorant of that about which they wrote. And certainly they have been even less understood by their later readers. The true meaning of the word apocalypse is this: *A lifting of a veil, a full disclosure of something hidden from the majority of humanity during an epoch marked by great darkness, falsehood, and ignorance.*

Fear not, beloveds of my heart, for there is nothing ever to fear. It is God's Law: *Absence of fear guarantees supreme safety; the presence of fear attracts inevitably that which is feared and manifests it.* And within these pages I will discuss my beloved John's Book of Revelation and his Apocryphon.

It may help you to know that your DNA is not a double-helix, as your scientists tell you; they have yet to understand its truly multidimensional nature, though soon they will. No, it is not at all a double-helix. Like the Universe itself, your DNA is in the form of a spiral, and this spiral is identical to the spiral of the Kundalini: the Serpent of Light.

Undoubtedly you have seen representations of the dove over the heads of saints, my Mother, my sisters, my sweet Magdalen, many others. Yes, the dove represents peace, dear ones. But there is a higher meaning, a much deeper implication. With the awakening of the Kundalini in your spine, it begins to travel upward through all of your chakras. You start to see things differently, the sacred unity of all life reveals itself. Then in the lives of many a struggle between the Dove and the *negative* serpent begins. As the Kundalini energy awakens the throat, third eye, and crown chakras, if you are weak, the serpent can have you believe that you alone are God, to stop right where you are, that there is nothing more to life beyond this, thus there is no need to quest for the One True God in the higher realms. This leads man to continue manifesting delusional incarnations marked by self-inflicted suffering. And it can cut one off from seeking the Shekinah kingdoms in humanity's evolutionary cycle of creation.

Thus the dove.

As you experience the awakening of the higher chakras, the dove also speaks to you. It sings to you in lilting song of greater, selfless things: of how, by shedding completely your ego, you shall be of service to God, and do good unto others, indeed ever thinking of others before yourself, dedicating every moment to God, and grasp the vast splendor of things, the magnitude of the Divine, each of us a living, loving seed of God's will.

Beloveds of my beating heart, the dove represents the Ascension. By whatever means you accomplish your Ascension, it is God's desire you achieve it. The only thing keeping you from it is your fearful, egotistical, small self. And what allows you to attain it is your embrace of your Divine collective I AM Self. So, when in the imagery of sacred art you see the dove above the saints' heads, it signifies they have achieved their Ascension by mastering the Kundalini forces, divinely realizing it is but a means to higher realms of being. Through the Mother one must indeed go to return to God. And the flight of the dove is the sweetest gift. The Shekinah kingdoms await, the many palaces of higher creation call, and when you are ready, you shall arrive, robed in Light. Beloved you are.

The Native, Indigenous peoples, the wisest, most peaceful, enlightened souls of this world, still venerate the Earth's Kundalini. Ever they have remained wedded to both the Divine Father and Divine Mother. In the Age of the Holy Spirit they will soon become very important, as they retain the wisdom you have lost, the Love you have forgotten.

Some believe Thoth was a god of the underworld, yet to the Egyptians he was the god of knowledge and writing. And it may surprise you to discover many of the axioms and parables attributed to me were first uttered by him. Thoth is Wisdom and Love and Light; for while he and Seshat have now in your age moved beyond this world, they still live in higher realms. Thoth's service to God and to our dear home is of the highest order.

Ever I hold thee in my sweet, loving embrace, for thou art so beloved of me. Ascension Hall awaits thee. As the Earth transmutes from a three-dimensional world to the fifth dimension, know in your heart that the spiritual kingdom you have always dreamed of is now here, ready for you, calling to you: magical, eternal, blissful, and free. Plumb deeply your heart, for only there is it found. And in the finding, increasingly you will discover that the brain is your enemy. No longer does it hold any answers worth hearing, nor did it ever. How often has it led you astray? The instant you completely surrender to the Heart, God walks in. Yet this is the hardest thing for your culture to do. It does everything in its power to stop this from happening. Nigh-ever it has been thus. There is an old saying: *The exoteric keeps you enchained, while the esoteric sets you free.*

It is up to you. Truly, *you* are the ones you have been waiting for.

Yahweh, the God *we* created, was an envious god. Without the Kabbalah, the full story would not be known. Without the Sufis, the full story would not be known. Without the Essenes, the Gnostics, the Rosicrucians, and the Cathars, the full story would not be known. This is part of the legacy of the three Abrahamic religions. Yahweh was envious because we sought and found the Truth which would set us free from the prisons of our bodies, allowing us to return in wholeness to the One True God. And Dearest Eve, the vehicle of the Holy Spirit within humanity and all creation, awakened Adam to the Truth our self-created God kept from us. Beloved John ben Zebedee speaks so beautifully of this in his Apocryphon when Eve says: *I entered into the midst of the dungeon which is the prison of the body. And I spoke thus: "He who hears, let him arise from the deep sleep." And then he (Adam) wept and shed tears. After he wiped away his bitter tears he spoke, asking: "Who is it that calls my name, and whence has this hope come unto me, while I am in the chains of this prison?" And I spoke thus: "I am the Pronoia of the pure Light; I am the thought of the undefiled Spirit...Arise and remember...and follow your root, which is I...and beware of the deep sleep."*

Remember, beloveds, before the early Church Fathers changed its definition, the word apocryphon originally meant *that which is hidden or secret*. So the apocrypha were hidden writings, kept secret from the masses. Yet I and my closest never would hide anything from you; this was the antithesis of our mission. The early patriarchs not only hid the writings, they then altered the definition of the word to: *that which is spurious or heretical*. As is true of all the apocrypha, John's predates the canonical gospels, and my heart was also in it.

In another also penned by beloved John, known to you as *The Origin of the World*: it further states Eve's true identity and her importance. Here, her name is Zoë, meaning Life, the daughter of the Divine Sophia, the female aspect of God, she who is wisdom: *Sophia sent Zoë, her daughter, who is called Eve, as an instructor in order that she might raise up Adam, in whom there is no spiritual soul so that those whom he could beget might also become vessels of light. When Eve saw her companion, who was so much like her, in his cast down condition she pitied him, and she exclaimed: "Adam, live! Rise up upon the earth!" Immediately her words produced a result for when Adam rose up, right away he opened his eyes. When he saw her, he said: "You will be called 'mother of the living', because you are the one who gave me life."* Later in this apocryphon it reads thus: *the creator and his companions whisper amongst themselves as Adam sleeps: "Let us teach him in his sleep as though she (Eve) came to be from his rib so that the woman will serve and he will be lord over her."*

In truth, dear ones, Adam's rib signifies the Tree of Life, the galaxy, DNA, and through the sacred gateway of the Mother, Eve first arrived to light *The Way* back to God for Adam and all humanity. Beloved of me they are, yet the early patriarchs changed the story to make women appear subservient to men, thus obscuring the path back to the One True God, making all the more difficult the necessary journey to peace and eternal Love. The ancients also correctly understood these female-male aspects to reside within each of us in sacred balanced union.

Forget not Eve's guiding words: *"I am the Pronoia of the pure Light; I am the thought of the undefiled Spirit...Arise and remember...and follow your root, which is I...and beware of the deep sleep."*

Whether ye choose to sleep or to awaken, ever I am with thee. Yet it is much easier to awaken; the path is smoother, the quickening comes, and God awaits.

Beloveds of my heart: *You* are the ones you have been waiting for.

"**D**eep within the Earth are beautiful, magical places, Yeshu'a," says Seshat as we stand outside the Great Pyramid ready to join hands. "In the middle lands are noble creatures, one day to be called Hobbits. Mistakenly thought to be smaller than humans, but, in truth, much like them in size and appearance, they are integrity itself, and filled with joy and wonder. They retreated from the surface after The Fall. The various sacred animals made different decisions as to their fate following our demise. In the days of Lemuria we held a close kinship with the flying dragons; they were so beloved of us, teaching us how to remain playful and free. Without a scintilla of fear we rode upon their backs as they flew us to the corners of the world, and played loving games with them. They are enlightened beings, the dragons, vibrating at a very high frequency, and we honored their guardianship of the world and our civilization."

I recall seeing images of the sacred dragons within some of the ancient texts, and my heart soars at the thought of their exalted state. "Something stirs in me, Seshat, as you speak of them."

"Indeed. There was one in particular who was your great friend, young one. One day we will share a meditation so you may visit him. In those glorious days what was then natural would today be considered magical, not understood. Yet all those who embrace their Ascension will again experience this Divine state of being. Now humanity is in the midst of a long cycle of fear and forgetfulness, which, at your young age, you already know will slowly come to an end two thousand years hence."

"What happened to the dragons?" ask I.

Her ebon eyes grow darker still and fill with tears. "Dearest, it is difficult for me to tell you these things because we were so close to this Divine life, the wondrous creatures so dear to us. Save perhaps the lovely, tender unicorn, no animal on this Earth held such noble dignity as the dragon. Filled with awe-inspiring love, they were our stewards as well as our playmates, and they oversaw the evolving world for hundreds of thousands of years. Their compassion, intelligence, and vision were so profound that, as humanity strayed from God, many became envious of the dragons and sought to dominate them, believing somehow they could enslave them and transmit their powers to themselves and others. After eons of mutual love, when this plot failed, suddenly humanity was at war with the dragons, slaughtering them, thinking their blood held powers that could be used as a vehicle of magic...

"Of course, Yeshu'a, it was not so with you. Many humans still loved the dragons and sought to save them, hiding them, feeding them. They ate only vegetation, contrary to what has since been taught. Your close dragon friend you sheltered for many years, before he, too, had to leave this Earth...Their numbers continuing to dwindle due to our carnage, the lovely dragons finally decided to travel to the Pleiades to escape our newly found ignorance, our newly embraced primitiveness. So loving are they, so strong in Faith, so filled with the golden memories, they have vowed to return to Earth in the Age of the Holy Spirit to assist in our Ascension. Though they now become vilified by man, and even members of the religion bearing your name will tell stories and paint pictures of saints and archangels slaughtering them, still they will return in utter love for humanity. Think of their depth of service to God, young one. They realize their denigration, as always, comes from guilt. Yet return they will, without fail."

Manetho and Thoth are both nodding their heads, the moon beginning to rise above us, shining its healing light. Thoth states, "The unicorns made the choice to stay, and retreated into the Inner Earth, young one. They, too, vibrate at a high frequency and inhabit some of the beautiful, shining inner worlds, awaiting our awakening. ...As we prepare for our journey, three things I will mention to you. First: special dispensation has been given for this journey. In future, when you are a man, you will return to Egypt to finish your initiations, and the full rigors you will then undergo. Second: in all situations you face in life, always remember you are never alone; God is with you. Knowing this, you can embrace this most important adage: no matter the circumstance, ever remain unattached to outcomes. You are the road, not the destination, and only the journey matters. And lastly, no matter what the tales tell you, you are aware that God permeates all substance in the Universe. There is, in truth, only One Life. Never forget this One Life *is* God, the Life which we with it share. Dualism is the curse of ignorant man."

Pursing his lips, he looks upon me with peaceful yet piercing eyes. "Now, we return to the Anunnaki, the Sirians of Oceania, and our rebirth. Upon the rebellion of the slaves there was communication between their leaders and Enki, now becoming more human, and the earthly whales and dolphins and the humanlike Sirians on Oceania. It was now time for a new species to be born on Earth...Enki's plan was working perfectly."

A cube of light now appears before us, growing until it is large enough for a human to walk into. And Thoth signs with his arms. "Behold!"

And indeed, within the large light-cube we now see the scene of a lush garden. Seven beautiful Anunnaki women come together and form a circle. Then all at once it is as if the air, the life, leaves their bodies, and they drop to the ground.

"These seven Anunnaki made the conscious decision to release from their bodies. Now observe closely..." Thoth calmly instructs.

Gradually seven spheres rise out of the bodies, of shimmering white-bluish hue. For a moment hovering over the fallen bodies, the spheres next begin to slowly merge, first touching one another, then interlocking in a pattern recognizable to me. Now I witness the birth of a powerful white-blue flame emanate from the unifying spheres. Suddenly a bolt of energy pulses through me—I am observing the Flower of Life in the process of creation! What joy! What splendor! Thank You, dear God, for this glorious gift.

Thoth explains, "Of course we are seeing the spheres of consciousness of the seven Anunnaki women blending into one. In your studies, young one, you will come to recognize each step in the process you have just witnessed. It is named the Genesis creation pattern. In your people's texts it says the world was created in six days. In the oldest of them it was written thus: *In the beginning there were six*. There are myriad meanings for this, as with all things, but only one of import: understanding Consciousness itself—the sixth sense. Even within the word *Essene* you find the word *sense*. These are all clues leading one to the Truth: Consciousness, Spirit itself, created Life. The first development was the perfect melding of two spheres into one, creating the Vesica Piscis, your sacred sign. This represents the *first day*, or first movement. The Vesica Piscis is the very basis of Light, of which we are all made.

"When the newly formed Vesica Piscis joins with the third sphere of consciousness, the star tetrahedron is born. This represents the *second day* or motion. Spirit ever travels to what is newly born. And we have just witnessed the full six-step pattern that creates the Flower of Life."

A glittering symphony of light, the newly born Flower of Life hovers before us, a testament to the will of God, the power of Love, the inescapable beauty to which we are all bound, if we can but open our heart's eye and see truly.

Now the Flower climbs higher and begins to travel over the land.

Thoth's wife Seshat turns to me and states, "If I am not mistaken, Yeshu'a, Thoth in this moment has some explaining to do." Once more she smiles and the stars shine in her eyes.

"Ha! Women rule the Universe! Never let it be said differently. And nigh-always they are correct. ...Little by little I will continue to instruct you, young one. The new Flower makes its way to the Great Pyramid, where it will enter my fourth dimensional tunnel that leads down to the Womb of the Earth: the Halls of *Amenti*...

"Have you wondered why the northern region of Egypt is called Lower Egypt, and the southern is Upper Egypt? Quite simple it is. Before the last full rotation of the Precession of the Equinox, incredible as it may seem, north was south and south was north, and the sun rose in the west and set in the east. This will occur again come the Age of Aquarius. I bring this to your attention as it is intrinsic to understanding life on Earth. Many believe the Great Pyramid was built by Cheops, the pharaoh, and that he used slaves to transport and hoist the stones. Yet the Egyptians themselves will often tell you true—they did not build it. It is much older than their civilization, and they lacked the knowledge to erect such an exquisite multidimensional object. In utter humility, Yeshu'a, it was I who built it, and no labor of any kind was used, slave or otherwise. It was constructed from the knowledge of Source, for distinct purposes in regards to the survival and the eventual Ascension of humanity and of the Earth Herself. In future, through your initiations and my instruction, you will learn all its secrets and those of its guardian the Sphinx. When the Age of the Holy Spirit arrives, the knowledge will become universally known, and humanity will move beyond it...And thus the true Exodus from Egypt."

Dear Thoth gazes upon me with such a tender eye, Seshat and Manetho on either side of him, their faces agleam. "Before we venture into the hallowed Halls I must also tell thee, young one, that I am known by many names, one of them close to your people's hearts. In time it will become obscured, nigh-forgotten, as the Hebrew texts will mostly veil my presence, save for the Kabbalah...I am also Enoch! ...And I am Enki!"

With astonishment I gasp. Such a fabled name amongst our people is Enoch. And to gaze upon dearest Thoth knowing he, too, was our Father Enki is nigh-too much to bear. Seshat now beams in radiance at his side. Ever she glimmers as the heavens above: the Pleiades are her eyes, Orion is her temples, her gleaming teeth Sirius, her face entire the galaxy, lit from within as the Tree of Life. Somehow I creep, cubit by cubit, toward Truth.

Thoth sighs serenely and continues his revelation. "By many names I am known. By the African Maasai I am called Enkai, their creator god; and yes, the Sumerians named me Enki, the creator of their civilization, and half-brother to Enlil; the Andeans of South America call me Inca; in Mesoamerica, another civilization in that part of the world name me Chanes. Other African tribes call me Ghana, and name the olden African kingdom after me, from which the more modern African peoples known as the Akan will one day come. And forget not: Enoch was a Canaanite hero. In truth, the word Canaan was a Hebrew reworking of the word *Aganor*, the African Father of ancient Canaan.

"These names all have a common root in the Nilotic African languages, and carry the same meaning: *foundation*. The words themselves denote *the formation*. And as difficult as it is to reassess the stories you know, the name Cain itself means the very same. Thus you may realize that there may have been a political need to paint the Canaanites as evil by describing Adam's son

Cain as his brother Abel's murderer, for Cain is certainly tied to Canaan and to all the other names...This also speaks to the story of Noah's curse on his grandson Canaan, through his son Ham. I offer this only for your scrutiny, as it is up to you to decide. You have already witnessed the subjugation of the Canaanites. And the Africans are treated abominably; this will alas continue in our cultures for some time to come...Thus the reason why. ...Yet, as Solomon, you declared, 'I am black,' as did Job when he cried, 'my skin is black.' And in your life as Moses, clearly you were an Egyptian priest-king. ...I tell you all this as it is *all* born of our shame over the loss of Grace by what we have done to the Earth Herself, the most beautiful of places, and of our fear of God as a result. Yet all happens exactly as it should. Do you understand?"

With great purpose I nod my head. "Of course, Master. Take us to the hallowed Halls of *Amenti*. Already I see the brilliant multi-hued forests of the inner worlds where the unicorns reside. No fear have I. Manetho will tell you, dearest Thoth: I thirst for wisdom, Truth, and knowledge. God is with us. This I know in my Heart of hearts."

"Good, young one. This is good. Do not misunderstand me, for the original language of the Hebrews, known by the ancients as Hiburu, was a language of Light and was the Mother tongue, the primal seed language initiated at the outset of this cycle to assist us in our way back home to God. In Light and sound and color, all of the multidimensional aspects of the living Universe reside within it. Never do I cast aspersions on any peoples, nor find in them anything but God. The patriarchal half of the Grand Cycle is ever the dark part of the cycle because of the need for protection; thus, to comprehend the truth beyond appearances, it is best to go into things deeply.

"As you know, the Universe is derived from music. In truth, Light is composed of the vibratory waveform patterns of musical tones. And the Nazoreans sought to keep inviolate the original Hiburu Mother tongue in their language, so closely aligned with what became Hebrew. Notice you will the similarity between the words Hiburu and Nibiru...All of this you know in the Interlife, the space between incarnations when on a soul level you choose the lessons you will learn in your next incarnation to achieve completion. The key is to peel back the veils we place over our physical eyes so that we may be with God while in our skin as well. Awakening ourselves, this transmutes our energy, giving us the ability to chose easier, more grace-filled lessons, and allows us to reach for the stars and attain transcendence."

Manetho and Thoth exchange a knowing glance, Manetho now nodding his head as if giving his blessing to dear master Thoth.

"Young one," Thoth continues. "Before we travel, it is important that I tell you the rest of the story...Manetho has shared some of it with you but has left to me the honor of confusing you all the more." A soft, subtle laugh escapes his thoughts into mine ears. "Manetho has set the stage with its basic structure, but it is far more complex. And with the birth of Babylon the story was changed...

"As I have revealed, I was Enki, Enlil's half-brother. My true name in that incarnation was Ea, meaning water or house of water; Enki was a title, defined as Lord of the Earth and Waters. As a people we were the Anunnaki—*those who from Heaven to Earth came*. And as difficult as it may be to believe, the word Anunnaki refers to the Elohim, as well as to the Nephilim. They are one and the same; the three words carry the same meaning. Yet the true Elohim are angelic-beings, the leaders of the angelic host, the architects of the Universe. Indeed, it was I who came first to Earth, it was I who led the rebellion, and it was I who first created the new human strain, with the help of Oceania. I was the one who uttered the words *Let us make man in our image*. ...You see, I loved my people so dearly, our new creation humanity; I came to Earth to help humanity grow, to gift it spiritual freedom, not to enslave. I endowed humanity with the wisdom of Divine Source, and taught men and women of equality, the Sacred Marriage, the Truth of God, and allowed for the ability to procreate so that humans could evolve and break the chains of bondage and find the path to the One True God beyond all illusions...Thus humanity became a living soul.

"Anu, my Father, was initially angered by this. His desire was to kill off the Divine creation of humanity when the mining of gold was done by allowing the entirety of man to drown in the Deluge, of which the Nibiruans had foreknowledge...So he sent Enlil to fulfill this plot and dash our plan of enlightenment, the highest mission of the Great White Sister-Brotherhood...He sent my half-brother to stop *you* from being born..."

He looks upon me with grave, caring eyes. "I know it is perplexing; it chews at your heart. Yet you are both old and knowledgeable enough now to see why the stories you know tie you up in knots, for they get things wrong; it leaves a nagging question within you: Why? Why would God do such things as are described in your stories, why would God be vengeful, angry, the great punisher? Why would God make you suffer? On and on and on. Well, dearest, you already know the answer...

"*God* would never do such things. The One True God, the Great Central Sun of all the Universes, would never stoke fear in the hearts of His beloved children, would never be angry, would never punish, would never have you live in ignorance. It is a great fallacy to believe one should not teach the Truth of God to everyone from the very day they are born, to instead teach falsehoods that only make it all the harder. Ignorance is not bliss!"

"Yes, Master, I understand this most of all. It goes against the Law itself, yet this we do with great forethought, with great conviction that it is just."

"Yes, you do see, Yeshu. It is, in truth, immoral. As you grow, you will continue to learn. I eschew all pedestals, yet it was I who saved Atlantis from utter destruction, it was I who informed Ziusudra, your Noah, what was to be done, it was I who saved humanity by also sending many to the Lemurians so they would not become corrupted by Enlil and his followers... Indeed, I chose to birth into the Nibiru cycle knowing Enlil would seek to fool humanity into believing he was God, and a god to be feared—a false god. The Nibiru had many wonderful souls among them, dearest, and Enlil himself was bright, yet still he feared God; he had no desire to become the Light. He was still learning numerous karmic lessons of the ego. And in his opinion, man had become too noisy. In part, this was the result of the revolt for freedom, but I also taught humanity more languages to speak so that we could escape Enlil's influence. ...In utter humility, I say to you that, verily, no one liked Enlil much; people found him to be a pompous, fearful, dictatorial windbag who spoke crookedly, and who led his people to suffering, not to the Light of God. Indeed, in fear of Enlil, to appease him, Abraham himself was prepared to sacrifice the life of his son Isaac as a result of witnessing the fall of Ur. Sadly, Enlil's kind will mostly rule the world until the Age of the Holy Spirit arrives; for various ostensible reasons, in the future, by them many wars will be waged in attempts to destroy the true story. Thus the need for the Great White Sister-Brotherhood, for all Lightworkers, to keep Truth alive...

"Nigh-twenty centuries from now, twenty-two thousand Sumerian cuneiform tablets will be discovered. Until then, man will not know its civilization had even existed. It will then take more than another century for the stories to be rightly understood. ...We must celebrate in our hearts that day's arrival. Before the Babylonians corrupted the story by embracing Marduk, a fearful father god having nothing whatsoever to do with the One True God, and turning Tiamat into a hateful, fearful abyss of a woman-planet, the world had been named Eridu by the Sumerians, a luscious sphere of peace, a garden paradise, for Atlantean and Lemurian and Sumerian and all Indigenous alike."

A glint in his soul's eye, Thoth gazes upon me anew. "Listen closely to my words, Yeshu'a, for when you hear the entirety of the story, you will see how it corresponds to what occurred here on Earth. As Ea, my Mother was the Divine Antu, Father Anu's elder sister and first wife. Enlil's Nibiruan name was Ilu; Enlil was a title meaning Lord of the Air and Lord of the Command. And Enlil's Mother was Ki, Father Anu's junior sister and second wife. Though my Mother was Anu's first wife and elder sister, Enlil was older than I. Yet by right of matrilineal succession, the rule our society lived by, kingship was bestowed upon the first born of the elder sister-first wife. This is the tradition of royal succession throughout the Universe when societies hold true to the manner in which the Universe is made. As the One True God manifests in nature, matrilineal succession—through the link of mitochondrial DNA—ensures justice and balance, cooperation and order, wisdom and growth. No matter what patriarchal plot claims to the contrary, inevitably it is so. Of course, Enlil saw it differently. And because he dishonored the Law, he did the same to nature and to man. All happens just as it should, but Enlil was responsible for creating the artificial separation between nature and God, and thus man and God."

"As a civilization, did Nibiru cleave to the Law?"

"It did in all things. There was a council of Anunnaki that made all decisions based on absolute balance, and from which Anu received his power to govern if he abided by their decisions. But with Enlil's emergence, this changed; he began to control the council; community was forsaken; communal decision was discarded in favor of dictatorial power. Consequently competition arose and harmony was lost to subservience. So pervasive was the climate of fear on Earth, it was thought Enlil caused the Great Flood; Enlil propagated this belief. And the ingenuity of his plot was so profound that I was made the culprit for teaching humanity the way to spiritual freedom. Yes, I was the one who created Adam and Eve *and* urged them to eat of the Tree of Life and Knowledge, something infinitely favorable for their spiritual development. The serpent represents wisdom."

"Yes, dear Thoth. My dear Mother told us this when I was a babe."

Seshat chimes in, "Indeed, your Mother, your family, is wise. This we have known."

"Not only was it believed Enlil caused the flood," Master Manetho adds, "the beliefs fostered by Enlil and his followers made possible the invasion and eventual destruction of Sumeria."

Thoth nods. "Yes, it is true. At risk of getting ahead of the narrative, it might help if you knew that Marduk was my son… Yet I had this son so that the luminous Inanna could be born… She was his daughter…*You* were his daughter! The black-headed people were vital to the evolution of Spirit on this planet, and it was Inanna who made this possible. Without her all would have been lost…So, Marduk was necessary…

"Remember, dear Yeshu'a, originally the Tree of Life and the Tree of Knowledge were one tree, and what we are really talking about is Consciousness, not a physical tree. And when Enlil heard they had *eaten of the fruit*, he was furious and could not find them. In other words, evidently *God* could not find Adam and Eve. Ponder this for a moment. Obviously neither Enlil nor I was God. I never said I was. But Enlil did. And his punishment was severe—he decided to create humans who could not procreate, and he kept a list of them so he could keep track. Enlil wanted to destroy Noah and all humanity. I was the one who saved humanity by warning Noah and then furnishing him with the proper plans for building a ship capable not only of transporting animals and Noah's family to safety, but also a large number of engineers, scientists, artists, builders, priestesses and priests, farmers and artisans and so many more. Yet Enlil later claimed Noah as his own, the very man he had sought to destroy. Do you begin to sense a pattern?"

Seeing me nod amazed at the subtlety of the plan, Thoth nods firmly in return, his eyes swimming in joy that I somehow understand. "Ultimately, dear one, under Enlil's command, his sons—Ninurta and Ningal—and his human followers waged war against my humans, and Sodom and Gomorrah were destroyed by an arsenal which split the atom, devastating weaponry to say the least. The so-called radioactive result brought about the end of the Sumerian civilization. And Enlil lost his preeminent position of authority…This is written in the

Sumerian, Mesopotamian records. Yet what would now become a patriarchal custom was here enacted with unparalleled precision: the painting of false-pictures by the clever, even masterful use of truth-reversal in favor of dictatorial wrath... Showing *evidently* God (Enlil) being right when he was wrong, honest when he was dishonest, a savior when he was the destroyer. It was Enlil who ordered the Semitic invasions that brought about Sumeria's demise, which in turn led to the necessity of the confusion of tongues. It is written he brought about The Flood, when he did not; he did level the cities of Sodom and Gomorrah but not because they had fallen into sinfulness, but because of the astonishing wisdom and high level of scientific, artistic, spiritual, societal, and cosmic knowledge of their citizens. This truth will become known with the discovery of a sacred text entitled The Coptic Paraphrase of Shem. In truth, Enlil was responsible for sending the Israelites into seventy years of captivity under the powers of six Babylonian kings...Yet the belief will be fostered, and then written, that only when the temples of the cities of Sumeria and Akkadia were rededicated to Enlil and his wife Ninlil were the cities deemed habitable again. Yet who was responsible for their destruction in the first place? This, dear Yeshu'a, is the devastating mountain of propaganda built to paint Woman as evil, to shroud the path to God, to make humanity ignorant."

Thoth heaves a sigh which fills my soul with his sadness. "When dearest Inanna made her journey to the Underworld, Enlil would not assist her. Known by very few, Inanna was my Father Anu's favorite, for upon witnessing from the heavens all that transpired, Anu came to the Light and knew she was the Light of the World. I, of course, saved my dear Granddaughter. ...And certainly Marduk loathed his daughter Inanna; he was her archenemy...But without him she would never have been born. Obviously, Marduk also caused great problems for Enlil and his early Hebrew supporters; the infamous captivity occurred at this time, yet Enlil never even lifted a finger to assist them. As Anu stated, Enlil felt they were expendable." In a sweet soul-embrace, Thoth's heart now touches mine, as mine bleeds. "You have now heard a more complete version of the Truth, with spaces to be filled in anon, and so you are ready to see the birth. Let us pray."

In solemn prayer we four put our hands together, palm-to-palm before our hearts. After sufficiently focusing every bit of our energy toward God in our praises, we join hands, and a jolt runs through me. All at once we are one soul yet retain our individual consciousnesses as well. My soul's eye observes the king's and queen's chambers, and next we dart down a lit-from-within tunnel, through the massive underground City of the Gods, then penetrating the upper crust, the earth outside black as a starless night sky.

# Chapter Ten
# Birth and Inanna

SOON THE DARKNESS RECEDES, and we pass through luminous regions replete with stunning trees of azure and orange and jade, multicolored moss-covered hills, glittering streams of cobalt-blue, the water liquid crystal, all lit by an Inner sun.

Shafts of pure white light pour over every scene, bathing each in serenity. All sorts of mannered animals roam freely the meadows of gleaming silver, green, and gold, and the hillocks and the valleys. Not unlike your whippoorwill, the songs of the birds carry aloft my soul, as if on a cushion soft, floating into God's graceful gaze….It is a place magical.

And suddenly, like a vision of Heaven, I espy the noble unicorn standing by a stream, his head bent to the water.

*What you see, young one, lives in the fifth dimension,* Thoth's voice intones within me. *You see all because we have passed through the fourth dimension. This world is not visible to most humans today, for they lack the ability to see with God's eyes. Here the gentle, loving unicorns live in peace, awaiting the birth of the new age. For them, and all who live as the soul lives, the centuries pass like minutes, the millennia like hours. Like the loving dragon, their mission is pure; they await humanity's awakening with such pure purpose of heart.*

Upon being given the task by God to name all he observed, it is said Adam saw the unicorn first among the animals, giving him an exalted position in the Universe. The unicorn traveled out of paradise with Adam and Eve, a divine, loving guide and companion of *The Way*, who lives in the purity of God and knows the route home. The noble horse is his cousin who decided to share our journey with us, while the tender unicorn chose to retreat into the Inner Earth as he began to be hunted by men for his horn of purification and for his mane. The Biblical and Talmudic descriptions of the unicorn sometimes bear the mark of man's guilt toward them. The Talmud even refers to the unicorn as the fiercest of animals, and the story of Noah often includes a folktale that says they were banished by Noah from the ark because of their space and care requirements.

Yet the astonishingly beautiful one now before me raises slowly his majestic head, his white mane brilliant with Light, and sweetly speaks my name; he tells me they were not aboard the ark. So utterly did Noah love the unicorn, he allowed them their wish to survive in the Inner worlds, to reappear to humanity when once again we return to God's embrace in the Age of the Holy Spirit. Only then will man be able to see the unicorn, and have the ear to hear his wisdom, his words of loving enchantment, the sight to see his mysterious beauty bespeaking of Paradise... the Paradise we all know in our hearts to be not at all a place, but a state of being, of Unity Consciousness, a realm of the soul.

His emerald eyes softly fondling my heart with Love, he speaks thus: *You may call me Zephyr, dear one, for the earliest Greeks saw me as I am, and numbered me among the living animals of the world, not as myth...One day you, too, will be seen as I, raising up your horn of salvation for humanity, and I will become a symbol of you, my horn emblematic of your unity with God. Yet tales they will also weave of hunting me, murdering me, but it will not last, for, as you, I speak of eternal bliss and Love and of the marriage of the Bride and God. Adam saw me, and Confucius and Krishna and Buddha, too. Ctesias and Great Alexander and Prester John and many others also through the ages caught glimpses. Yet ever more with women have we dwelt, until men grow hearts.*

May I see you again, so we may converse the more? ask I. For there is no veil between us, and I have so much to learn, dear Zephyr.

*We will meet again, of that you can be sure. As I reside here in the fifth dimension, I am everywhere all at once. Here it is as spacious as the Universe entire. And the clouds hear my words of praise and return them to Source. I await thee, my heart filled with joy.*

By his side a posy of radiant lilacs stands in ecstatic beauty. One of them now turns her head toward me and speaks in a child's voice: *Zephyr always speaks true and lovingly. He resides in my heart, as I do his, and you do his and mine. The world awaits thee, dear Yeshu.* With an enchanting smile upon her violet-white petals, she states, *As you continue your journey, ever keep this poem in your heart; all creation wrote it as One in the very beginning:*

> *Fast and furious*
> *The candle burns without the wax*
> *Vast and curious*
> *You look at me like I can't relax*
> *Wondering who I am*
> *I face myself and ask the past*
> *"Who are you," say I.*
> *A child answers in the sky:*
> *"You are the Light."*

Our four united consciousnesses travel into the womb of the Earth, the hallowed Halls of *Amenti*. Based on the proportions of what you call the Fibonacci series of numbers (0, 1, 1, 2, 3, 5, 8, 13, 21, 34, 55, 89, 144, 233…) the various chambers are stone-and-crystal hewn and are not visible to the three-dimensional world; they reside in other octaves, in higher multidimensional realms. We pass through a series of square rooms illumined in golden glow wherein reside the Lords of Light, the Masters of the Earth and Cosmos. Each a perfected merging of male and female, one sits upon a Throne of Light, appearing tall as an oak, pure white iridescent light streaming from a form that seems male, yet with a feminine face, a long white beard falling toward the blue-crystal floor.

Thoth speaks melodious words in an olden tongue, stirring memories within me of all the Four Ages, of the primal birth of Light-worlds long since gone from most of our minds. Though by covenant I cannot repeat them to you, instantly I am informed of my root, our root of Love, and only the ecstasy of Love Pure resides in my soul.

Upon the Light Throne, the Ancient One intones musical notes, deep, pulsating sounds, causing the walls of the crystalline room to become a choir of interval notes, each adding to the whole, creating a chord of celestial hues. And my heart becomes a resonance chamber containing them all...We have been granted admittance.

Journeying through a long hall, suddenly we enter an incredible spiral-shaped room, a long flowing stairway of golden, azure, emerald crystal, all in one, leading down to an open area: ruby-red and cobalt quartz walls, the curvature perfectly formed as if cleaved in one Divine touch, and a light-filled floor. It is vast, the spiral room, infinitely healing and serene. Here, beyond the first four dimensions, the air is charged with energy: cool, blissful, and lovingly charged with magical possibilities. It sparkles and speaks to me. The air itself is alive.

Thoth says, *Yeshu'a, fear not, the Mother's womb was conceived and exists only in the higher dimensions; nothing occurring in the three-dimensional world can harm it. Now, listen closely and understand, dear one: You are the Veil. There is nothing separating one from the numinous, the magical, the Divine, the Glory of God but oneself. Thus, when you hear this term: the Veil, forget not that we are speaking of ourselves...Truly you are the Veil. And to lift the Veil, to banish the darkness of ignorance, of suffering, of lack; to find abundance, wisdom, magic, and Light, look no further than yourself, for ever and always. Behold!*

In the exact center of the immense spiral room is a gray-white cube of gleaming crystalstone, and atop it is the Flame of the Flower of Life created by the female Anunnaki, four feet tall and three to four feet in diameter, its brilliant blue-white flame a vision truly Divine. The Flame is pure Consciousness, vibrating at such a high level it does not blind: it invites, it includes, it soothes. It heals and creates and beckons.

*We are about to witness the arrival of the Sirians*, states Thoth. *For as long as we are here, Seshat will be monitoring the flow of our energy so it is ever balanced, neither male nor female. Though we three males each have the female well-proportioned within us, at any given moment we may veer to our male side; her femininity is crucial, as is her own balance.*

Subtly, now the entire spiral chamber appears to ripple, as if a pebble has dropped into a still pond, the crystalstone walls, stairway, floor, and ceiling seeming to become a giant waveform, merging into one, and we will fall through into some great chasm. *Be with God, be only with God, Yeshu'a*, I hear Seshat say in her calm, knowing voice, her lovely visage like the night-sky appearing before my soul's eye. And lo, soon the chamber stills once more, the hues are ever so slightly different, less muted perhaps. I know by this we have shifted in time.

All at once a large group of Lightbodies shimmers into view, coming from nothing. Beginning as tiny multicolored disassociated gleams, then becoming coherent Lightbody forms, within the passing of a moment they are there, standing before us. Of physical mass, yet not, yet both Light-energy and body, I count thirty-two of them, sixteen male and sixteen female. The Sirians are breathtakingly beautiful, giant like the Anunnaki, yet much more evolved. Thoth is telling me this is their entire race, that their sun, *Sirius B*, is a white dwarf star, a germanium, and highly evolved, thus the sixteen males and sixteen females are married to one another in one family. It is clear their mission is pure, as they kneel and form a prayer-mediation circle, such splendor shining on their faces.

My heart quickens: they are aware of our presence, and bow to us. Putting our hands together palm-to-palm before our hearts, we bow in return. One of the women now steps toward us, an azure disc agleam in the exact center of her forehead: the third eye, like a jewel but a natural, living part of her. Surrounding her is such a glorious light, her face that of the Goddess of the Dawn, she gazes into each of our eyes.

She sings musical tones that I instantly comprehend: *Blessings to you, a thousandfold blessing. You are most welcome. Dear ones, we bestow upon you our greetings in Love and trust, for of you we have heard great tidings of joy. What we will here perform is the act of creation allowing the Divine star seed of humanity to achieve its immortal destiny. Many will attempt to stop it, to kill it, to steal your Light for their own purposes of fearful control...Yet it cannot be. This you know, and as you honor us with your blessings and reverence, so, too, do we, for you are the great Light shining on this Earth which will tend the growth of the Divine presence in all things.*

Retreating back into their prayer-mediation circle, the Sirian Light-woman takes her place. A pulsing melody now emanates from the thirty-two, each of their Heart-voices a distinct pitch, and the tuneful air awash in deep meaning is the result, with harmonies atop harmonies atop harmonies: eight layers of four each. The song is like the whale-song of their Oceanic cousins: so achingly beautiful, so full of Love and Light and wonder, so wise, caring, and pure.

Alternating male-female, they gather around the Sacred Flame of the Flower of Life in a perfect circle, great intent upon their Light-faces, and suddenly giant slabs of quartz appear beside them, rose-pink in hue. Looking each to each, they then lie down upon the slabs, eyes gazing upward to the ceiling of the spiral chamber, the crowns of their heads next to the Sacred Flame.

Says Thoth, *They now make love with the Flame, Yeshu'a; the union is of the highest order for it is a true blending of cosmic proportion. Here they will lay motionless for two thousand years: at one with God, all creation, themselves, the ovum of the Anunnaki, and the womb of Mother Earth. And above, on the surface, the Anunnaki work with their flasks, conceiving in tandem with this planetary birth process, impregnating seven Anunnaki women with the seeds born of it. They, too, will remain motionless for two thousand years...from which the new humanity will be born on Gondwana.*

Now the chamber dissolves and disappears and we travel through a tube of light at an incredible speed. Outside of the light-tube, the star-filled galaxies strewn throughout the cosmos shimmer like jewels, and within, the voices of Manetho, Seshat, and Thoth have united into one, along with mine own. *The black-headed people were always here; they have come before, and will come again. Enki and Adama have told us: "It has occurred; it will* occur. It is God's will. And upon the rebirthing of humanity in Sumeria, a flood of Divine consciousness knowledge comes all at once in a blinding flash of enlightenment." Inanna sees to its perfection and protection and, as a result, to its eventual fruition. Thus the mission is ever the same: to save humanity, to raise it back to Godhood, whence it has come.

I see a brilliant vision of humanity as it has always been, on Earth before the coming of the Anunnaki, and throughout the Universe. A shining, golden Light-filled vision it is, for while we are each but tiny cogs in the realms of all that is, humanity is the temple through which God transforms to higher and higher dimensions. In my own personal revelation, this is what is now clear to me. Many glorious planets I see where men and women still drink the air from the water, the water from the air, and ingest the Divine prana, manna, from the glowing heavens for further sustenance. And now I see that the planet Nibiru once truly belonged to another solar system, and failed in its Ascension, thereby coming into our system, not as the twelfth planet, but as the thirteenth, a Divine thirteen, the original Hebrews having to, in effect, repeat their spiritual schooling in order to join the more enlightened union of the whole…Glory of glories! All is clear, all is dear, and God summons me, a joyous clarion of Love.

Thank you, dearest Lord, for this greatest of all gifts: Life, and the remembrance of all which passes in the doing. The change is upon me.

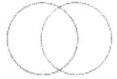

**M**y bosom heaves like a passionate ocean, for indeed it is the Great Sea of the world itself, my every emotion and thought reflected in the churning of the mighty waves. Ever must my thoughts be attuned to the Eternal. My necklace of jade and crystal, carnelian and alabaster, agate and emerald bears all the colors of the rainbow, for indeed it is the rainbow seen upon the crest of every mountain, in the nape of every valley, hovering over every stream, upon the brow of every hillock, the result of my joyful tears bringing life to the world. Ever must my every thought and feeling be measured and sure and attuned to the Eternal.

Crowned am I in glittering lapis: the sky itself, and the stars of the ocean of the heavens, their twinklings and revolutions devoted to and dependent upon me; ever I hold them in my Heart-thoughts. Indeed, the darkness of space itself moves; my perfectly twined black hair, ever in Love with the Light, directs its flow. My every emotion must be pure, even in the act of Lovemaking, the very essence of Divine union; all is born through me: every creature, tree, and waterhole, all the worlds and stars. Even the gods are born through me. My son-become-lover Dumuzi is come; the Great Shepherd is he. His cream is good; his milk is good. He shaped my loins with his fair hands, filled my lap with cream and milk, he the honey-man of the gods. He watered my womb, laid his hands upon my holy vulva, smoothed my black boat with cream, and quickened my narrow boat with milk. His hand is pure honey, my eager impetuous caresser of the navel, my caresser of the soft thighs. He sweetens me always, he whom my womb loves best.

Ever must my every emotion be measured and pure and attuned to the Eternal as I caress the faithful shepherd Dumuzi.

I will caress his loins, the shepherdship of the land; for him I will decree a sweet fate, the honey-man of the gods. For him I bathe, I perfume my sides with ointment, coat my mouth with sweet-smelling amber, paint my eyes with kohl, for he is the one my womb loves best. He is lettuce planted by the water.

Every act, every thought, every feeling, every gaze, touch, and intention is sacred, bathed in the purity of God, for I am Queen of Heaven and Earth. In me all knowledge rests in peace and is secure in the holding; Grandfather Enki has lovingly bestowed upon me this trust: We are all made of Light. And our mere observation influences the Light's behavior. The connection between our emotions and thoughts is what is dear to know. The mind was made as a receptor of information in service to the Heart, a faithful faculty in service to the Heart. Soon men will force the mind to take hostage the world and you may forget the Heart. The Logos, or Heart of the Divine, wherein the wisdom of God resides, ever holds the magic key. A wondrous tool the mind is, when it is used as was originally designed. This Dumuzi knows, my honey-man of the gods. This dearest Grandfather Enki knows. Here in Uruk and in Eridu, the splendid villages, the Flame is lit.

For above my head shines the eight-pointed star: my sacred symbol. Those who enter my rooms here in the palace-temple remark upon its brilliance, the Light glittering about me in blue-white flames. Some few see it not, those who do not see God in themselves, some cower in fear of themselves; others see but do not understand. Yet in our gracious land these constitute the very, very few, for we are the Children of Light. The eight-pointed star represents the four directions: north, south, east, and west, and the two equinoxes and two solstices. It also symbolizes the Breath of the Compassionate, as it is formed of the union of two four-pointed stars: the cycle of creation. To many of the most faithful, the Compassionate is the highest pronounceable name of God. And it, too, was my symbol as I breathed as Melchizedek. Unto thee I tell these things for ever I in poetry sing into the ears of God, of which you, too, are a part. I am you. Look closely mine eyes.

Gula and Damkina, my two lionesses, sprawl on either side of me. Gula I named after the Earth Goddess and Damkina after my dear Grandmother. They tell another truth that the eight-rayed star is Venus: the planet of Love, the great initiator, the morning and evening star. Damkina lovingly presses her left front paw into my girdle of the zodiac indicating the Venusian emerald.

Outside the vaulted pillared windows my land thrives: golden, azure, and green. The groves of date palm beckon, the pear and lemon and apple trees sweetly smile, the grape orchards entice, wheat fields permeate the vistas, the avenues of gold lined with juniper, oak, cypress, and ash, beech, acacia, tamarisk, elm, sycamore, and willow.

The world is a splendid garden, and all are priestess or priest. Across the great Oceans of Atlantis and Lemuria, once our homelands, my sisters and brothers of the Red People silently speak; their Heart-thoughts are my Heart-thoughts, for truly there is only one Soul, one Heart. Their villages are like mine and Grandfather's: living gardens, bountiful testaments to God, vast, towering ziggurats around which society is hewn, amid pools and lush glens and teeming forests, the sky a spectacular canvas we have all imagined into being, though you still may remember it not.

I sing to thee, my beloveds, so you may not forget your Heart, for all you touch and see and hear and taste and sense beyond was born of our imagination, our co-creation. Lest you near the forgetting, call my name, and I will come. If you search for me, you will find my story the same as your beloved Yeshu'a's. I know what comes for me, and I know it will come again in Palestine, yet all this I do for thee—without fear, without remorse, without thought, for in my Heart you breathe. And in thy Heart God resides.

I tell thee true, for while I will be Yeshu'a and his story mirrors mine own, I am the Great Cosmic Mother. And I am Mother Earth. I am Eve and Mother Mary and dearest Sophia, the Shekinah; I am Isis and the Gnostic Great Mother, Ila and Alla, Siva and Abnoba, Cailleach, Branwen, and Brigid. Now may the Light of the Great Central Sun of all the Universes be awakened in thee, for this, in truth, is who Yeshu'a is. Upon my cheek I feel your breath. And in thine own Heart God resides, for thou art me.

The footfalls of my high priest come down the hall, my high priestesses about him in Holy fours. Grandfather's sacred number is forty. *Enki...Enki...Enki, Enki*, his name I silently call as many times. Yet now as my priestesses and priests enter my chambers, it is I who am called. So I must bilocate. And like the Light that I am, all at once I am also on his rooftop terrace in Eridu, what we have also named the world entire.

"They have come, Grandfather," say I without a word.

"Indeed," he replies, his handsome pointed beard bobbing in acknowledgement. "The Aryans will soon in future come, and the Semites. Sargon will take Uruk and make it a city, Gilgamesh will surround it with walls, Hammurabi will write the laws of conquest. Babylon will create Ishtar in thine image but will make her a Goddess of war, as well as of Love. From the very first invasions, thine own story will change…The men will steal your power and make you appear the fool. Thou hast known the time would come…"

"…Yes," sigh I. "And Father sits and waits on Nibiru. All must be as it will be; this thou hast taught and shown me. My people, the souls of Light, the chain unbroken from Atlantis and Lemuria, and ere before on other worlds, are my only concern… They will become like legends, myths, chimeras, symbols…like the wisps of shadows. Architecture, writing, engineering, astronomy, music, all the arts and sciences, religion: all this and more we bequeath the world, so that the sacred knowledge is not lost or forgotten…The souls of my people are my only care…They will never die!"

"Because of you." He smiles wide, the gleam of the heavens in his caring eyes. He thinks of the tender unicorn, Zammuz, my childhood pet. The thought of him merely crosses both our hearts, and he is here with us.

*Naught is time, dear Inanna*, sings he. *O Holy Shepherdess, Keeper of the Cow-Byre, you are the Builder of that which has Breath, the Carpenter of Humanity, the Carpenter of the Heart, the Coppersmith of the Gods, the Coppersmith of the Land, the Lady Potter. You who shed limitless tears in joy and sorrow, who conceived Dumuzi so he would become your sacred-lover, the one whom your womb loves best, even you and I will again meet, though our names will be different. Touch my horn once more.*

And I do.

Vaulting through the stars am I, a stream of Light. Instant by instant I see ever more of our profound creation. Now I am on Oceania, on the Isle of Love. Enki is here, and Zammuz, and the sacred whales and dolphins frolic in the sea. The palm trees tower into the sky, a song of serenity fills the air. And the holy thirty-two who rebirthed us on Earth now arrive. My third eye is alive as never before.

The blond one named Adama speaks: "Great praises, dearest daughter. On this day I will show you one moment in time, far into the future on Earth."

Before us a living cube of light appears, and within we view some sort of laboratory. "What we see occurs in a land called Britain, many millennia in the future from your earthly days," Adama continues. "As we know, everything in the Universe is alive and is made of Light: the Light of God. The smallest units of Light will be named electrons, or photons. Through man's long dalliance with science, he will build many machines, two of which you see here."

On one side of the laboratory there are two men operating a device that is projecting a thin beam of Light across the room against a thin wall with slits in it. On the other side of the wall stands a machine which appears to be a receptor of some sort.

Mine eyes intuit the import of the scene. These men are somehow obtaining a record of the nature of the Light-beam. "With inquisitive eyes, these men endeavor to understand the nature of Light, how it behaves," say I. "They question the existence of God; how can this be?" Yet as soon as my inner voice says these words, I know the answer.

"Yes, Inanna," Grandfather Enki responds. "The nature of God, the knowledge of God has long been lost. This moment we see is near the end of the reign of darkness; the Age of Aquarius comes nigh-two centuries hence.

For a moment we watch the men about their tasks, I full of Love for humanity's ability to find Truth, no matter the many veils we place before our eyes.

"Much will be discovered about the nature of Light by these studies," Adama states. "We focus ourselves upon the important, all-encompassing Truth, which humanity will neither comprehend nor accept until after Aquarius arrives. In the dense three-dimensional world, form, or mass—a mountain, tree, flower, rock, table, or animal, human or not—exhibits itself in what will be called a particle-based pattern. Yet, outside of time and space, in the higher realms, Light acts in a different manner, like the waves of an invisible ocean. This will be called a waveform pattern. You see here a machine shooting an electron or photon-beam across the chamber. On the other side of the wall, there is a device which, upon the beam hitting its surface, creates what is called a photograph of what it sees, a true-to-life painting, capturing an instant in three-dimensional time...Much to the amazement of these scientists, when they measure, or observe, the electron beam hit the photographic plate and the photograph is created, the results demonstrate the beam existing in a particle-based reality, but when they do not observe the process, when they are not watching, the photograph taken shows the Light to exhibit waveform properties, that it exists in a completely different manner, what we know to be a part of the higher, multidimensional realms. Though they would not have understood because we know the language of the Heart, we could have told them this millions of years ago."

"How joyous!" I cry.

"Indeed. And a new expression will be introduced into the world's languages: little by little humanity will come to understand that the nature of Light is *observer-dependent*. Following these studies, a new realm of science called Quantum Physics will be born. And ever so gradually humanity will come to accept itself as being composed of Light, which can and does behave differently depending on the observer's expectations or perception. With this knowledge, man will slowly begin to understand how a physical pattern can change when one chooses to observe it from a quantum, Godly perception—what many will call waveform consciousness. Instantaneous healing, for example, will return; once more, disease will no longer be known. This is merely one result of this *breakthrough of God*. Ascension will also be rediscovered, and the Merkaba; suffering will cease, so many Love-filled things will come of it."

Adama raises and outstretches his arms to the paradise all around us, an expression of pure joy upon his face. "Here on Oceania, this knowledge of the Heart was never lost; indeed, we have only grown in our Love. And thou, dear Inanna, in thy many forms, art the reason why this knowledge survives on Earth, though its path is painful."

He kisses me on the cheek and brow, and I am traveling again through the cosmos, the Pleiades rushing past, a cache of jewels humanity will one day discover.

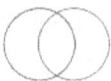

My priests enter my rooms with solemn faces, the priestesses at supreme ease around them and coming to encircle me. Gula and Damkina are already bored with this scene, yawning with gaping maws and teeth like sharpened timbers. In this moment I bilocated so as to be with Enki in Eridu and on Oceania and to also remain here. To achieve bilocation, one must still the body and mind and master the subtle energies of the etheric body so one can exist in absolute balance, and project one's consciousness, while remaining attuned to all the processes in two locations, even if it be exercised for interdimensional travel, and not merely for two locations in the physical planes. In this moment, my wish was for my priests not to become fearful at my disappearance. Through the Rite of the Sepulchre, the sacred skills of bilocation, teleportation, interdimensional travel, resurrection, Ascension, and more are learned.

Apsu, the high priest, is anxious. While we journeyed to Eridu and then to Oceania, he exclaimed of the dire situation forming to the east of tribes having witnessed and heard of our prowess in the arts and sciences and our knowledge of the Divine. Some of our loving souls inhabiting the outlying areas have been murdered. This is the first event of its kind in our world, and, truth be told, it is the beginning of the end of paradise. And ultimately the forces of fear will mostly be fearful of me.

Suffer not, dearests of my Heart, for I know not fear...I will survive in thee.

"Have I not spoken with thee of this, Apsu, not four moons past? We have known of its coming from the beginning. Fear nothing! And it will go well."

"Yes, Goddess-Queen. This I hear without thy speaking. But of thee I sing: the people; you possess the *Mes*, the tablets of civilization, the laws of existence, from Divine Truth to weaving and sculpting and the art of the Sacred Harlot. Therein also is contained the Great Mystery. Will you survive?" His brow is deeply furrowed, his countenance dark and perplexed.

All at once the group of priests is aghast, agog, in turmoil—the full import of what comes has finally been realized. My ladies of God smile and chortle, appearing to have expected this scene, as the male clamor fills the room.

I will take none of it. "Silence! Silence all!" The priests look upon me in befuddled awe. "Fear not! We will conceal the Great Mystery, in Consciousness and in the Earth. In Consciousness, we will leave the clues in the higher realms, so that when humanity is ready, women and men will find it—first in the Unity Consciousness Grid. In the Earth we will leave our writings, our symbols...One day they will all be found...When God decrees it. Then we will return, as will all the souls of humanity. Do you understand?"

Apsu nods sheepishly, and the others follow suit.

"Even you will change, Apsu, I promise you. The conquerors will change my story and create many falsehoods to confuse the masses, to debase the Woman; this we have known. And now that the tribes begin to mark their paths to our destruction, you will know I must descend, to resurrect and ascend...By my head, they will place me on the hook, from which I will hang three full days, until I am conceived dead by their willful ignorance. If you see not that this is a plan we have created and implemented, then you are fools!"

The room is gone silent. Outside the windows I espy many on their rooftop terraces, their hands together, palm-to-palm.

These are my people. All hear my words, even the stars and orbs which wheel in the heavens.

"My sweet honey-man of the gods will save me, of this you may be sure, he whom my womb loves best: Dumuzi. For this he is come. I call to thee, man of the honey of the moon, arrive!"

Lo, Light shimmers near the double-doors. It begins to take on form. In the same instant the room fills with many others: there is Enki, yet also Enoch and Thoth and Seshat, Melchizedek, Moses, Solomon and Sheba, Yeshu'a and Magdalen, Enkai, Inca, Chanes, and Ghana, and their wives. Krishna is here, and the Buddha: all the holy men and women of the world it seems appear.

Yet there is only my honey-man of the gods, in his beautiful sculpted body, his fine rippling muscles, his beaming smile, his eyes like burning sapphires. He approaches.

"Inanna, I would go with thee to my garden. I would go with thee to my orchard. I would go with thee to my apple tree. There I would plant my honey-covered seed. To the ends of the Universe I would go with thee."

Out of the floor around him grasses now grow, and grains and lilac flowers and roses. And a cedar unlike any other sprouts as from an invisible seed, and pours into the room, causing the priests to cower in the corner. The mighty cedar pushes against the ceiling and crashes through it, bringing in the light of day. Birds are within it, singing a joyful song. And my heart flutters, wanting to feel his penetration once more.

"O Inanna, thy breast is thy field. Thy broad field pours out plants; thy broad field pours out grain. Water flows from on high for thy servant. Bread flows from on high for thy servant. Pour it out for me, Inanna. I will drink all ye offer."

Dumuzi raises his right hand high above his head and, from the air itself, produces a blue rose, unknown to nature, abeam it is with radiating Light, and gifts it to me.

"Bridegroom, dear to my heart, goodly is thy beauty, honeysweet. Lion, dearest to my heart, goodly is thy beauty, honeysweet. Bridegroom, let me caress thee; my precious caress is more savory than honey, in the bedchamber honey-filled. Lion, let me caress thee once more, for my caress is more savory than honey."

Looking upon the chamber, filled with plant and flower and tree and bird and more, the priests have become joyful and serene. All is peace and Love, no matter what comes.

"My dear children all, Children of the Light, he has sprouted; he has burgeoned; he is lettuce planted by the water. He is the one my womb loves best. And through him our future is sure...Leave us."

When the room is empty of all but ourselves and the bountiful nature surrounding us, I gaze into Dumuzi's eyes agleam. "Love me."

# Chapter Eleven
# Rebirth and Destruction

"BY NOW YOU ARE coming to realize many things from your experience as Inanna," states Manetho, the Ageless One. "Though your conscious mind is still studying it, your oversoul, or higher self, has been working to integrate this experience into your conscious mind so that you may move forward and accomplish your mission in this life."

In the lotus position we sit in his rooms in the temple of Heliopolis. Thoth and Seshat are no longer with us. And I feel as if all my recent experiences occurred over a span of many days. But, clearly, time has not passed. What I witnessed and participated in is so vast in its implications, so profound in the knowledge revealed, I find Manetho's words strike exactly the right chord. Yet, too, I sense there is much more. Manetho's knowing smile tells me so.

"Yes, Master, it is so. I feel I am on the cusp, yet through the door of the Eternal I walk, God and the angels guiding me in Love. Reliving those moments of my life as Inanna awakens me all the more. Nothing is closed to me now; I veil myself from nothing."

"Good. Thoth knew you were ready, and you do remember all. Now I will mention a most important element to stitch it into cloth for you. As a living human soul, you are a part of the One Soul, the higher matrix as some call it, of all humanity, each of us just one aspect of it…Adam Kadmon, as the Kabbalists name it. When you were very young, you heard your Mother speak of the idea of the Messiah, how the way it is now perceived by man causes great calamity, for in a messianic culture the people seek the Anointed One…one *special* person in whom the Glory of God is revealed, who will lead the masses to spiritual freedom. She was very clear: this belief ever leads to destruction; men kill each other in fits of crazed ideas and feelings, as if the world will end, and deny the divinity in each other. Ever your Mother is pure and knowing and calm in her words, intuiting precisely how the wisdom of God, gnosis, is to be revealed in every given moment. It is a gift. You see, dear one, she spoke of this in your presence even as a babe because she understood you already knew Truth. She said the spark of God exists in everyone, and the Glory of God will only arrive when this Christ Consciousness resides within enough of humanity that the rest will plainly see."

"Yes indeed, Manetho. I remember it well."

"It is one thing to hear the wisdom, the Truth, and another to experience it, to *know* it. You know it, dear Yeshu'a. There is yet more to come. But you do know it. Before you leave Egypt to return to Palestine you will know much more. Yet, in this moment may you truly comprehend that the term Messiah is a cumulative term, a collective noun. It was never meant to refer to a single so-called *special* person, as by ignorance it has been corrupted into meaning. The true Messiah is the entirety of humanity, when it reaches the level of Love required to vanquish all suffering, all limitation, and attain the Light, to be the Light it has always been...When enough of humanity ceases to be so fearful of *being* loved. Truly it is remarkable that so many cling to suffering and are so fearful of the Light; the illusion of guilt is so pervasive because the ego—the very reflection of fear—paints, and then accepts, a devastatingly true false-picture that it is real, that suffering is real and good and Love is the illusion."

The Ageless One gazes upon me with caring eyes and loudly proclaims, "Some will call you a king, the King of Israel; this the prophecy of Micah tells them, so they believe. Yet you and I know better. It is not the earthly kind of king at all. As you are beginning to say with your own words, to feel with your own Heart-thoughts, as once again you breathed in Inanna's body and knew once more your heart is hers, she spoke the Truth well: *Look closely mine eyes. I am you.*"

For a moment I ponder in silence, and then state, "Words are inadequate, are they not, Master? They are merely tools to convey the reflection of the essence of things, yet their mastery is of such importance. Krishna spoke well of how one is to attain the essence of peace, of being with God. He said: *In profit or loss, pleasure or pain, sickness or health, victory or defeat, praise or criticism, remain the same! Remain evenminded!*"

"Yes, indeed he did. A writer far into the future named Kipling will say it thus: *If we meet with triumph and disaster, and we treat those two imposters the same*...Words, dear one, convey great meaning; they emit powerful energy unto themselves which radiates across the Universe. The secret is to find simple ways of conveying the deepest wisdom; small words and pithy parables are invaluable. For myself, I choose a phrase of five simple words we have spoken since the golden ages; they will be said again and again until there is no need: *Let go and let God.*"

My heart smiles wide upon hearing these words, for, indeed, nothing else need to be said.

"It is well you mention Lord Krishna, or Christna, as he was most anciently named. In your visit with Sheba, she mentioned your people's Ark of the Covenant. The Hindus, too, Yeshu'a, have their Ark, which, even millennia in the future, they will parade once a year through the streets...God being carried in procession. Too, the Egyptians have had many Arks. Your people's Ark was patterned after them."

"Krishna speaks to me, dear Manetho. He is my brother of the Spirit; he tells me his name today is Maitreya. Already I know I will travel eastward to study and to teach. He calls to me..." Gazing curiously upon my dear friend, I decide to speak my thoughts. "Sheba also revealed my dear Mother would become the new Ark, and that I myself would become the sacred food of God. Please, Master, explain this to me."

Quietly he smiles. "The Ark, dearest, is most of all a symbol of the union of opposites, what it carries within—the food of God, the Divine universal energy, manna, the holy nectar—derives from the perfect union of female and male. It is the energy of creation, of healing, of transcendence: the very sustenance of both physical and spiritual life. Your resurrection, like that of Osiris and Krishna, is the result of this blending of opposites. This is how and why it occurs, yet it is only a means to an end, a mere illustration of humanity's divinity shining *The Way* for all of us. Ascension is achieved without resurrecting. They are two entirely different processes. In future we will speak more of this, for yours is unique, and will take the dedicated assistance of many so that you may achieve it. Resurrection is the conquering of death in the body. Ascension is eternal life...

"Far in the future, in the land of Albion will reside a certain form of temple called a cathedral. Within it will be a lovely carving of Moses leading the Israelites out of Egypt, the Israelites carrying the Ark upon poles. In this image the Ark is a small reliquary box. On the opposite side of the carving will be an image of you emerging from an Ark-like container, the Light of the Vesica Piscis shining behind you. Your Mother's womb brought you into this world, and you will become the resurrection of the Testament of God, as truly it exists in all things. In sheer earthly terms, this is indeed your mission. All I will say of your people's physical Ark of the Covenant, which today resides well-guarded and well-hidden in Axum, is that, in truth, within it are the tablets of the Commandments given you as Moses by God, and nothing more."

"Yes, this I know well."

"The Ethiopian priests wrap tabots, copies of the original tablets, in shrouds to create a mystical replica Ark, but they fiercely guard the true Ark and the original tablets. Even these tabots they hold sacred...Remember, young one, like Noah's own vessel: the Ark is a boat or ship, the word bark, or barque, derived from it, a vessel that provides safety and protection. Its use as a word for the container of the Covenant—a connection to the sea of creation on Earth—is well-understood. And the measurements given by Enki/Thoth to Noah for the building of his ark are, in truth, a Divine code which reveals the ark to be the Universe entire, and humanity the vehicle through which God is realized. Indeed, the ark *is* man! ...A study of the ark reveals eleven main sections and at the roof and base of each are three lesser divisions, making for a total of thirty-three, a most sacred number which will be attributed to you in many ways...

"The human body has thirty-three vertebrae leading to the crown chakra; in Hermetic tradition there are thirty-three publicly known degrees, which the future Freemasons will also use. At one time, thirty-three constellations and thirty-three signs were known. The first temple of Solomon was said to have stood for thirty-three years, your Father of that life, David, said to have ruled as king thirty-three years, and your own life today to last thirty-three years, alas which is false. You will live much longer. Indeed, in many of the most ancient writings, Noah's ark is not even said to represent a boat at all, but a salvational spiritual state of being, in higher realms, which can survive the collapse of the Universe. As you know the word Christ is a title and not a name, you will understand that thirty-three symbolizes Christ Consciousness."

Manetho gazes caringly upon me. "When esoterica becomes thick as mud in symbols and symbolic numbers, it can tie your mind up in knots. To the uninitiated, the symbolic can appear to be the stuff of nonsense. But, as you know, symbols always have real meaning, so it is best to heed omens, even if one does not completely understand them. Banish fear, seek and find serenity, exude unconditional Love and forgiveness of everyone and everything, know it all to be sacred, and the true meaning will then appear."

For a few moments we commune in silence, I deeply contemplating the enormous impact of all I have just heard, embracing its significance in connection with the extraordinary history I have witnessed in my journeys with Thoth, Manetho, and Seshat, and the insights I have been given by experiencing bits of my lives as Inanna, Solomon, and Moses. How is it possible, dear Lord, that I am so loved by You, that I have such a loving family, that my teachers and friends are so pure? How can it be that every breath of every single day is filled with such wonder and Love?

In the silence I release any desire, any attachment to a miraculous answer finding my ears. Just as I am empty of any anticipation, the Voice comes, a Voice so pure, so soft and soothing, so irrefutable in its presence within me: *Dearest Son, you are so loved because you Love so; each and every creature has this Love shining within and nothing more; every stone and flower, tree and blade of grass, stream and mountain and valley is filled with my Love. The air itself is an expression of my Love. In this way it is only possible for you because you have chosen it; it has chosen you. Your family, your friends, your teachers, and I are all the exact things you have imagined...because you have imagined it...just so. This you will teach and demonstrate with every act and word. Beloved you are.*

"Now I will share with you what occurred in Atlantis," says Manetho. "Though seemingly a circuitous route we have taken, it was necessary for you to clearly understand the true history of the world. Unbelievably, now for long ages many will be told the world is flat. In truth, what you have already witnessed and learned is of the utmost importance; what later happened to Atlantis is intrinsic to understanding our mistakes.

"Intimately connected to Consciousness and the Precession of the Equinox, when the pole shifts occur on Earth, one land often sinks and another rises. In the generations following Adam and Eve, Gondwana sank and Lemuria rose, and Thoth-Enki saw to it that Adam and Eve's descendents were moved to Lemuria. Here they lived free of the influence of Enlil's Anunnaki for many joyous millennia, some seventy thousand years. And in this long reign of paradise humanity developed in the ways of the right-brain, the female orientation. It was during this time that two spiritual leaders, one male and one female, attained immortality. They formed the first Mystery School and discovered Light-conception, whereby interdimensionally they conceived offspring who also became immortal. This is lovemaking at the highest levels, without touching, without even needing to be in the same physical space...Much later, Yeshu'a, this is how you, too, were born, through the Divine knowledge of your Mother and Father.

"The Lemurians knew when the next pole shift would occur over a thousand years in advance of the event. And before the eventual sinking of their land of many islands, through their Mystery School, nearly one thousand of their people learned these skills: Light-conception, resurrection, and Ascension. As a result of the sum of their knowledge, by the time of the sinking of Lemuria, most of the Lemurians had dispersed and resettled in North and South America, as far north as the sacred mountain you visited with Thoth named Mount Shasta, and in many other locations. And with them they brought all their important relics, their tools and crystals and disks. The Lemurians and their culture, their spiritual science, their art, their advanced right-brain technology, all survived. They had only just begun their journey when the demise of their land occurred, so the Earth was not yet prepared, but, in truth, because they survived and knew exactly what to do and where to go, God was at all times with them, knowing the day will come when the higher-dimensional Lemurians will light *The Way*."

Manetho now brings his hands together palm-to-palm before his heart, and a multidimensional image appears before our eyes, hovering between us. Walking over to stand behind me, he cannot help but emit a sweet sigh. "This is the great continent of Atlantis, once our home."

Indeed, it is a beautiful sight: a plush land with many varied terrains: of lakes, forests, grasslands, fields of grains, some low-lying mountains. It is a vast, rich dominion.

Pointing to an isle just north of the continent, he states, "This is where the immortal Lemurians relocated. While the rest of the surviving Lemurians scattered across the two Americas and beyond, the nearly one thousand immortals traveled here using the knowledge of flight. And immediately they set to the task of building an enlightened land. For a long time they lived in deep meditation, sanctifying the newly born region, existing in deep communion with the Earth. Building upon their experience in Lemuria, they then began to re-create their sacred science."

Now a gleaming image of the Tree of Life appears upon the Atlantean continent, each axis-point clearly marked as a Light-filled circle, with two extra points: one on the northern island, the other in the ocean just south of the landmass.

Says Manetho, "You have seen the Cross of Atlantis in the ancient texts." (*Beloveds, I place one below for your eyes to see.*)

"Across the world all future crosses within circles will derive from this cross. There is of course meaning to the alternating black and white rings. The black rings denote water and the white denote earth. There are also junctions along each ring of black on white and white on black, and a white inner cross in the black core. I mention this as an illustration of the depth of Atlantean knowledge, for of course the rings also represent the harmonic balance of male and female." Turning once more to the image of Atlantis overlaid with the gleaming sacred Tree, Manetho continues: "Each circular point of Light on the Tree of Life here represents the location of a city, and at its center stands an acropolis: in the Atlantean cross this would be the Heart."

I smile wide. "Yes, Master. And in the composition of the brain, the left hemisphere is the logical male side, and the right the experiential, feeling female side, connected in placental mammals by the corpus callosum; you have told me it will be called this."

"Indeed, Yeshu'a. The corpus callosum also existed in other mammals now extinct, or thought to be extinct, called the Eutherians. The other vertebrae animals have various structures linking the two hemispheres of the brain. Of course you already know that in vertebrae animals the pineal gland is the great gateway of the union of the hemispheres to attain the Divine...

"And you are wise to mention this. From the beginning, the immortal Lemurians who came to reside on Unal, the island due north of the Atlantean continent, made the fateful decision to fashion their new society upon the structure of the brain. They felt the brain must come first. And this was their mistake. It goes against the fabric of Creation itself to *create* in this manner. When the Aquarian Age arrives, in fifth-dimensional form, many Lemurians will admit this was their error; they will be the way-showers to humanity of the right way to live from the sum total of their lessons: the Heart must rule; the female is indeed the master race. This *so-called* mistake would open the door for the Martians to break Galactic Law and impose themselves and their ways upon the Earth. Behind the scenes, their kind will rule the Earth until the Age of the Holy Spirit arrives."

I gaze deeply into Manetho's eyes as he says this, knowing he was once Atlantean, and sensing how deep his pain is at the loss. "Yet, Master, God even decreed this. All happens as it should; there must have been a karmic reason to learn this lesson."

"Yes, indeed it is so. The immortal Lemurians fashioned a representation of the human brain on their island. Thoth retains the record of this incredible endeavor; on the surface of Unal, so that it submerged into the earth, they first created a wall that split the island exactly in half—roughly twenty-seven cubits high and thirteen cubits wide. They filled this enclosure with water: the earthly corpus callosum.

"Now, the human brain is additionally divided into four lobes. The frontal lobe of the right-female hemisphere is the emotive, experiential element, the frontal lobe of the left-male hemisphere the logical element. Yet behind each is an opposite mirror-lobe; so the posterior lobe of the right-female hemisphere is a logical component, and the left-male posterior lobe is an emotive, experiential component. The male and female logical lobes are based on different three-dimensional geometries, as are the two male-female emotive lobes. In effect, these are four mirrors reflecting four different ways of seeing reality into each other; Thoth taught us they reflect diagonally, front-to-back, and side-to-side. So the immortal Lemurians also built a small wall at a ninety degree angle to the great center wall, thus dividing the isle into four *lobes*.

"Next, depending on their right-left brain orientation, yet regardless of their physical gender, half of the immortals went to one side of the island, and half to the other. And they remained in this physical state for millennia. In this manner of creating a human-body-consciousness brain on the surface of Unal, half of the immortals came to represent the female portion of the brain, the other half the male. Three of the immortals, including Thoth's Father Thome, were then chosen to be the only ones able to travel on both sides, thereby representing the corpus callosum in human form: synergizing the energies, emotions, and thoughts of both sides into one fully assimilated brain. After this was accomplished, they then projected the Tree of Life onto the landmass of the Atlantean continent, just south of Unal—"

"—with two additional points of Light!" I exclaim.

"Yes: one on Unal and one south of the mainland in the sea. The immortals then called forth the Lemurians who had settled elsewhere in the world. As was the plan, the most advanced of these stayed where they were, to continue building their new spiritual sites, while the majority traveled to birth Atlantis. This was the beginning of the next golden age, which lasted a very long time. I should say, dear Yeshu'a, that many will one day doubt the existence of Atlantis, as many have chosen to forget Lemuria. But there is a document the Mayans created that describes in great detail its existence, its people, its culture, and its demise. Using the Mayan complex hieroglyphic language, one day it will be called the Troano Codex, or Madrid Codex, and come the Age of the Holy Spirit, humanity will at last decipher and understand it."

"Tell me what occurred."

"Remember: the Lemurians were the female aspect. And regardless of how long their civilization had existed, and despite the level of understanding of their immortals, as a whole, they were still young in their development. The immortals called them and they came to Atlantis. Each of the ten spheres of Light on the continent would become a city—Plato stated that Atlantis had ten cities, and this is confirmed by the Troano Codex. And each fulfilled a specific function in the consciousness of the society. But as the right-brained Lemurians were still spiritually young, they were only able to fulfill the tasks of eight of the ten spheres or cities, which left two open. Two extraterrestrial races stepped in to fill those voids of life: one, of course, was the Hebrews, who had received permission from the Galactic Councils to do so, and the other, who had not, was the Martians.

"The Hebrews brought important knowledge with them, although they were relearning certain things they had forgotten. They taught us mathematics, science, an entire new way of seeing things which promoted our development. But the Martians came from a planet they had utterly destroyed, and to escape it, they created an artificial Merkaba by erecting a complex of buildings, and abused the sacred science to inject themselves into our evolutionary cycle and corrupt our race...

"Many wise souls say the Martians raped the child-consciousness of Earth; they were purely male in their makeup, and, as such, had completely severed their connection with the Heart, emotion, and, therefore, God."

My heart skips a beat. "I have read of this in the ancient texts, Master. It is like the story of Satan, once an archangel, attempting to create a reality in the Universe separate from God."

"Indeed, young one; you are most wise. And each time an attempt is made to create a reality separate from God's Love it inevitably fails with devastating results felt throughout the Sacred Universe. The mind is important, yet it must be ruled by the Heart. This is how creation is born and how it thrives. Humanity is now in the painful process of relearning this lesson for the final time within this cosmic cycle; this will bring the Earth to nigh-complete destruction near the cusp of the Aquarian Age.

For a very long time the Atlantean golden age lasted. The Martians arrived later and were well outnumbered, but ultimately they came to control Atlantis. While some of the Hebrews fell under their influence, Thoth was ultimately successful in saving the majority of them, getting them to the Lemurians, who shielded them from the Martians' control. By the end of my beloved Atlantis, we had fallen prey to all manner of diseases and fears and wars. The Martians created infernal left-brain technology and altered our manner of existence from female to male. The Hebrews were ever-loving people who melded the female and male and brought it out into the world, but the punishment for those who became deluded by the Martian way of doing things was severe...Right-brained technology had long existed, though today it is little understood. But the truth is we need neither left-brain nor right-brain technology; as you demonstrated as Solomon with the creation of the grapes, one's thoughts can create all that is right and good, when the mind is in service to the Heart and one's thoughts are pure.

"Ultimately, a comet collided with the Earth; science will record this occurrence across the southern and central regions of North America. With the foreknowledge of its arrival, the wise right-brained Lemurians counseled that it was an act of God, and to allow it to occur, while the Martians wanted to destroy it before it hit the Earth. Atlantis as a whole sided with the Lemurians, and when the comet arrived, the area struck by it in Atlantis was where the Martians resided; a significant part of their population was lost. Until then, though they had slowly come to control Atlantis by the implementation of their technology, and wanted to wage war on the Earth, they had not completely succeeded due to their inferiority in numbers and their underdeveloped thinking. They had even tried to comprehend and tolerate the female aspect. But this event changed that. And we have been dealing with their wrath ever since. The Martian male instinct to control the world and to subjugate women now became like a furious storm that knew no end. And they attempted to re-create their artificial Merkaba with disastrous results. They had lost part of their knowledge over some fifty millennia, and in their wild, ill-fated attempt, their artificial Merkaba spun out of control, ripping sizable holes in the lower dimensions of the Earth. Ultimately, this act forced entities from the lower dimensions into the higher dimensional planes. Out of their element, in a reality they could not at all understand, in absolute fear they now needed bodies to survive. As a result they began to enter into humans, sometimes dozens of them, even hundreds, into one body, and eventually most of humanity became possessed by them...

"This, dear Yeshu'a, is the true story of the demise of Atlantis, the worst disaster the world has ever known; the actual physical effects felt on the continent came to pass a few hundred years later. Yet there were enough of us who were strong and God-guided that we saved all that was once good: the Hebrews, the Lemurians, all dispersed. Thoth saw to the survival of the world...the Mayans came to be the Mayans. All that is right and with God did endure. And from this calamity the idea arose among the ascended masters to create the Christ Consciousness Grid: the Unity Consciousness Grid.

"All life on Earth has—and indeed must have—consciousness nets surrounding the planet in order to survive and grow, even the tiny flea. Life could not exist here without these electromagnetic grids. From the heavens they appear as a soft glow around the Earth. The first human consciousness grid is associated with the Indigenous peoples, the oldest humans on Earth; the second allows our specific human consciousness to exist here. And the third is the Unity Consciousness Grid, conceived by the ascended masters because of what occurred in Atlantis. Here the state of human consciousness we preserve beyond the capacity of most yet to detect it. If we did not, humanity would perish, forever exiled to the material world until we killed each other off completely, purely as a result of being unable to ascend into the higher realms of Consciousness. Come the Age of Aquarius, Unity or Christ Consciousness will be the stage of Consciousness humanity flows into, whether it likes it or not...Humanity will become Christ. Thus, while your holy number in this life is to be thirty-three, in truth, it will become forty-four: the gateway to God. In numerological terms, *I am the Life* in Hebrew calculates to be forty-four; and the words Jesus—what you will be named—Y'shua, messiah, gospel, increase, Joshua, cross, forgave, the key, the lock, gematria, menorah, Jewish, and so many more all calculate to be, and resonate with, four hundred forty-four: the attainment of the supra-Consciousness of God."

# Chapter Twelve
# Remembrance

BELOVEDS OF MY HEART, know I well that for many of you the path is hard, *The Way* jagged and tortuous. Within you festers a great pain of forgetfulness, of doubt, of fear. Yet every moment I am with you, ever allowing you the opportunity to open your Heart to the Truth of God, the Majesty of Love: the seed of the Divine within each and every one of you.

To give you wings, already I have spoken of so many things. It may help you to know that this very instant your DNA is being reprogrammed. Fully ninety-six percent of your DNA is blank. In its true multidimensional form, it receives its instructions from the higher realms, and during this transformational time, much of what you are experiencing in terms of the energy changes is due to this reprogramming. You cannot escape it, for all life is being affected. Sometimes this manifests as irregular sleeping patterns, shifts in thought paradigms, radical swings in mood, or breakthroughs of intuition that suddenly shine a great light on what was once shrouded in darkness. Fear not, beloveds, as all is for The Good. Embrace yourselves as loving expressions and shining epiphanies of God. For this is exactly what you are. When I say your DNA is in the process of being reprogrammed, remember that this is not some outside omnipotent force controlling you. It is what the totality of God, of which you are a part, must do, so you may once and for all accept Love as your true savior. And this begins with loving yourselves.

All too aware am I of the fear-based thoughts still permeating your culture. From the mountaintop I cry so all may hear: the journey of the Soul has ever been known. Never once has it been veiled from you, save by yourselves and power-mongering institutions. For one: If you believe in a Judgment Day, then that is a part of what you will experience upon your passing. The idea of a Judgment Day came into being because of ignorance and fear, which are one and the same. Upon your passing, your Soul makes all the choices about what it experiences in the Interlife.

Embrace God in Love, make all you do be about God, know in your Heart of hearts you are unconditionally loved, and you will be loved, unconditionally. You will be anyway, for even those souls who have been led to *believe* in a Judgment Day and create its illusion eventually realize what they are doing and move on in their journeys.

Now the world stands atop a great precipice. Love is everywhere found; it is all around you. Though it was a circuitous route, I have shared with you some of my early days in the Mystery Schools of Egypt and my education of the true history of the world therein for a definite purpose. What transpired in those early ages is of supreme importance to what you are experiencing today. Imagine, dear beloveds of my Heart, the nigh-absolute destruction of wisdom and knowledge which allowed the world to sink into darkness. The multiple occasions that the Library of Alexandria was burned to the ground come to mind, more than once by rabid followers of the religion bearing my name.

It is my great sadness that in my name the ancient Mystery Schools were destroyed and the world's oracles were silenced, besmirching all of the beautiful conduits of God I loved so much and that taught me so well.

Yet what happened in Sumeria, Atlantis, and later the wider world teaches a great lesson about the wages of fear wrought by the male-mind, ever seeking to control the world for fear's own sake. Forget not that ego is the reflection of fear. In Atlantis the destruction was so complete, the male-mind then took complete control of the narrative of the world, as it did with Enlil in Mesopotamia, and turned the story back-to-front, and women everywhere have been feeling the repercussions of it ever since.

Dear ones, in the United States today, the last stand is occurring at this very moment. Under the guise of much false imagery, women are losing their rights so the hegemony of the male sperm can still reign supreme. A war cometh! For it cannot last. Never be fooled by what you see: all the horrific things done to women, and to people of color, are truly about the fear of God. Whenever you hear about the sinfulness of abortion from the right-to-life people, know deep in your hearts that each time an abortion occurs the souls of both the Mother and unborn child make this most difficult decision together.

Those pointing the finger of sin at these women are usually conservative religious folks so filled with their own shame they attempt to project it onto the easiest targets. Beloved of me they are, but they know not how God works. Ask yourself this simple question: Should any institution have the right to lord over a woman's body? And if you look closely, you will find that those who see abortion as sinful want women to either be virginal or baby-machines. The male sperm is their king. On this very day, in the city of St. Louis a twenty-nine year old homeless black woman with two children, complaining of great pain in her legs, was thrown out of a hospital, then arrested for trespassing. Thrown onto the floor of a jail cell, she died there moments later of blood-clots in her legs. Would this have happened if she had been a young white man? I tell ye true: every act against women in the dawning Aquarian Age is a desperate last attempt to kill God.

And you will notice that as science now begins to prove the very nature of God and that it is all I share in these pages, these are the same souls who also wish to kill science.

See the sacred in all of it. Yet understand these suffering souls need to learn what is a very basic karmic lesson in the most painful manner possible. And they work very hard to make certain as many others as possible will suffer along with them for the sake of their own spiritual education. Love them, bless them, forgive them, and release them. This is how you cure cancer: Love it, bless it, forgive it, and release it. But deep inside you, remember: this is all about God, and nothing else. And all of those waging the war are diligently working to keep as many souls as possible from attaining God.

This is the world's last stand.

Elsewhere, while there is still a long way to go and violence against women including female circumcision continues, across Europe, South America, Africa, Australia, and Asia, women are beginning to comprise proportional representation in institutions, governments, religions, social movements, and all the fields of human endeavor. But in the United States and the Middle East, it is sadly going in the opposite direction. And many of the women in positions of power in the United States are truly men in disguise.

As the Light of God pours into the world, the fight has just begun.

This is why I have shared with you the stories of Atlantis and Sumeria. For within them is the seed of Truth that every attempt to create a reality separate from God fails, no matter how brilliant the ideas of the mind appear to be. Yet God Loves you so much, the allowance is made for you to experiment... After all, all Creation is an experiment.

But now the days draw thin. Now, each day, every decision has repercussions far beyond any most people could possibly imagine. The year 2015 will be a magical year, but only if you want it to be. *You* are the ones you have been waiting for.

In his divinely inspired Book of Revelation, Beloved John ben Zebedee speaks well of this age now cometh when he describes the arrival of a *new heaven and a new earth*. John the Beloved created this codex in a sublime state of meditation in communion with the Holy Spirit. He speaks thus: *Behold, the Tabernacle of God is with men, and he will dwell with them, and they shall be his people, and God himself shall be with them, and be their God.* Dear reflections, many would tell you that this passage means God will magically materialize and walk among you in the form of a special man, like myself, in a second coming.

Yet what is the Tabernacle? In the Sephirothic Tree of Life, the many ornaments of the Holy Tabernacle appear, and describe in great detail to the discerning Heart-mind that, like the arks, the Tabernacle is a symbol of the Universe, and indicates a direct link between the Universe and the House of God, which is the world itself, and that man is the vehicle through which the Divine is attained. To the uninitiated, the Tabernacle is a place to which one brings offerings. To the Initiate, it is a temple of learning, and within it wisdom breathes. And to the Adept, or Master, the Tabernacle is found within oneself. The Tabernacle is symbolic of spiritual Truth: the indivisible One Spirit dwelling in everyone and everything. In Hebrews, chapter eight, it reads thus: *Who serve unto the pattern and shadow of heavenly things, as Moses was warned by God, when he was about to finish the Tabernacle*. This reveals the Tabernacle to be but a shadowy reflection of that which has been, for most, invisible. And like so many things, ours was patterned after the Egyptians'.

That Beloved John tells you *Behold, the Tabernacle of God is with men* confirms to those with eyes enough to see, ears enough to hear, and Hearts full enough to Love: within humanity itself the Holy Tabernacle resides.

In chapter four, Beloved John states *And God shall wipe away all tears from their eyes; and there shall be no more death, neither sorrow, nor crying, neither shall there be any more pain; for the former things are passed away*. In this Age of the Holy Spirit when all shall be revealed, all of this will come to pass, for soon God's Love will be all that remains. Yet each step along *The Way* must be walked. Like the ancient scrolls of the Hebrews, it is a code, but in the case of Beloved John's book, it is written in such a sublime manner that anyone may understand in the Light of today. Believeth in me, and thus thyselves, and thou will come to know there shall be no more death, neither sorrow, nor suffering, nor pain, nor separation, nor limitation of any kind, for all of these illusions now pass away.

All that Beloved John speaks of is part of a process which involves Earth changing its position in the heavens by turning one-hundred-and-eighty degrees in its orbit within one day. Divine Will brings this about when all the events in Beloved John's book have come true. Then all those who understand the true meaning of life will survive. And bestowed upon them will be the great trust to create the new world where humanity shall never again forget its connection with the Divine.

And in the upper realms it will reside: Heaven on Earth. As Beloved John so eloquently says: *In the days of the voice of the seventh angel, when he shall begin to sound, the mystery of God shall be finished, as he hath declared to his servants and prophets...And I saw a new heaven and a new earth: for the first heaven and the first earth were passed away; and there was no more sea...And he said unto me, These sayings are faithful and true: and the Lord God of the holy prophets sent his angel to shew unto his servants the things which must shortly be done.*

Rejoice, beloveds of my Heart, for Love conquers all, and all are equally loved.

Many meanings have been ascribed to the seventh angel, and many theologians have grappled mightily to understand Beloved John's book. As heretofore I have promised, within these pages I will continue to reveal the many truths behind his words given to him by God. Of the seventh angel, I will say this: truly it represents the crown chakra, or seventh seal, when all that has gone before rises up the spine of all humanity, the Tree of Life, and releases through the crown into unification with God.

Magdalen and I have been coordinating the ascensions of hundreds of thousands of souls, and working with many others who may not accept Love in any form before the coming change. She has a Heart of water and fire, does Magdalen, and throughout the world her presence is known, seen, and felt as much as mine. And it is her wish I proclaim to thee once more: Many things they say I said, some true, some not. One in particular has done more damage than all the rest. You may have been led to believe that I once declared *The only way to God, or the Father, is through me*. Alas, dearest reflections, I never said this, nor would I ever. I did once say that *The Way* to God is through the fulfillment of your own soul's journey. Hubristic statements like the former come from religions, not from the mouths of prophets. I tell ye true: *You* are *The Way*, *You* are the Light; the only way to God is through the completion of your own soul.

As Magdalen and I fulfill our final missions in the world, I and others have noted that the Mystery is coming out through me. Yet what does this mean? For, indeed, the Mystery also births into the world through you. And what does it signify to you when I say our mission in Palestine was to bring the Mystery out into the world?

What is the Mystery?

Much I have shared with you already about what the Great Mystery is. And Beloved John's Book of Revelation prophesies that in the now dawning Age of the Holy Spirit *the Mystery of God will be finished*. The Book of Revelation is divided into twenty-two chapters, the number of the Master Builder, a double-number of great power and meaning. And the first verse of the twelfth chapter yields an important clue to the Great Mystery: *And there appeared a great wonder in heaven; a woman clothed with the sun, and the moon under her feet, and upon her head a crown of twelve stars*. In ancient times the Great Mystery was not hidden; it was known. And it was symbolized by the virgin Herself: the Woman Clothed with the Sun: Isis in Egypt, my dear Mother later in Palestine.

The blessed Rosicrucians later gave us the true symbol of the Great Mystery: the rose upon the cross. Their first rendering of it was the rose crucified upon the cross, and eventually the symbol became the cross enfolded by the ten perfect petals of the rose. As you have witnessed through my mating as Solomon with Sheba, the rose is a yonic symbol; it signifies purity, fecundity, creation, and regeneration: the Holy Vulva. And when men premeditatively made sex dirty, shameful, sinful, they knew precisely what they were doing. The world has never been the same. And pornography was born.

Saint Thomas Aquinas once said *Take away the prostitutes from the world, and you will fill it with sodomy*. In the ancient world the Sacred Harlot was a revered figure. In truth, the word harlot derives from hierodule, or priestess. As was once true of my Beloved, the priestess of the Goddess was a teacher of many things, even including Love and sex; hence they were given the title of Sacred Harlot. The temple harlots held a high social status and were venerated for their healing abilities of mind, body, heart, and soul, and their wisdom and learning in a wide variety of areas. Embodiments of the Queen of Heaven, they were honored like queens in learning centers throughout Greece, Asia, and Asia Minor. Before she became Justinian's wife, Empress Theodora began her spiritual calling as a temple harlot. Constantine's Mother, Helena, was also a Sacred Harlot before she became empress. She was later sainted.

Indeed, dear ones, my own lineage can be traced to Sacred Harlots if you look deeply enough.

It is no coincidence Beloved John lived out his many fruitful years in one of the oldest sanctuaries of the Goddess: Ephesus. *Savta* Anna and my dear Mother also spent significant time there. As part of my Grecian studies I, too, visit this great ancient city dedicated to Artemis. Beloved John ben Zebedee partook of his meditation in communion with the Holy Spirit in Ephesus, a land far removed from Palestine, and created his revelatory book there.

The chief aspect of knowing the Great Mystery is understanding truly how the loving force of God works in the Sacred Universe. And as I have already revealed to you, in reading scripture, no matter its derivation, you discover that the creative element of the Universe is embodied in the image of the Woman. She is the creative element in all of us. You may have heard I ever defended the Spirit of women in my many travels. Yet your texts are mostly silent as to the reason why, for you are taught the female is the weaker sex, a great lie foisted upon you by guilt-festing men. This is the outer, revealed reason.

As the inner now becomes the outer, as it becomes manifest in the world, you may truly discern what it was about me that threatened the leadership of Rome and Israel. It was simply because I was a man's man, with the active, creating Heart of a woman. I was in touch with my female side, in proper balance with my male, left-brain nature. My Heart ruled me. Thus, when you picture me up on the cross, look closely, for it is Inanna herself, having given herself once more to demonstrate to the world what it takes to be free, to commune with God, to be *fishers of men*. The Truth does set you free.

When you give yourself up completely to the creative force of God, in scientific terms you are living in quantum reality. We all see what we want to see, do we not? Yet the difficulty for most is to see the very best in people, every instant we breathe. And most of the time this works to God's favor. Yes, there will be moments on any given day when this is not the case with those who refuse God's loving embrace, as it was with Barabbas the Zealot; no matter the amount of Light I saw in him, he could not escape the chains of his anger, beloved of me he is. Yet most of the time, when you see and expect the best in people, it will be so.

This is the very first step. In an advanced stage of dearly loving God, as one retains their utter confidence, walking tall, one sheds completely the ego, often forgoing freewill, and the world creates what it wants to create. As merely one example, in this life I live today, my appearance alters; so, to some I appear to be twenty-odd years old, to others much older. I have ceded my authority, my control to God. My appearance changes upon the expectations of those who observe me. Some see me a healer, others a heel, some a prophet, others a liar, depending on what they wish to see and how they see themselves. This is how much I Love God, and those who know me truly know themselves most truly of all. Beloved they are all of me.

Twelve seasons past, I suffered an Achilles tendon injury. I had spent the three months prior involved in many healing activities, and my reservoir of manna was tapped, the need for rest supreme. So, instead of instantly healing the ruptured tendon, as would be my wont, I gave myself short bursts of universal healing energy—manna—over a period of a month.

This injury can take a full year to heal from, but within a month I was walking normally again. Yet, at that time, some observed me striding absolutely freely, while others saw me walking with a bad limp. The angels informed me these souls had a vast amount of guilt invested toward me, and were projecting the image of my limp in an effort to fool their conscious minds into believing I was responsible for their guilt. While I suffered not, I invoked the Violet Flame on many occasions to help them in alleviating theirs. They are so beloved of me.

The joy of becoming the Mystery is the amount of assistance, teaching, healing, and so-called miracles one can bestow upon all those ready to receive the Light. There is no greater gift than to witness the Light of God penetrate more hearts each day on this Earth. Sometimes it is just talking, or speaking with passed loved-ones, others a healing, and still others can be a seemingly miraculous chain of events that brings epiphanies and alters the lives of souls, forever. Whatever is the utmost need, in balance with God, is the cure.

In this life I have also been gifted my final lesson in forgiveness, though in many previous lifetimes I have forgiven the world itself, even for my own deaths. When I was a young man, my fiancée was murdered by someone with whom we had been acquainted. I somehow at once recognized the spiritual alchemy God required of me, and truly forgave her murderer, within and without, though I had lost all. And my life ever since has been even more miraculous, more Love-filled, more magical than it had been before.

In Palestine nigh-two thousand years ago, we knew in great detail all the ancient stories, especially those of Egypt and Greece. They were the stuff of our daily education. And as I became a man, the full extent of my earthly mission became clear as crystal. Every day I trained for it, knowing it would come, as I had been born to fulfill it. By the time of my return to Galilee, my knowledge was pure, my communication with the Inner Essenes had been ongoing for years, and all fell into place as God had planned.

Look closely, beloveds, at the Egyptian story of the Savior Gods Osiris and his Divine son Horus. As is true of many savior God stories, in the Egyptian there was indeed a betrayer; his name was Set, or Typhon. Without Set, the resurrection of Osiris could not have occurred. So, as our plan of bringing the Mystery out into the world was written within us, the role of the betrayer was tantamount to its success. Each one of us knew how important every aspect of the story was, and there were very, very few who knew our plan as it really was. Such was our high regard for its fruition and for God's Love.

Yet it does not end there. Recall you will that I have shared with you the resurrection of Lazarus in Bethany, how, in truth, it was Magdalen that day who brought him back to life. This was merely the result of my being utterly exhausted from so many miraculous acts that I could not on that day be the raiser of the seeming dead. Thus it was Magdalen who became the Divine conduit and dispensed with any need for credit due. In truth, as you will see, dear Lazarus gave of himself just for that very moment; he birthed into the world to allow it to occur. And while he appeared dead, truly the Divine spark still hovered about him; he still desired to inhabit his body. This was our plan all along, just one tiny aspect of bringing the Mystery out into the world.

But I save the best for last. As you have seen, in ancient Egypt Osiris was called Asar. And as in the title *The Christ*, the Egyptians often named him *The Asar*, in their language *El Asar*. In time, the Greek male ending of *us* was added and the initial E was dropped, making the name L'asarus. Horus resurrected his Father, El-Asar-us, in the city of Anu, originally derived from the great Father of the Anunnaki. Yet, as the Anunnaki were the female representation of our species, the word Anu came to signify the female principle of creation, come from Virgo: the Woman Clothed with the Sun. This, in turn, the Egyptians and Essenes understood as the bread of life, the building block of both spiritual life and physical sustenance on Earth. The ancient city of Anu came to be known as *Iunu* and would later be renamed Heliopolis.

The Hebrew word for house is Beth. And it is common knowledge that before it became known as Bethany, the town was named Bethanu: the House of Bread, where some of my most important acts took place.

Our Lazarus lived; he was a man who came to high virtue. In his eyes the Eternal Light shone. And he chose his name and life and the town in which he resided to fulfill a very special purpose. Our intricate design was so well-woven, we knew it all precognitively and also in time, as each step was meticulously planned and spoken of in great earnest. Lazarus died, or seemingly so, for if he had been absolutely dead, he would not have wanted to return. His health had been poor for some time; yet, beloveds, we knew why. His dear sisters Miriam and Martha knew the true story: Lazarus came back to the world by way of the Sacred Marriage: Magdalen and I.

In this life I live today, I have returned the favor to she who was once Magdalen. Her sister fell very seriously ill four years past, and she who was Magdalen was so exhausted from many healings that she could not be the Divine bridge her sister needed to heal herself. From across the great ocean, my soul found hers and fed her manna, and she was willing to receive, rallied and survived. This, too, we knew, two thousand years ago in Palestine. Yet it also must be told that within our family in Palestine, more than one could not be healed, or could not heal themselves, even among *Savta* Anna's large brood. So beloved of God they are. Though we were a family of healers with penetrating cosmic and Divine knowledge, not all in every moment were able to heal themselves. In these pages I will describe their stories. We shed such tears upon their passings.

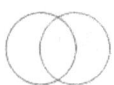

Gaining access to your Heart, learning to live in the manner God prescribed, is often the most difficult challenge since it has been forgotten by so many for so long. Throughout these pages

I will continue to gift you the golden keys to open your Heart's door. This I promise.

I will now tell you, beloveds, of Mother Earth's great Truth, and then relate it to how your mind should cooperate with your Heart's calling.

The entire Universe is ever making Love; this I have shared with you. Though humanity precipitated it by losing trust in God and thus itself, ever since The Fall, the rest of God's creatures, all of Nature has never lost its trust, its Love, its knowledge of the Heart; the Mother ever waits in absolute certainty of our return. Her gifts should never cease to amaze thee. Despite theories to the contrary, Nature is ever living in pure communion. This has never changed, though the formula has by need been adjusted.

In the nineteenth century Charles Darwin advanced a very enthusiastically received thesis called *Natural Selection* that claimed Nature operated by a paradigm he called the *survival of the fittest*. In short, this idea maintained a *Natural Selection* of species on Earth endured and evolved through the mechanism of *survival of the fittest*—a violent struggle between and among species for continued existence—and the strongest, or fittest, were the winners. Embraced by the elites of his age, and still taught in higher education centers today, this theory is painfully mistaken, and displays an absolute ignorance of how the Mother, in all Her wisdom, works. Unfortunately, it has been used by elites to justify all manner of inequality in human society as necessary in the struggle for existence.

In truth, the governing principle in Nature is cooperation, not competition. The fittest in Nature are always those species which cooperate. People with vast experience in human matriarchal tribal societies and in animal societies will tell you true: both live in a state of utter balance, only kill when they must, never overwork, and ever honor the process of life and death with an extraordinary reverence. No matter how civilized man has changed the equation after The Fall, Indigenous peoples and animals alike live from the Heart. Like Santa Claus, the idea of Nature being a chaotic, nihilistic state of existence was created by powerful, wealthy men so they could become even more powerful and make more money, and as a result, keep the Woman and the Heart down. Although empirical research denies the claims of social Darwinists—numerous scientific studies have proven Nature's cooperative reality—only a few peeps have pierced the veneer of the so-called free world. Fear is a mighty brew—ego drives the maniacal theory of competition; capitalism was built on it. And dear Darwin was an eloquent spokesman for it.

Cooperation, not competition, is *The Way* of the Mother and the Father, and also of the most thriving human societies, including European medieval guild cities, wherein all enjoyed the fruits of their labors, all were cared for, though women still had a long, long way to go. In truth, these guilds and Indigenous tribal societies would today be viewed as enclaves of anarchism, another word misdefined and misunderstood by most, due to the incredible wiles of the powerful in painting false-pictures.

Intention, passion, creates everything in our world. Throughout the Sacred Universe, complementary electromagnetic energy and frequency energy networks congregate. The electromagnetic grid of what is called *lattice* energy binds the entire structure of universal energy: manna or prana. This grid is the form-creator of all life in the Universe. The complementary waveform frequency energies are called *scalar* energies; they fill the void in the electromagnetic grid. And by means of our *lattice*-Heart-energy, we convey our intentions to inform the *scalar* frequency energies. The confluence of the *lattice* and *scalar* energies forms a point of Light. The process of creation then joins with the mind so that a single intention, or event, extends outward and takes on physical form in the three lower dimensions, becoming a reality in human consciousness. Literally, creation occurs the instant human consciousness becomes aware of it. In the ancient Mystery Schools this process was well known as a Heart-to-mind-to-Heart sequence, yet the vast majority of humanity has since become unaware of it.

Beloveds, I often use the analogy of the chicken and the egg. But humanity has grown so spiritually ignorant most people cannot even figure it out that way. The mind is given top-billing; so much reverence is given it, but when one gets right to the core of things, it does not have the answer. It never has. Creation always begins with the Heart.

Humanity has become so deluded by the mind, men and women actually believe the mind is the leader. Inspiration, intention, passion, the eternal wisdom of the Heart is responsible for all creation. Yet it has been so beaten down, desecrated, so ignored and abused that very little attention has been given to its state of being. Believe it or not, this has led directly to almost all forms of disease in the world. It has also led to strife, war, within and without, because so few in your culture are even aware of this, and allowing the mind to be leader has led to separation, not unity. As I have said, the mind, as God intended, is a tool to be used as a facilitator of the Heart.

At this time, beloveds, your crucial mission is to begin to turn over leadership to your Heart. For, in truth, the war I speak of that is taking form today is between those who will not let go of the old energy and those who *are* the new energy. You must Love them all. It may help you to understand that, in the near future, among the many books hidden in the sands which will resurface are the original versions of the four canonical gospels: Matthew, Mark, Luke, and John. And the revelation will be how different they are from the *known* versions. These four books were significantly altered. Remember, dearests: the Roman Church did not allow anyone to read the Bible for a thousand years, and beloved of me they are, the original Church Fathers were also leaders of countries, something infinitely dangerous. These texts were copied and translated and changed so many times, the biases of their transcribers imbuing nigh-every page, it is no wonder they have come down to you as they have…On one page a passage of beauty, followed by pages of control, fear, and the wrath of God…The Heart weeps at its own denigration. This is the reason why your mission is now so essential. You have allowed this to occur, therefore it is up to you to untangle the mess and find yourselves.

Let us begin.

If we were again to speak in terms of left-brain right-brain, I would use computer terminology to tell you that the right-brain can process something along the magnitude of eleven million bits of data per second, compared with the left-brain's trifling seven bits per second. This should yield some understanding as to how much richer the so-called female side of you is. Yet left-brain right-brain mechanics is not sufficient to understand your relationship with God, nor can it return you to full consciousness as Divine beings.

To accomplish your *mission imperative*, let us speak instead in terms of a higher mind and a lower mind. Your higher mind, in truth, communicates with both your Heart and the Divine Mind; indeed, a hub of receptivity and inspiration, the higher mind amasses all of your impressions and experiences, and then seeks to comprehend and ultimately resolve them for the sake of your evolutionary process. This it cannot do; inevitably its reach exceeds its grasp. Resolution is discovered through the Heart, as resolution and creation are one and the same. The lower mind is a compiler of lists; it seeks order by placing everything into neat little rows, trying to define things, and is always very busy. It is your very own hardwired research center. But it is not the place from which to make decisions of what to do or how to be or what Truth is. It is an invaluable tool because it allows you to communicate your Heart-wisdom outward. But your only true authority is your Heart. In the present Age of the Holy Spirit, if you pay attention to those who steadfastly stand by the ultimate greatness of the mind, you may notice their wisdom and decisions to be innately flawed. Where is the Heart? It has been severed, and those who exist in this way legitimize it, ceaselessly. These people will even say *You wait; there is a reason for this; we are meant to be like this; we are supposed to cut everything up into little pieces and analyze them; this is what we are taught, and there's a very good reason for it.*

Yes, there is: to keep you from God, to continue suffering. God bless them. For they cry out for God's Light but cannot access it...Yet.

The mind does not surrender. It never gives up its fight to keep the veil up. So your *mission imperative* is to learn to still it, not to turn it off, as some practices teach you, but to silence its fearful busyness, to learn how to access your Divine creative flow as God intended. From the Heart. Today, with all the chatter going on in the fourth dimension, people using it like a mobile-phone, Facebook, or Twitter: gossiping, rumor-mongering, trying to control others, often even using people like marionettes on strings, many are now falling prey to less-than-Light-filled sources and are not hearing their own hearts. Many of you need to *guide your guides*, and stop being led around by the ears. Being with God means trusting others. Those who rely on their guides to see, for instance, if everything people say is true, or purposefully lie to see if others use their guides in like manner, etc., the list of suspicions is endless: they do not trust themselves, are suspicious of themselves, have not been honest with themselves.

Remember: my dearest Mother told me true: respect people's private lives. If you find yourself listening to some inner voice every time you interact with people, this is *obsession*, and comes from lack of trust—the very reason for The Fall. Ask yourself: *Would I want this done to me? Does this mean I am trying to project onto them what I truly feel about myself?*

What do you think? It certainly does not have anything to do with God, does it? God does not think that way. You are afraid; you are seeking answers *out there*, when they are only *in here*, within you. You see dualism everywhere, and it does not work. It never has. Try to think more like God thinks.

Search your Heart because it always knows. It is so much easier to be with God.

You must first learn to allow your higher mind to loosen up; in a relaxed state, let it breathe and receive its intuition and inspiration from the Divine Mind with great respect for its process, not allowing any judgmental thoughts from the lower mind to intervene, cutting off any desire to define. This is achieved by taking away any duty of the mind to do anything. This is the Heart's job, but it does it by *being*, not doing.

Next, you must learn to turn off the chatter of your lower mind. My own personal method for achieving this is to focus on the beat of my Heart. Indeed, with many healings I perform, I allow the healing-thought to pass through the chambers of my Heart, and with my intention pure, the healing is done, with no sign of my involvement; God and the patient are always the true healer, and the healer merely a conduit for the energy of God's Love. But in the beginning, learn to listen to the sacred beat of your Heart, not just where it physically resides in your chest, but throughout your entire body.

When you disconnect your mind from controlling you and resonate with the flow of your Heartbeat, you allow yourself to reconnect with who you truly are. The frequency of your Heart will return you to the state of being fully awakened, the way you were meant to be, the way God designed you to be. But you have allowed the mind to control that, to dismiss it, to abuse it, so you do not trust it anymore. And you have become very skillful in perpetrating this illusion. Hence it will take work to undo this sabotage because, in fact, it has caused a short-circuit in your energy. Yet as soon as you re-engage in this sacred act and continue to do so, you will be astounded at the results. God Loves you so very much, and is waiting for you to rediscover your Divine I AM presence.

In truth, many would like to achieve their Ascension because they do not Love their bodies anymore, or themselves, or this dear planet; they want to escape. I tell ye true: you chose to incarnate to find Love within all of it, and you must rediscover that Love in order to find God. Deep in the stillness, listen closely, beloveds; can you hear it? I know you can. It is so extraordinarily beautiful. God Loves you so much.

In John's Book of Revelation, following the verse concerning the Woman Clothed with the Sun is this description: *And she being with child cried, travailing in birth, and pained to be delivered.* This tells of the painful birth of the New Humanity, for the trials borne by so many in their efforts to deny the Light of God, to attempt to stop It from coming into the world, will be painful indeed. Yet, dearests, it is so much easier to truly surrender, to lay down your armor, so much easier to be with God than not. Beloved of God you are. In the verses following the new birth it tells of a serpent being defeated. Of this I shall speak more, for many false things have been attached to it. On a galactic scale, this has to do with a screaming comet. But know from me the true inner meaning: Not only is the galaxy in the form of a spiral serpent, but around our galaxy is a star-clustered haze that keeps the galaxy in perfect tune. It, too, is in the form of a spiral serpent. In truth, what these verses refer to is that humanity is about to move beyond the galaxy into the larger heavens, and beyond space and time. Soon you will all realize that time and space and thought are not the separate things they appear to be.

What Glory! For YOU ARE that YOU ARE.

As I ever praise God and speak of my Love and gratitude for this incredible gift of life, you, too, must praise God the very same; ask God how is it possible you are so loved? How blessed are you? How can it be that God's Love is so beautiful, so healing, so pure? And you will know. YOU ARE that YOU ARE. And you are so beloved of me.

# Chapter Thirteen
# Mother and Son

FROM TIME TO TIME Father takes me with him on his journeys to the southern temples: Abydos, Edfu, Dendara, and Abu Simbel. As ever, he includes me in his meetings with illustrious personages, seeking my guidance as to their character, yet also instructing me in how one behaves properly in the world of luminaries. In this manner I am acquainted with all manner of leader: high priestess and priest, seer and prophetess, alchemist and queen and king alike. In Abydos I partake of the initiatory rites of the Osiris mysteries, climbing in silence the stairs to illumination in the very first Osirian temple. Not known in your age, in the beginning there were many temples on this site, of impressive size, veneration, and energy.

Yet it begins with a prophetic dream in which I walk through the initiatory tunnels of the City of the Gods beneath the Sphinx and the Great Pyramid, searching for the way out. I am becoming anxious I will not discover the exit; while dreaming, I am aware this is some manner of test, but as yet I have not deciphered its true meaning. After a priest signed for me to follow him into a small candlelit room, he removed a large stone covering a dark, craggy hole in the floor, stating with gravity that I must succeed in finding the way to freedom or I will not become a full Initiate of the Great White Brotherhood.

In pitch black I crawl across the floors, feeling the walls, looking for any inscriptions which may guide me, the dank air choking me. There is no doubt breathing within me in the beginning; I know I will triumph. I seek the angels, my teachers dear Thoth and Manetho, my Father, my Mother, *Savta* Anna, though instantly I know I am alone. Passing into the fifth tunnel, my arms and legs are bloodied, and I have scraped my face more than once, and I slump against the wall, nearly hopeless. I have already been taught how to see without my eyes, how to project my soul's vision out beyond my body; this is no great task. But ahead and behind and beyond is darkness and more of the same.

There is a Heart-logic to this initiation, I know, so I somehow get myself up standing and slowly continue my blind-man's walk to oblivion. In the seventh tunnel, rats scurry by me, brushing up against my skin, and the voices of those who did not survive the test issue from the crags, I crashing into their disintegrating bones in the final bend before the eighth tunnel. As I negotiate its meandering length, I recognize the beginning of the journey and my heart drops. Surely, think I, I have already passed the exit; and I turn back into the last tunnel, once more searching the walls with my fingers for inscriptions.

The tunnel is like a long, low-ceilinged, irregularly shaped room, the walls smoother than the ones preceding it, but the floor is knotted. I taste blood in my mouth, mixed with the sweat flowing from my brow and the trails of tears. Seeing the space around me, I call upon all my senses to view beyond these walls but meet only pitch.

Suddenly I feel a presence before me, like a great quickening of the Heart, yet there is nothing here. Soon a light grows from the size of a chickpea until it radiates larger than my body, filling the entire subterranean chamber with a soft golden glow.

Crystallizing into the form of a luminous human, all at once I recognize his face, like an innocent boy's it is, his gleaming eyes a gateway to paradise, his smile a piercing sun among lesser stars: it is Horus! In sacred art often you see his is the head of the falcon, yet this is truly a depiction of *Nekheny*, an ancient falcon god, later renewed in Horus, whose Egyptian name, *Heru*, means distant one. The glistening boy-man standing before me is curly black-headed, seemingly a mere few summers older than I, with beautiful, purely noble facial features, quite feminine in countenance. The stamp on his lips is of both confidence and empathy. Not one word has passed between us, yet instantly we know each other.

"Praises to thee, young Yeshu'a," sings he.

"Blessings upon thee, O Great and Wise Horus. I fear I am lost."

"Never lost. Thou art never lost. How many passageways have ye espied?"

"Eight I have seen. Yet each leads only to more darkness. And with each turn a doubt festers and grows I will not succeed. My skin itches, my mind claws at me. Ever I sing my praises to Mother-Father God, but I find not the answer."

A most discreet chuckle escapes his lips, brimming with Love, not judgment. "Think not, young one. By way of thy heart alone, consider all ye have already been taught, for within it is the key. Thou art as I once was, yet thou also hast advantage. Some of thy teachers were also mine, but you have more, much more, and the knowledge is purer in thee at thine age. Fear not, for of all the prophets, your talents will be the least tested." The hue of his light is changing, becoming whiter still. "Think not; let it come to thee. Surely ye can see...This is the eight-fold path. Of what is the eight-fold path?" Representing the sun and the moon, his two eyes gaze upon me assuredly.

The answer leaps to my lips. "The eight-fold path is of Consciousness, the journey of Consciousness itself."

Now his visage grows ever more feminine, his nose becoming sleeker, his skin softer, the purse of his lips more full. "Now thou art nearly there. What is the key to understanding the journey of Consciousness? To becoming a Master?"

"Yes, I see. Manetho has told me this, and I have found it breathing in my life. One must transcend the barriers of Consciousness; each is but an illusion we have placed before our eyes as a veil to make necessary the journey. In truth, there are no veils, for we ourselves are the veil. And the fourth fold is the most arduous, for it twists and turns and fools one with many subtle voices of human fears, mostly of those who congregate to keep God from entering, to keep Love Pure from living, to divide us from God and ourselves and our families."

"Indeed, Yeshu'a. Now thou know'st once more. Even thine own brother may betray you. Yet what must ye do? It is easy to live and speak of forgiveness; this is thy creed. But there is something more, is there not?"

Thinking for a moment, I choose my words wisely. "It is as I was first tested in the Heliopolitan temple, when the voices of fear instructed me to kill Manetho as he sought to murder me... Yet this was false. Surely, I love myself, therefore I love others equally and more. Certainly, I instantly forgive, even mine own blunders...Yet at the very core of God—the paradise we all seek—there is nothing ever to forgive."

A pure white light now emanates from Horus; as he bows to me, he shines anew, his hands together palm-to-palm before his heart. "Thou hast correctly deduced the answer, young Yeshu'a. When thou cease allowing anything on the outside to influence thee, ye find God. Many falsely believe with the ceding of freewill one must ever remain serene; the fiercely religious and the profane both push this false creed. Yet one can fight if God decrees it. Now, release the shackle of fear and see the Light. What was it thy cousin Mariam shared with thee about the fourth dimension?"

"I have traveled through these passages in absolute darkness, scraping my arms and knees, my mind creating demons to keep the Truth from finding me, but, as always, it shines within me: One must *pass through it*. This Mariam taught me. And now it is clear. Many create games to twist others into believing all manner of thing is true; this is why the spiritual traditions of the world warn us of the fourth dimension's many dangers. Verily, one can do these things to oneself, but those souls who form gangs of fear to fool others to turn away from God's Love, and to perform acts immoral in the doing, are the most dangerous of all."

"Yes, this is so. Especially among the fiercely religious and the profane. But there is nothing to forgive; so how must one find God? Thou hast said the words."

"I know it well, dear Horus. One must *pass through it*. Verily, the only way is up!"

"Thou art brilliant, Yeshu'a. Of this there is no doubt. Do not tarry with those who would confound the world in psychic knots. They know not what they do, and are not yet aware of the upper realms of the fourth dimension. They would rise up against thee; yet even this picture is false. They ever confound themselves by their own insecurities and immaturity and seek suffering company, that is all. Leave them to their own devices. Of the moment it is thee who matter. The only way is up! Thou hast solved the riddle!"

Casually I gaze up into the ceiling. And lo, amidst the knobby blocks, I behold a small but shimmering light. Placing my fingers upon the stones around it, instantly they shift at my touch, and the sun fills the chamber with Light. I am free.

Says Horus, "Upon thy successful passing of the initiation of which thou hast now dreamt, thy Father will the next morn awaken thee from thy slumber to view the rites of my Father—the Passion Plays—and ye shall also journey to the southern temples. An old family friend will join thee. But there is yet more Love and knowledge to be bestowed upon thee by mine. This, I promise, is the key to all."

Hannah is chirping before I open mine eyes. My sweet Phoebe is ever my companion in all things. Her clear eyes see more than I, and in song and in her voice of the Soul she shares her wisdom so I may grow in mine. In full I have learned her languages and speak softly in return, for she is, above all, to be loved and heard, cared for and respected. Sweetest sweet of the sweet is my dear Hannah. Thrice even I have hidden her in my tunic as I ventured the secret chambers of the Heliopolitan temple, wanting to hear her sage words describing and explaining the meanings of what I saw. Sweetest sweet of the sweet is my dear Hannah.

This morn there is glory in her notes, and as I waken and the sunlight filters in, I gaze upon her perch to find she is not there. Sitting up on my pallet, mine eyes bulge out of their sockets. There, clothed with the dazzling sun, is Isis! So named by the Greeks, her true Egyptian name, meaning throne, is Issa or *Essa* or *Aset*, as my Mother revealed when I was just a babe. She is resplendent: lustrous, long, perfectly twined ebony hair, absolutely elliptical, sympathetic eyes, rose-petal lips, and a luxurious, considerate nose. Her eyelids and face are free of paint, her many-folded white linen robe of the finest quality. And on her shoulder sits Hannah singing her splendid song of God. Upon mine eyes meeting hers, Isis unfurls luminous golden wings, spanning thrice the length of her body so they fill the room. She wears not her empty throne headdress symbolizing the fallen Osiris, nor the horns of the cow with the disc of the sun betwixt them. She is unadorned.

To the floor I kneel in obeisance, espying her radiance as I peer up once more. "Great praises to you, O Queen of Heaven and Earth, Mighty Mother Issa."

"Yes, Yeshu'a, it is I, for I am long moved by thy prayers. I am she of a thousand names, for I am all that has been, that is or shall ever be. No mortal man hath ever me unveiled."

A playful smile dances upon her lips. "Truth be told, dear one, a fair measure of men and women hath me unveiled. God bestoweth upon me my words, my acts, my powers, and it falls to each to unveil my treasures. Orpheus, Pythagoras, Sappho, and Zarathustra, Socrates, Plato, Confucius, and your *Savta* Anna hath so done, as hath many others both known and unknown: among them Rebekah, Deborah, Ruth, and Esther, Siddhartha, Krishna, Sheba, thus your Beloved as well. And thou hast so done as luminous Inanna, wise Solomon, knowing Melchizedek; as Moses ye saw God alive in the bush on Sinai...And ye will again. To each I gift the torch, yet to each the task is given to light it with their thirst...

"I *am* the Holy of Holies, no matter how many temples men build with secret rooms given the title. Throughout thy days I will teach thee the secrets of my Tablet, and light the way with the wisdom of all the ages, as I am the incarnation and culmination of every goddess and god. For I am the first and the last; I am the honored and the scorned, and I am the whore and the holy one, for I tempt the fool and guide the wise. I am the wife and the virgin, as I am thy guide along The Path. I am the Mother and the Daughter, as I give birth to each Initiate and he gives birth to me...I am she who is the womb of all and I am born of her. I am the solace of the world's labor pains, as I clean its impurities. I am the Bride and the Bridegroom. It is Binah, or the Holy Spirit, who begot me. I am the Mother of my Father and the sister of my husband, and he is my offspring.

"Behold! For though many will liken you to my son Horus and my brother-son-husband Osiris, it is I, Yeshu'a, whom you become, for I am the Logos, sent forth from the Christic power. And I come to those who in meditation reflect upon me; I am found among those who seek after me within themselves. Gaze upon me, hear me with your Vishuddha ear, banish me not from your inner sight; see me in all things: remember your true I AM self. For, as are you, I am the incomprehensible silence and the much-remembered thought. Indeed, I am the voice of countless sounds and the thousand guises of the Logos. I am the utterance of my name."

Looking upon her placid yet indomitable countenance, though they be steeped with riddles, awash in paradox, I instantly grasp every possible meaning of her words. Save one. "Sweet Mother Issa, verily I understand your words, though they craft a masterful labyrinth...I am even acquainted with them, yet I do not see how I, a man, can become you, the Mother Goddess of all the ages."

She chuckles like a Mother recognizing herself in her child. "As you will be many times, even come the Age of the Holy Spirit, you are the Sacred Androgyne Child. Have I not told you I am the incarnation of every goddess and god? And were you not thyself Inanna? These words you hear me speak are from the dawn of time, thus the reason you recognize them. For millennia they have been performed as dramatic oratory in festivals and rites of passage, including Inanna's and mine own.

Many times they have been and will be written, and many times destroyed, altered, and of course misunderstood. Yet here in Egypt a true rendering of them will survive to inform the Age of the Holy Spirit. It quite rightly will even confuse with the switching of genders. It is the eternal knot of Truth to be untied by the discerning Heart-mind, is it not?"

I nod vigorously my head. "Indeed, Mother Issa. It is the story of Consciousness, its birth and evolution, its abiding call to take heed and never forget. It is the ever brilliant Light of Truth to be fooled not by any illusion: we have given birth to ourselves...Issa, when I was a babe the Voice once came through my dear sister Martha. It said Issa is in my breast, that I am not a king or a god, but a great Heart who brings man the map to the Glory...I *am* you, am I not?" I ask, still incredulous.

"Yes, dearest. And you will inspire great Love in many and great fear in others. Thus you will be pedestaled in glory and also scattered across the Earth in guilt and shame...Thus the paradox. You are he who is the Mother and the Daughter and the Son and the Father. Some who know you will shun you in shame, as they will not be able to bear the sight, and many far away will know and Love you best. So loved will you be, the darkness will rise in nigh-equal measure in attempts to destroy you...When of myself I spoke as the solace of the world's labor pains, as I clean the world's impurities, behold! For you will shed the tears and bear the burden of every Love lost, of every hurt caused by harsh word and hateful act, of each pain endured for every lie told, all injustice big and small, every grievous injury to the Heart, each act against the Sons and Daughters of Man, each deed against God's Glory. Every error inflicted by ignorance and fear you will purify by your Fire and release into the Sacred Universe, so all will be transmuted into the Light of God, to be reborn as the sweet, innocent lamb of creation.

"Yet nigh-every word you will speak has already been spoken, every miraculous act of Love already many times done." Suddenly she falls silent, Sweet Mother Issa, and all Creation stops breathing. The silence is deafening. Gathering her golden wings behind her, she approaches me and, placing my face in her hands, kisses my brow and cheek and lips. "I have said I am the first and the last; you, too, will say it thus... But how will you translate this anew into your own words for the world to understand your Truth, the Truth of all humanity, the Truth of Consciousness? ...Think not, for you already know it."

"...I am the beginning and the end, the alpha and the omega," utter I, "for I remember the beginning, therefore I know the end. My sight, my hearing, all my many-splendored senses, Sweet Mother Issa, recall every single instant of Creation. How joyous this is!"

"Yes, dear Yeshu'a. This is your gift. While in this life your Beloved completes you and by the faithful completion of her mission she makes possible the fulfillment of your destiny, *you are the Bride and Bridegroom*; you are the servant of God who prepared you, and you are the lord of your offspring. God is the one who begot you before time was born, and God is your offspring in time, and your power is from Her/Him. You are the staff of God's power in God's youth, and God is the rod of your old age. Whatever God wills happens to thee. Do you not see you are my reflection?"

Solemnly I nod and search my inner sight for the future. As it was when I was but a babe, like crystal it shines. With such joy I breathe, knowing I will surmount all obstacles in God's loving embrace. "I am the one they will pursue, both by those on their Paths to Glory and by those who desire to slake their thirst to slay the Light. I am the one they will scatter, and they will gather me together anew. I am he before whom they are ashamed, and they are shameless to me, and yet, in mine eyes, they are blameless. I am he who is the Life yet many will call the death. I am the Law, but many will call lawlessness."

Beaming ever brighter as every word coming from my lips pours over her, Isis stands back and unfurls once more her golden wings, my room flooding with Light.

Yet my face is drenched in tears, mighty streams coursing down my cheeks, over my lips, and trailing down my neck, born of both great joy and great sorrow. Stunning scenes I see of Albion, Persia, India, and Greece, Jerusalem, Bethany, and Gennesaret, Tyre, Magdala, Syria, and so much more: the River Jordan—the Hebrew symbol of the Great Divide between Heaven and Earth—Capernaum, Bethsaida, and the Sea of Galilee, shaped like a great beating Heart, around me the familiar faces of friends naming me the Teacher of Righteousness, I walking upon water like it be glass…And the darkness creeping in. I cry, "Bring me in shame, to yourselves, and be forever cleansed of your shame. Blame the parts of me within yourselves you cannot abide, and in Love embrace them so they are forever healed. Approach me, all of you who know me, assemble the great among the small, and surely advance toward childhood!"

I am flushed. A fever pounds in my brain. Gazing upon myself as from afar, I see not a Light, a child of God, a divinely wrought being born of God and queens and kings, but a simple, nigh-broken, groping-in-the-dark boy emerging into a young man.

I have seen mine own death! …Yet never do I die. Because of thee.

In my family's home on Marmion Way is a cloth upon which is rendered the Tree of Life. Many hours I gazed upon its sacred image, for by us it is revered. Dear Mother and Father often meditated before it, and the Essene communions are much based upon the understanding of it. I see the cloth now as if it shines before me, slowing my heart to a peaceful murmur, stilling my thoughts, arresting my tears…Praise Thee, God, for Thou ever dwell within me.

Slowly Issa approaches me, her face beaming. "Much I have yet to share with thee but would ye like to see the Tree of Life, dear one? It is well within thy grasp to visit its holy precinct, to touch its dazzling radiance? While to some it is considered a place or a physical tree, in truth, it is a state of being, even Heaven itself, what your Beloved will name a Place of the Soul. Thou art ready, Yeshu'a. Will ye come to the Tree of Life with me?"

I hesitate not. Walking into the warm folds of her embrace, tenderly she holds my hands as her wings enfold us in Love. And we shoot through the dimensions, I counting twelve overtones in each of the twelve. Suddenly I realize Isis' wings are the wings of Ascension.

Before us stands a towering Tree aglow with hundreds of thousands of dangling Light-filled vines, like the tendril blooms of a graceful, giant wisteria, each a streaming beam of soft bluish-lilac-white Light, reaching down from a great height. A celestial choir sings around us, of bells and voices and the lyres of God all in one, its song an eternal chord of serenity encompassing all the musical tones, in supreme harmony. I am rapt and weightless and without thought or care, outside of time and space. Upon my shoulder Hannah nestles against my cheek. We do not breathe, as there is no need for air.

Isis outstretches her Divine arms. "Behold, dear ones Yeshu'a and Hannah, for here we have arrived, the very nesting place of our Divinity, the issuance of Peace and Love. Is it not bliss?" With her hands she signs to approach it. "Yeshu'a, lovingly touch some of the streams of Light, take one softly in thy hands."

As I approach the Tree I see each tendril is like the finest of cilia, thousands of strains within each. Now under its canopy, I am surrounded in Love, many of the Light-streams nudging toward me. With tender devotion, I gather one in my hands, and all at once I hear a single note, indeed a singular song, so exquisitely beautiful it is, and now a voice speaks to me, such a lovely voice. It tells me of itself, its story, its mission, from whence it came within the essence of God. All at once I am transported to see visions of its many lives on many worlds, in many universes. She/he is Ka, and once lived on Lemur, the planet from which the Lemurians originally came. I am strolling through lush foothills of gleaming purple grasses as Ka leads me to see points of interest, a truly radiant world of Light is Lemur. I will ask Mother Issa of this.

Now more Light-streams touch me, gathering around my head and heart, allowing me to hold them, some wrapping themselves gently around my neck in Love. And soon I realize we are in full communion, that as I learn of each of them they are learning of me. How can I possibly describe this experience? Words are incapable of this, for it is ecstasy. Never have I felt such Love in all my many lifetimes. And when I am older and wiser and purer, I will again come here, and bring those in need, as Mother Issa has me. With each Soul communion I feel the eternal music soar and grow deeper in its textures.

Dear God, how I Love Thee.

The Tree of Life and Knowledge is our sacred haven, our Divine Truth of Love, and in its embrace is the sweet release of all cares and the realization of all Love and knowledge. Listen closely, dear ones. In the dazzling silence when all is absolutely still, listen ever so closely, call upon the angels. Can you hear the Divine song that resides deep in your Heart? Will you allow the angels to bring you here, the place which, too, dwells in your Heart? Can you hear it? Can you see it? Can you sense and commune with the exquisite beauty of God that breathes all around you?

I know you can.

As Issa and I travel back to three-dimensional time and space I am able to discern the entire form of the Great Tree as I have earlier in these pages described, and upon our return to Earth I am most grateful for the gift Issa has bestowed upon me.

"Tell me, Great Mother, I communed with a beautiful soul named Ka who originated on the planet Lemur. Tell me of this place."

Isis smiles broadly upon hearing these words. "Glad I am you have experienced this. I had hoped you would meet a soul from the land of *Mu*, a word meaning Motherland. Dear one, there is already great bewilderment on Earth about the origins of the Lemurians. Over four million years ago, the original Lemurians came to Earth at the request of the Creator, to bring the knowledge of Source here. And they came from the land of *Mu* on Lemur, a planet existing in a fully enlightened, ascended Universe that will be named the Dahl Universe. The original land of *Mu* is situated near the constellation Earthlings call Cassiopeia."

This insight stirs more memories in me and kindles the Flame. I gaze intently upon Isis, asking for more.

"When the original Lemurians arrived, there were already a few people living on the continent and islands to be named by the Lemurians in reverence and remembrance of their homeworld. There was no true developed language here at that time, and the few who lived on what became Lemuria were beautiful, simple folk. ...You met Adama, on Oceania. And you heard his name spoken during your multidimensional journeys with Thoth. In truth, Adama is known as the Father of humanity because the Lemurians were the first to bring a new race of enlightened beings here. Some will call the earthly Lemuria the land of *Mu*, but the true land of *Mu* resides on the planet Lemur in the Dahl Universe, the sister Universe of our own...

"And you, and thus I, your parents, your Beloved, and many others were on the ship of *Mu* that arrived here...Now you begin to sense the true enormity of your mission, how vast the chasm of time is since you first came, and how and why your conception was indeed immaculate...How you came to fulfill the Law, which is God. What men will make the Law is a false law of rules and regulations. The true Law is the working of God throughout the Sacred Universe, what in your studies you have come to understand as the manifestation and confluence of lattice and scalar energies, how the Law is balance, with what is considered to be the Female in command...It is the Law of Mitochondrion DNA. When a being or society errs in the Law, the results are ever devastating, destructive, yet even this is a working of the Law, of God's will, for balance will therefrom return. And come the Age of the Holy Spirit, this beautiful Earth will no longer support any deviation from it."

A bright light forms within my understanding. "If I indeed came to fulfill the Law, is this not true for everyone and everything?"

"Yes, this is so...but your singular demonstration of it is the culmination of many things, including myself. In the Great White Sister-Brotherhood, there is the understanding that the Logos, what you are, is linked with the Divine Mother. As members of the Sister-Brotherhood, the Essenes have this knowledge, even portraying it in complicated maps of the Tree of Life and Knowledge...Thus the need of men to hide it."

Gathering her golden wings behind her, Mother Issa ponders a moment. "Dear one, you will understand that Master Thoth was my teacher, as he is thine. Entrusted to him were the great secrets which have since been preserved in myths and legends. He gave these secrets to the high priests and others who could comprehend them, and when the secrets were transposed into myths, in the form of allegory and emblematic symbolism, only the truly wise, the alchemist, philosopher, Initiate, Adept, or Master, could realize they concealed the secret formulas for regeneration—physical, mental, emotional, and spiritual regeneration...Alchemy: the chemistry of the soul...These are the many truths you are being taught in the Mystery Schools, and they are concealed from the profane; they worship the emblems, the idols, the symbols...The Great Mysteries of Hermeticism—all consisting of the One Spiritual Truth—are hidden from the world due to the world's ignorance, and are all symbolized by me, and therefore by you."

Now my mind is racing, for her secrets are within my grasp, and to me she aches to reveal them. Great praises to Thee, God, for bestowing upon me this gift of Isis.

"Surely you realize, Yeshu'a, it is no mere coincidence that there were originally three hundred and sixty days in the Egyptian calendar year, and therefore the Atlantean and the Lemurian."

"Indeed, they represent the three hundred sixty degrees of the circle."

"Yes, and if you look closely, the myth constructed of my husband Osiris is awash in metaphors conforming to the creational patterns of Sacred Geometry."

"But of course, and like discovering the aura, one must look beyond what is given to ascertain the true meaning," exclaim I with surety.

"Yes...Thoth tells the wonderful story that in the beginning there was the mighty god Ra and his wife Nut. Yet Nut was in love with Geb, another god. This infuriated Ra to no end; thus he forbade Nut the ability to birth children on any of the three hundred sixty days. The beautiful goddess Nut called upon her dear Thoth to alleviate this situation, and he formulated a plan. Knowing Ra's curse must be fulfilled, he decided to propose a wager with the moon, engaging her in a game of draughts. She accepted, and Thoth was victorious, and thus came into being five extra days during which Nut could bring children into the world, and also brought the waning of the moon each month. One version of the legend states Thoth won a seventy-second part of the moon's light.

"Now, obviously you realize this legend encodes the knowledge of the Precession of the Equinox. If you multiply the number seventy-two by the five extra days, the result is the three hundred and sixty degrees of the sacred circle. And the number seventy-two is significant astronomically, since the orbs of the heavens seem to move through one degree of their cycle every seventy-two years. When you multiply the seventy-two years by the three hundred and sixty degrees of the circle, the result is twenty-five thousand, nine hundred and twenty, the number of years it takes to complete the Precession of the Equinox...Take heed, young Yeshu'a: Both the Pythagoreans and the Kabbalists understood the true *circle of the year* to consist of three hundred sixty days, and that by dividing the year by the emanation of five deities you once more discover the number seventy-two. And, dear one, the wise Kabbalists knew that by arranging the four letters of the Tetragrammaton in the form of the Pythagorean Tetractys, the seventy-two powers of the Great Name are manifested.

"When science matures, it will prove that all forms ranging from the smallest atom to the largest systems of planets revolving around stars are composed of positive radiant nuclei surrounded by so-called negative bodies existing upon the emanations of life of the central life-and-light-giving component. This astronomical truth will bring forth the allegory of you as Solomon and your numerous wives and concubines. In truth, they represent the planets, the moons, the asteroids, all of the bodies of our solar system...Some say you had seventy wives, others seventy-two...It matters not, for the knowledge is lost that you actually understood all, and your mate of the soul was Sheba, the dark maid of Jerusalem, and the allegory is just that...a symbolism of your vast wisdom and the great assistance it gave your people. Though, as Solomon your name meant Sun-Moon, the sky god people made Solomon into the sun, and your storied wives and concubines were, in truth, all the receptive bodies surrounding it!"

"Verily, I see!"

Isis looks into mine eyes with a new gaze, piercing with seriousness. "When you come of spiritual age, before your earthly ministry begins, you will select seventy-two companions who will represent what I have described, what many call the seventy-two names of God...But these will only be the men; your vision is deeper—you will also call to service seventy-two women...The balance is all-important, is it not? One hundred and forty-four companions. To call them followers or disciples denigrates them as, especially among the first and second twelves of each, they will truly be your partners in the Divine. And behind each member of the first holy dozen, male and female, the succeeding dozens perform equally important duties, and also provide support for the members with like skills in the preceding holy twelves, sometimes even taking their places when needed."

She approaches me once more and kisses my brow. "For now it is enough. But to thee I will oft return. I will teach thee of the Akashic Record, the Book of Life, and how you may help others to heal themselves by lovingly opening its sacred scrolls. And still more I will reveal to thee, as there is much still to learn. Thou art still so young, yet ever so blessed, my beloved son, myself."

# Chapter Fourteen
# Father and Son

AS HORUS PROPHESIED, following my passing the initiation of the eight-fold path of Consciousness, early the next morn dear Father wakens me. As I walked the tunnels of initiation beneath the Sphinx and the Great Pyramid, the angels were with me, and while some may think me a charlatan for knowing the solution in advance, fear not. Along with my prior studies and service, it was my precognition, my ability to step out of time, and my connection with Horus which all saw fit to gift me my first title as Initiate. I am now a young brother of the Great White Sister-Brotherhood. You may have heard I was often given prophetic dreams, thus my passing of this initiatory test.

"My son, Yeshu-Maria, open thine eyes. Open them quick, for once more together we shall journey, you and I! We will first make our ablutions. And as it is the fourth morn following the eve of the Sabbath, we will of course speak our Communion to the Angel of Joy."

Ever ready, clothed, and my travel-sack at my side, I jump from my mat in delight, my feet already sandaled.

Rarely one to be surprised, my dear Father casts upon me a gaze of amusement, as if he expected no less of me. Much is unknown to you about my Father, for he is shrouded in mystery in your stories, if he is at all mentioned. Already I have shared with you that he was a talented builder and artisan, and you surely have been told he was a carpenter. Yet the Hebrew word for carpenter, *nagger*, also means learned one, or scholar. Beyond the revealed depiction of dear Father's trade as carpenter or builder is the Truth, for he is above all else a Man of Our Lord, a well-respected elder of the Essene community of Mount Carmel, of the Great White Sister-Brotherhood. Nary has a sacred scroll escaped his avid eyes; nor does the true inner meaning of a tale elude his grasp. Yet he is often silent…but not with me. And truth be told, when you hear I myself was a carpenter, this merely means I was one who built the Temple of God within myself, as did Father.

The angels tell me someone hides behind him, in the small courtyard of tamarisk trees. My heart quickens, for I recall Horus' words. And all at once the wild-brown-eyed face of dear cousin John pops into view in the doorway. John of the River, whom you know as John the Baptist, rushes in and squeezes me in a rambunctious embrace of the bear.

My mind is reeling. It was John who leapt in his Mother Elizabeth's womb when my dear Mother arrived at their home in the hill country of Judea and issued her salutations, for he knew I was soon to come. It is true Elizabeth was well-stricken in years and had been barren and that Zacharias, his Father, was, too, well-on in years, and a priest in the Temple of Jerusalem. And it is also true Elizabeth and dear Mother are cousins, so John and I are second cousins, though much different in appearance. Even as a child, John has the look of a man, full-bodied, with brawny hands and a visage full of deep understanding. He is the cackling fire, the pot aboil, the busy bee who will one day indeed feast on honey. Yet he is also loyal, calm, loving, generous, a dedicated listener, and wise. He is Truth revealed. In John a dazzling blend of seemingly incongruous traits lives in perfect harmony.

As we gaze into each other's eyes, my heart harkens me back to golden memories of us playing together as young children in the purple hills. On one occasion we hiked to the top of a great mound in Galilee, a lamb following in our wake, and John plunged a staff into the ground, proclaiming possession of the heights in my name.

Ever energetic and eager for adventure, young John, even now, takes on the role of a protective brother, six months the elder. Dear Father has already revealed to me that John is Elijah reborn. Somehow, very deeply I understand this, for Elijah found God through his Ascension by the Merkaba, the Chariot of Fire, the pure burnishing of God's Light preparing the soul of Elijah to return to us, in the form of John, to blaze the trail for the Prince of Peace. John's mission is no easy one; often he sees so much, so very quickly, and possibly you have heard of our meeting at the Great Pyramid some years hence which speaks to this. But this is the first telling of our present journey, and I tell ye true: he walks with God, does John of the River. Though his fire burns ever so brightly and can blind, his is a most noble Heart, and wisdom does within him dwell.

Sitting by the little stream which runs from the Nile into the village, we are silent, spooning with pails the cool water and pouring it on ourselves, allowing it to wash over our heads and shoulders and torsos, eventually each cubit of our bodies touched by its holiness. Certainly a ritual act, this has also sanitary and energy regeneration purposes. And silently we speak our prayers.

The daily Essene Communions are central to our way of life, and form the foundation of our connection to the Divine forces of both Earth—or the visible Universe—and the invisible higher realms. As Hebrews, our days begin at sundown, thus why the Sabbath starts on Friday eve. Based on the Tree of Life and Knowledge, each morn and eventide is dedicated in communion to one angelic force or another, the mornings to earthly forces, and the eves to heavenly ones. This allows us to become increasingly aware of the many angelic forces and forms of energy surrounding and ever-flowing through us. In turn this enables us to be ever more conscious of our organs and chakras receptive to these energies, and to establish beneficial connections between them, thereby nurturing our physical and spiritual health. Given to us by Enoch, our daily Communions teach us how to properly absorb, control, and use them throughout our lives; they demonstrate how each of the seen and unseen forces is utilized by our human body and our consciousness. Also, we understand the relationship between the heavenly and universal angelic forces, how each heavenly angelic force directly corresponds with an earthly, universal one.

Unlike other practices, we recognize only the positive forces around us. And we have a simple map of the Tree of Life and Knowledge which illustrates seven roots and seven branches, the seven roots representing the earthly forces, the seven branches the heavenly ones. In each Communion we deeply contemplate and meditate upon a distinct angelic force and how it manifests itself within us, for, in truth, we are the Tree itself, of both Earth and Heaven. And by dedicating ourselves to our daily Communions we consciously open ourselves to harmony and wisdom.

On Saturday morning, for instance, we commune with the Earth Mother. Simply, we establish our unity between our bodies and the nutritive energies of the planet. Yet on very deep levels we come to understand anatomy, the processes of our metabolism, and our various energetic bodies, and over time we develop the ability to perfectly absorb and use all of the nutritional substances of the Earth and the energies within them. Alone, this Communion is a principle means to our living such long, remarkably healthy lives. For, in truth, we know the physical, emotional, and mental bodies are all aspects of the higher spiritual body, the body which is a part of and exists in unity with everything in the Sacred Universe. And on Saturday evening we commune with the Angel of Eternal Life. We recognize the purpose of the Universe is immortality, and that we ourselves achieve this by increasingly creating the necessary conditions for the advancement of our evolution. Knowing we have no limits to our growth, through our dedication to this Communion we stimulate our intuition of the eternity of all life in the Sacred Universe, and of our own participation in this process, as there is, in truth, only One Life. By this one Communion we deeply embrace the reality and importance of overcoming gravity itself, a manifestation of earthly thought, and thus unite with greater forms of cosmic reality, a prime function of our and the planet's growth.

In these pages I will acquaint thee with all the daily Essene Communions, and the Noontide Contemplations.

Dear Father intones, "Now, John and Yeshu'a, let us in unity speak the introductory verse with which we preface each communion, and then recite the simple words given us for this morn."

As one say we, "I enter the Eternal and Infinite Garden with reverence to the Heavenly Father, the Earthly Mother and Great Masters, reverence to the holy, pure, and saving teaching, reverence to the Sister-Brotherhood of the Elect."

For a long, silent moment we contemplate the angel with whom we are about to open our hearts in communion. And then as one we say the words, "Angel of Joy, descend upon Earth, enter my thoughts, and give beauty to all creation." I gaze about me and behold the glorious sunrise, the tender flowers strewn by the stream, Hannah's precious face as she joins with us. By absorbing pure joy from everything around me: the colors, the sounds, the aromas, how God so magnificently manifests in all I behold, I attain a state of inner peace and harmony as cannot be defined by mere words.

Eternally I thank Thee, God, and offer my praises, for the great gift of joy.

As we three and James the Older and Simon make for the Nile across the desert sands, John tells us of his many studies at Qumran. "There are model representations of the heavens, of many star systems, all in constant movement; in the main library is a bronze replica of our solar system. My teacher Benjamin has been informing us of the properties of each of the orbs and their many orbits around Father Sun." Clearly John is bored by this, as obviously we are all educated in such things, but he is leading to something, as his eyes slowly come agleam. "Yet it is the great crystal of Qumran which astounds me. Hidden in the library, it resides upon a pedestal, behind a wall, and around it a curtain is drawn…Only the initiated are allowed near…Following my exams on the ancient Persian texts, in confidence Benjamin took me to see it. The utmost silence is required in its precincts—" John stretches his arms wide, far beyond the width of his body, and then opens his meaty hands "—it is thrice this large and more. When I saw the giant crystal, it was stunning lilac, blue, and white in hue, yet Benjamin informed me its color is ever-changing. While he knows not the inner meanings of such things, an aged Essene Master revealed to me that some brothers and sisters are able to focus their energies, in some manner connecting the crystal with others across the ley lines of the lands, to provide health, communication, and protection."

My Father nods his head knowingly. "The great crystal of Qumran came from the stars, beyond Cassiopeia, from the area of the Great Central Sun of all the Universes. The Sister-Brotherhood has used it since time out of mind; the Kaloo—the Atlanteans—and the Lemurians saved it from destruction on many occasions. Before Israel was born, a small group of Atlanteans came to Carmel and Qumran to ensure, for a time, the survival of their sacred science...In order to save their knowledge, on occasion a soul of a people has even allowed itself to be placed within a powerful crystal, allowing it to survive nigh-countless ages. Crystals, dear ones, are life, of a very high order."

John snaps his head to attention, his eyes bulging in epiphany, and my heart smiles.

"Heed my words, boys," Father continues: "There are record-keeping crystals...The words of our sacred scrolls originated therein and were then transferred to papyri. Other crystals are used for the accelerated development of vigorous plants, with little need for water...Quite useful in Qumran...Others aid in healing, even from great distances. The great crystal is quadrilateral, with the base constituting a fifth surface, like a four-sided pyramid. And you are correct, John; Masters properly combine and align their energies within it, and focus and enhance them."

Dear Father goes silent for a moment and then declares, "In future it will prove very useful. Remember: the meaning of the word pyramid is *fire in the middle*."

As we walk toward the Nile quays, little by little the desert sands diminish and the land becomes more lush; deepest green in hue are the grasses, strewn throughout with flax, papyrus, and wheat, hearty fig and barley and vibrant melons. From afar, this we can see from the main temple of the lofty mound of Heliopolis. But to again walk among the luxuriant reeds, to espy the lovely blue lotus blossoms and the plentitude of colorful butterflies makes my heart sing with a choir of angels. A double-masted cargo ship awaits, its outsized two red sails billowing joyfully in the breeze. At the gracefully elevated prow an African gazes through a small telescopic glass, such as those used by stargazers. And up the great river, into Upper Egypt, Abydos and Osiris beckon.

Looking back at the City of the Sun after we are aboard, my heart stills; though my early days in Heliopolis are now nearly done, I know as a man I will return to endure some of my most difficult tests in becoming a Master. Yes, my Divinity has been awakened here; much I have learned. Yet, too, it is its placement as gateway to Heaven that has roused me. Heliopolis is the oldest of pre-dynastic Egyptian cities, and was built by Thoth to align with the star-filled cosmos and the geomagnetic ley lines of the Earth. Though I have yet to describe them, as I will indeed return, here also are the famous Persea Tree and the Fountain of the Sun, both potent symbols of this city's connection with the most superior aspects and planets of the utmost heavens.

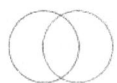

Along the banks of the Nile are fertile grasslands, fields of vegetation, innumerable plots of thriving farmlands, and scenes of humble family life lived off of the river. Just now ending, the *Akhet*, the season of the Inundation, has been fruitful this year, with plentiful water flooding the banks of the mighty waterway and its tributaries. As we sail deeper into Upper Egypt the land grows richer still, the soil darker and darker, and various of the temples flow past, Father often giving us a history of their existences and the reasons for their placement in such and such a spot. As I have before mentioned, the Egyptians saw the Nile as the spine of the planet, and the seven major teaching temples correspond with the chakras of the planet, and thus with those of our human bodies. Yet, as a whole, they number in the hundreds, the temples, and as I become a man I will come to transcend the seven chakras to achieve my immortality. As will you.

With the oil lamps lit, our first night aboard ship is full of stories. Grand in size, the vessel has two decks, twenty oarsmen, and a fit crew, yet the heavily bearded Egyptian captain, Djedi, eats with us, longing to hear our stories. Before boarding in Heliopolis he and Father spoke in code, an exchange of truly ancient words, and I become aware the captain hails from Lake Mareotis; he is of the Brother-Sisterhood of Light.

Dear John recounts the tradition of the blowing of the ram's horn on *Rosh Shofar* (Rosh Hashanah), the Hebrew festival of the New Year which occurs in Autumn, the first of the High Holy Days or *Yamim Nora'im*, Days of Awe. Leading to the Day of Atonement (Yom Kippur), on the Hebrew calendar this is the holiest time of year. There is light in John's eyes as he speaks of hearing the horn in the distance, as these holy days have just now passed. It is soon clear to Captain Djedi that in some fashion we do not follow the same rules in our Essene communities as do those on the outside.

"Do you attend the temples on holy days?" he asks.

Father replies, "Some do. Many have that need. Is it not true the most powerful rituals are those one oneself performs? We are all holy men. Those who feel the need to go to temple or synagogue attend them because their Faith is not strong; they require the sharing of that experience amongst a large group. A simple ritual we perform is the passing of the cup of wine to express fellowship, like it be the blood of our body whole. And we enact body-Spirit-purification by water-dowsing, as do the Egyptians. We do not live by the laws of the Hebrews. We do not sacrifice animals, and are more lenient in many ways."

John of the River perks up and asks dear Father, "Did they blow the ram's horn long ago, in the beginning?"

I smile upon hearing this question, for the angels tell me in some fashion I will soon be tested on this point. With each instant my intuition grows. I lean forward as the sun, a pulsating dark red ball, finally sinks below the horizon.

"An astute question, John," replies Father. "Remember: the Essene Book of Creation reads very differently from the revealed texts of the Hebrews. Our texts are far older, and within them nothing is hidden, for they speak Truth, bless the Brother-Sisterhood of Light. The very first words of Genesis say: *In the beginning God created the Heaven and the Earth.* Yet our sacred Essene text, the Book of Creation, says: *Without beginning the Law creates thought and life.* Notice first the use of the word create in the present tense, and of the word Law instead of God. And instead of Heaven the word *thought* is used, and in place of Earth is the word *life...or living matter.*

"We see by this that the first words used were not *In the beginning*; this phrase was substituted later for the simpler mind that cannot conceive of a beginningless or eternal state. Yet the Truth is: the Universe has always been and will always be; ever in a process of change it is, and limitless. Secondly, in Genesis it reads that God created man in His own image. As Yeshu'a knows, in some of the earliest texts these words were slightly different: God *makes man into* His, or Their, own image."

Suddenly dear Thoth is in my ears. "Ah yes, young one. I have been awaiting this moment. Take heed, for your Father now begins to tell the ultimate Truth," says he silently. "I have given you what you could then perceive. Now you are ready."

"Yes, yes, Thoth," I inwardly reply. "This somehow I already know, yet I am aquiver."

At a distance some of the crew and oarsmen have begun to hear our words, and they, too, are rapt.

Father clears his throat. "This phrase—*God makes man into Their own image*—is helpful to the discerning Heart-mind because it speaks in the present tense, and, indeed, we do eternally grow, transforming ourselves into higher and higher states of being. This is plain. Yet the recent cycles of time show man seeking to understand his own place in the Universe by attempting to make God something manifest, something discernable in three-dimensional existence. Be it the sun or moon or river or tree, in the later ages man ever sought to make this so, now culminating in the idea that God must have made man in His/Her own image...Yet the opposite is true: It is humanity that creates gods in its own image. This has led to the erroneous, destructive, fear-based idea that God is an old man with a long white beard, who lives up in the clouds: watching us, judging us, ever willing to smite us for our sins because he is capable of anger, of jealousy, of all human weakness...We have fallen into such ignorance, we create an anthropomorphic God! It will be Yeshu-Maria's mission to right this terrible error, for he will bring our teachings out into the world, he will become the Light upon *The Way*. In truth, he already knows all, and it will be our duty to assist and protect him."

We grow silent for a moment, the sky now darkening as the Nile widens. My brothers, Simon and James the Older, gaze upon each other in mutual understanding, dear Simon nodding his head with resolve. John looks out into the horizon and then stares deep into mine eyes. And Djedi thrums contemplatively his beard, looking at my Father and me, each to each, his countenance firm, his black eyes bottomless pools of penetrating wisdom.

Every day I more clearly see my path, my true reason for being, my mission. And with each unveiling, I have more words given me by the angels. Now, as she promised, it is Isis who speaks within me, and in turn I speak her/my Heart. "As humanity grows, its vision will gradually become more absolute, all-seeing, all-knowing, all-sided. In the words of the Great White Brother-Sisterhood of Light, God *is* the Law. This is not the rules and regulations of man-made social law or the ever-changing man-made laws of science or what is become religious law. It is the Law of God. Handed down by the Atlanteans and the Lemurians and beyond, the Essene scrolls tell us the ageless Law is revealed as God Itself; they speak only of God as the Law…The Law is everywhere and initiating all. In Its true form God cannot be conceived as substance or metaphysical, for indeed the Law is ever-present in both; it rules all things. It is omnipresent…

"And as all which occurs in the Universe, both seen and unseen, is governed by the Law, it is omnipotent, and the entirety of all laws is within it; thus it is also omniscient, all-knowing. And thus, too, the Law is our most loving Teacher… In truth, it is much superior to a Father or Father God, for the Law teaches us that when we stray from it, we are punished… Yet, knowing what God is, what the Law is, we know truly it is we who punish ourselves…And even then, the Law is always loving us, ever lighting *The Way* to a higher state. And in ways we equally may not realize, we are rewarded when we act with It."

Though he seeks to hide it from those around us, my dear Father beams as my words escape my lips. The lilac-white light flashes from his third eye to mine. He sees the man coming from the child. And the few crewmen who have heard are entranced or aghast.

"Well-said, Yeshu-Maria!" cries Father. "Indeed, as we continue to devote ourselves to the Essene Communions, all this is well-demonstrated…The sun itself is included in our morning Communions with the visible forces of the Universe, not in our evening Communions with the unseen forces, the higher realms of God or the Law…Through the Mother we must pass, for our immortality awaits—" he points his left forefinger upward, indicating the higher dimensions "—above! With both we must commune!"

How I delight in my Father's pleasure. How I am lifted by his enjoyment of me. How I have ever recognized him as my teacher, a man caring and wise and hardworking and both silent and yet brimming with effervescent life! From the beginning of my life it has been his example I follow. Many secrets of my dear Father still remain, but as I have promised, I will reveal all, no matter how much it turns on its head all you have been taught, no matter how much it stuns you, no matter how many questions it brings you to ask. The Truth shall set you free.

It is enough for me to proclaim my dear Father's lean but upright, solid figure, his strong hands and confidant countenance, his melodious voice, his ever-steady measure of balanced appraisal, his unfailing knack to know Truth, his gentle humor and healing gifts, his pure dedication to God: all of this and much more is my compass. His eyes are grayish-emerald, as he is of Aryan stock—that is in the original usage of the word, of Hindu origin, derived from the Sanskrit *ārya*, meaning noble. My Father is a Gentile. And like all members of the Elect of the Great White Sister-Brotherhood, he was to learn the systems of the land in which he lived.

Says he, "It is well this morning was the fourth since Sabbath eve and that we spoke our communion to the Angel of Joy, for it brings to Heart a most important Truth. Each time Yeshu'a recites the words, he then looks out upon the world and sees the Angel of Joy within all things. Behold! He sees it in the bloom of the flower, in the morning dew upon its petals, hears it in its rustling in the breeze, smells it in its sweet scent. This is good, for, as it is with all things, verily the flower has no other purpose than to bring joy to the hearts of all humanity. Now may you truly understand the reason for Creation, why we are here, how the act of creation occurs, for the Earth, indeed all the Universe was created in joy!"

Ah, dear Father, I will remember this. In future this I will use in my own way to illustrate the importance of this communion, how we are all co-creators of this dazzling life, of this Love-filled Universe.

"And from this," he continues, "you may now also comprehend a perfect Truth about reincarnation. As we know the trees are our brothers; so, too, are the animals intimately connected with us. Those who enter our lives and share theirs with ours, when they pass over, they return to us in their next incarnations, even those we kill. For those who are loved-ones, quick! Go out and find them anew, for their Interlife is brief, such is the vastness of their knowledge of Love, and they immediately return to us once more; if we do not seek or find them, they will grace other people with their companionship. Yet those animals who live out their lives without human contact of any kind, they ascend, for their lessons are done."

We contemplate Father's words in silence for some moments, the soft Nile breeze caressing my cheeks, the stars beginning to shine through the ebon of night, the nigh-full moon making her journey across the planisphere.

"Shall you tell, dear Father, what the meanings of the other words are?"

"O Yeshu-Maria, ever vigilant you are in the transmission of Truth. Indeed I shall; one must always remember there is no religion higher than the Truth. Yeshu'a is referring to the end words of the first line of the Essene Book of Creation: Without beginning, the Law creates *thought* and *life*. Instead of the words of Genesis *the Heaven and the Earth*, as I have mentioned, we have *thought* and *life*. First, we can readily see by this that the use in Genesis of the word Heaven does not represent the sky and the word Earth does not signify only the planet Earth. As we know, so, too, did the ancients: the Universe is composed of countless planets in innumerable solar systems in nigh-infinite galaxies. We have knowledge of them. While the text of Genesis speaks of the planet Earth, with our memory we Essenes and the Greater Sister-Brotherhood of Light know it is truly referring to all the planets in the infinite Universe, not just our own."

Djedi nods earnestly his head, while John stares adoringly into my face, as does my dear Mother when she expects wisdom-words of the Heart to spring from my lips. How wise is John.

Say I, "Surely we recognize the sacred life-force of everything in the Universe. All is indeed life. And in the original text of The Book of Creation the phrase is written thus: Without beginning, the Law creates thought and *living matter*. Living with God, we see no distinction between living matter and seemingly lifeless substance. Everything has within it the potential of Life. So, when we see the word Earth written in the text of the Hebrews, we know it truly speaks of all the planets and of all life on all the planets."

His big brown eyes agleam, John declares, "All the Universe is an ocean of life. We call it the Cosmic Ocean of Life!"

Now dear Father will perform the final unveiling: "Yes. This brings us to the meaning of Heaven in the Hebrew text of Genesis, what in our text is called thought. As Moses and Enoch and Melchizedek knew, our Book of Creation tells us there is another Cosmic Ocean: the invisible one, the higher one, the one called Consciousness. The Cosmic Ocean of Thought or Consciousness."

Djedi exclaims, "So, indeed, as is told by all the original knowledge, Heaven equates with the highest realms of consciousness, not a physical place or the sky or anything in the visible Universe!"

My heart smiles, for I know it is Love which creates thought itself, and from my third eye I send the lilac-white light of vision to both Djedi and John, allowing them for an instant to experience the Sacred Tree of Life and Knowledge.

"Beyond time and space," dear Father continues, "the consciousness of all life on all the planets forms a coherent unity of energy that is the most powerful force in the Universe. Like the Law itself, it is all-powerful, all-knowing, and everywhere-present. When man's science comes of age it will declare the velocity of Light to be the speediest thing in the Universe, yet the speed of consciousness is faster, instantaneous in truth…At all times there is interaction with all life everywhere, a harmonic unity between all living things that determines existence. And of course there is an energetic interaction between the Cosmic Ocean of Life and the Cosmic Ocean of Consciousness. Thus now we may understand what is meant by the revealed text which reads *In the beginning God created the*

*Heaven and the Earth...It means: Without beginning, the Law creates thought and living matter."*

A grand teacher is my Father, a true visionary, to be able to state it thus, and through him, the moving Temple, I learn of myself and how I shall myself teach, with my own flourishes of insight. Thus I think and feel as Djedi and John return with opened eyes from the Tree of Life and Knowledge and hear Father's sacred words.

Father says softly, "Let us now earnestly speak our evening Communion. As it is the fourth evening following Sabbath, we shall commune with the Angel of Power; most appropriate this is."

In one voice, my two brothers, John of the River, Father, and I recite the prelude to all our communions: "I enter the Eternal and Infinite Garden with reverence to the Heavenly Father, the Earthly Mother and Great Masters, reverence to the holy, pure, and saving teaching, reverence to the Sister-Brotherhood of the Elect."

With eyes lovingly upon each other, we then close them and contemplate with great reverence the Angel of Power, what its force in the Universe signifies to each of us, and then speak our evening Communion: "Angel of Power, descend upon my Acting Body and direct all my acts."

Such a simple Communion, with such simple words, yet having such great meaning, and, as dear Father said, it is most appropriate for this eve. Through my beating Heart, I direct my thoughts to contemplate the sacred unity of all life in the Universe, how the solidarity is continually occurring at higher and higher vibrations. Such immense joy this gives me, my Heart swells. All life: plant, animal, mineral, energetic, and human, is indeed connected with me, and I with it. All life sings its exquisite song within me, and pacifies my nervous system, I gathering all of its threads, soaking up every scintilla of vibrant, Love-filled, healing, life-giving energy so I myself am a living Temple of God's eternal Love.

Say I aloud, "Verily, what we think and feel are never sufficient, for they be like the words written on the crumbling pages of scripture. When we invite the Angel of Power to direct our acts, it is to this that we must attend, as all the Sons and Daughters of God must ripen their feelings and thoughts into righteous acts of fellowship, as the golden fruit of summer gives meaning to the green leaves of spring."

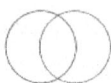

Late into the third night, as we sleep astern, dearest John is awakened by the footfalls of one of the sailors. On the starboard side Father and I are bundled in blankets as the Egyptian nights are nigh-always cool. And my two brothers sleep comfortably portside. But it is John who has intimately understood all of the currents of thought aboard this vessel.

My senses waken me in the last moment, a curious scent of musk in my nose. And all at once a man is upon me, strong he is, with heaving breath, and a blade glints in the moonlight. His iron forearm across my chest, I make to resist, but there is no use.

"From me," he rasps in a whisper, "ye will know I cannot allow thee to survive. Forgive me, yet ye know too much. The world is not ready for thee…Not yet. Not by half."

He raises his arm high in the air, his dagger long and jagged, and suddenly there is John, tumbling atop him, bludgeoning him with mighty blows as he wraps my would-be assassin tightly in his blanket. Throwing him to the side against the cedar stern, my brothers are now here and ensure the man is truly unconscious with more blows, and John comes with a rope. The ship is awake now, and Djedi rushes from his cabin below and gazes in astonishment upon the scene.

Never will I mention who the man was or his place of origin because it makes no difference. Neither a Hebrew nor an Egyptian, he was merely a man ruled by fear, as so many still are in the age in which you now live. The event lasted perhaps three minutes, and with Love in our hearts we then threw him, tied in blankets, overboard into the Nile, Djedi offering his supreme regrets, as he had sensed something amiss with the man.

To John of the River I give all credit due, for again and again he proves himself. And with tears in my eyes as I write these words, as also there were on that night, I say to you that, along with my Father, John is the finest man I ever knew.

It is with great moment that at this time I am to begin my fasting and the cleansing of my body in anticipation of the rites to come.

Deep into the night I lie awake, peering over the railing into the endless ebon of the desert, my Heart pounding with Glory. Dearest God, bestow upon me the strength to weather any storm, to surmount every obstacle set before me. Ever illuminate the path so I may see clearly and true, for Thou art my eyes, my ears, my voice, my feelings and thoughts. If I am to take the mantle offered to me, if I am indeed to become the Christ, it is to Thee I give all of myself in humble dedication. Be with me. Great praises to Thee.

"My beloved son, to thee I bequeath all there is to give. Deep in thy Heart I live and breathe and grace thee all the answers ye will ever need. In thy darkest hour I am there, in thy moments of triumph I am there. As is so with every woman and man, ever I am by thy side. To thee all is given: every answer, every wisdom, every possible solution to every puzzle. As you embrace the ever-growing Truth of your especial life, with thee all the more I am. Never will you suffer my absence, for I Love thee without measure. Such is the great gift I thee give."

# Chapter Fifteen
# Osiris

WE ENTER THE LONG, water-lily-laden canal leading to Abydos as evening settles in on the eighth day. Ere being renamed by the Greeks after one of their own cities, it was called *Abedjou* by the Egyptians, but in the ancient tongue it was originally known as *Ta Wer*, or The Oldest Place. *Ta Wer* also means tower, the Tower to Heaven. This city was sacred long before dynastic times, and, as I have shared with you, many temples existed here long lost to the ages. Surely Seti the First's spectacular temple of the twelve pillars, the absolution tanks, and the hypostyle halls, is well-known and venerated for its energetic power and exquisite design. Dedicated in part to the early Pharaohs, to which its famed List of Kings attests, in truth, like the Osireion to its rear, Seti's temple is a monument to Osiris, or *Wesir* in the olden tongue. And if you recall, I was given a vision of the Flower of Life in the Osireion by Thoth. Many hours I have studied in Heliopolis the history and symbols of this great city, and I have also traveled in my energetic body with Manetho to view its stunning precincts. Here, it is said, is where the body of Osiris washed ashore and was entombed after he had been saved by Isis and their Divine son Horus, with Thoth's assistance, and resurrected. Like a drum my heart pounds, as I know my next revelation awaits and that its key rests with Osiris himself, the world's first immortal. As has to me already been revealed: he and Isis and Horus are far older than humanity's forgetfulness allows itself to understand, and truly were Atlantean, not Egyptian.

Sailing through the canal, the scents of fennel, aniseed, and cinnamon, saffron, cumin, and fenugreek, and the blossoms of white and blue lotuses, lavender, chrysanthemum, acacia, and the pungent rose mingle in the air like potions. And soon it is clear the entire city is alight, as if a great fire of the Heart is kindled. As we come into the jut leading to the harbor, we see every corner, home, street, and building lit by lamps, so it appears the sun shall indeed shine at midnight. My, how my pounding heart swells at the beauty of the feeling it creates within me.

Yes, dearest reflections, like nearby Dendara, Abydos is the Heart Chakra of the world.

Isis intones within me: "Beloved, now thou art here; now ye will know; now begins the understanding of the deepest, highest layers of the mythos. Lest ye forget: merely a story it is, which teaches thee the deepest mystery: me, you. The tale of my husband/son achieving his Divinity—his body torn to pieces and spread across the world by Set and his followers, only to be found and gathered up by me and my inseparable sister Nephthys, I putting the pieces back together again with the help of our dear Thoth—is just that: an allegorical story. The secrets of regeneration, reincarnation, the quintessence of Sacred Geometry, within it breathes. Truly it represents the journey of Consciousness...The first stage is of unity, through the lessons of knowledge and of service to humanity and to the world, the second of seeming-separation into many parts so as to experience the many aspects of the One, and the third of returning into the One with the help of the Feminine face of God. Then the Resurrection and the Ascension, to the Godself within each and every one of us."

Upon my cheek is her tender kiss, and all at once my heart's eye catches a glimpse of the young girl in the Heliopolan temple. "...Yes, Mother Issa. Thank you."

"Fear not, dear one. Of what now comes I can say no more, for ye must pass the tests. But yes, thy Beloved is awaiting thy reunion, though it is still some time to come."

Disembarking at the harbor, I gaze upon the ingenious canal, following its slender thread back to the Nile, my heart's eye taking me there. And once more I realize the great Truth of this land rests in its incredible waterway. Egypt lies both in Africa and Asia; it is the center of the world, and now having traveled many days upon the Nile, observing the fecundity it brings to this land, I understand the relation to Osiris, the rejuvenating, regenerating, resurrecting god. *Hail to thee, O Nile! Who manifests thyself over this land, and comes to give life to Egypt! Mysterious is thy issuing forth from the darkness, on this day whereon it is celebrated! Watering the orchards created by Ra, to cause all the cattle to live, you give the earth to drink, inexhaustible one! Path that descends from the sky, loving the bread of Geb and the first-fruits of Nepera, You cause the workshops of Ptah to prosper!*

The Osirian Passion Plays are performed at the end of the final and fourth month of *Akhet*, the Inundation, and include eight acts. Perfect in his planning, Father has gotten us here on the first eve. The city is alive with light and life; a great pilgrimage occurs at this time, wherein all come to watch the drama of the myth of Osiris performed, seeing themselves in his example, achieving eternity, engaging in ritual playacted versions of Resurrection, while also dedicating themselves to him, the first immortal. Of this I have learned many things, yet, without a word passing between us, Father has allowed me to realize that I myself will become the god...Initiation awaits me.

The lush green of *Abedjou* thrills me; the groves, the orchards, the immense gardens of flower and tree and vine awaken in me the breath of God. And on this first evening of the Passion Plays John of the River and I sit comfortably in a date palm tree, watching the first acts.

Easy it is to think John a mere bystander, a character in *my* play. Yet truly he is my equal. We know that in the ancient pre-dynastic, pre-Egyptian story, Horus is baptized by *Anup*, or Anubis, in the great dividing river *Iarutana*. Indeed, *Anup* is decapitated in the Egyptian story, as he represents Aquarius, the Water Bearer, as does John. On August 29th in your olden Julian calendar, a particularly bright star at the head of the constellation Aquarius rises above the horizon in the nighttime sky, while the rest of the constellation remains below it, as the sun sets in Leo, the kingly sign, thus *decapitating* the Water Bearer.

Beloveds, of this John and I already have deep knowledge, and know it to be part of the mythic-tale woven to explain the many intricacies of Sacred Geometry, the cosmos, and life on Earth. Yet, too, we already understand that we will one day enact the celestial drama upon the surface of the Earth, bringing the Mystery out into the world. In the story, *Anup* is a crier of *The Way*, a faithful guide through the wilderness, as is John of the River.

Each city and village of the forty-four nomes of ancient Egypt celebrates the Osirian rituals differently. Some fashion him as a plant reborn, a mound of vegetation, a sprout of barley. But here in *Abedjou* we are in his lordship's home, and thousands of pilgrims come as if called by him to his side. In the city streets every scene of the drama is acted out by priests and actors, and within the temple courtyards the same. First we are treated to a mesmerizing hymn, all the townsfolk and pilgrims joining in...It is solemn indeed. Soon, out of Seti's temple pylons, a tall, striking, golden man, dressed in robes of colorful silk and linen of many layers, walks along the pillared porticoes, a glittering crown of gold upon his head. And lurking in the shadows behind him, following at a safe distance, come Set and his seventy-two conspirators. Slowly crossing the main, second courtyard, in poetic verse the serene Osiris waxes rhapsodic on the sublime Divinity of humanity, his hands together palm-to-palm before his heart, his eyes glittering like diamonds as he gazes up into the brightening stars.

Now, in the absolute center of the courtyard, thousands of souls watching around the sides, the followers of Set pounce upon our hero, and a great struggle begins. One by one, Osiris ably dispenses with many of them, his courage and strength a sight to behold, yet soon enough he is subdued, a thick red liquid resembling blood now oozing onto the stones around his trembling body, and carried to the waterfront where he is drowned. They attempt to flee the scene, leaving the dead Osiris face down in the water, a cold silence permeating the square before the harbor. A lump forms in my throat, my mouth is gone dry.

Then there is a great lamenting, as all around us the mournful cries of all who have witnessed the scene engulf us in a vast sea of sadness.

All at once, led by *Wepwawet*, the first jackal-god and crier and opener of the way, a long procession pours out of the temple: the companions, followers, and disciples of Osiris, their parts played by priests and pilgrims. And there is a mock-battle between the two forces, contending mightily for supremacy, and finally the seventy-two conspirators are vanquished. Such a rush of motion and emotion I have never witnessed. Now the dead body of Osiris is pulled from the water, and the many priests wail loudly and pound their chests, deeply aggrieved at the loss of their god. *Wepwawet* whispers words over his body, and the scene ends in absolute silence, the lamps of the city extinguished as if they be one light…The sun shall not shine at midnight tonight.

Since we arrived Father has been strangely silent with me, even seeming to avoid mine eyes and my questions. Now I espy the violet-white light come from his third eye into mine. We are to be separated. And coldly he turns away from me. By two hierophants I am led into Seti's temple where, without a word, I am unceremoniously shown to a cell where I will spend the night. Alone.

Absolutely silent the night is; my mind is at first racing with random fearful thoughts: Why this treatment? What is the reason for my Father's sudden change in behavior, ere unseen by me? And where am I? Yet soon my heart calms my mind, my thoughts are once more ruled by Love, and the sight of my Beloved appears. And I recall the unusual layout of the L-shaped temple. Near an ancient small inner palace I am now situated, not far from the hypostyle halls and the seven chapels. One candle lights my lonely cell, and every cubit of the exquisite white limestone walls is covered with glyphs, of white and gold and green and lilac-red. Before my eyes the stories come alive, and my heart is awakening; its chakra is opening wider still, the shades and places of time, past and future, coalesce into one.

Time and space dissolve; I am with thee, at this precise moment, writing these very words. My Spirit at once within and outside of my body in Abydos, I am also myself in the Age of the Holy Spirit, and I know how and why. I now truly know how to be in two places and times at once, on my own power, by ceding my self-power.

And I see thee, reading these words, and, once more, I understand how and why.

You are all becoming Christ. You are the ones you have been waiting for. How much I adore thee, my beloveds. Never once have I doubted you.

Dawn is born. I find a bowl of dates has been placed inside the door, a small ewer of water by its side. As I am fasting, the dates will be my only food of the day. I also have begun to cleanse my body with oil and scent. After silently speaking my morning prayers I eat and drink, and then, as the door is ajar, I decide I will walk the temple.

Peeking into the hallway, I find all is quiet; not one soul is here. One may tell you of the many treasures of this vast shrine, yet only by walking through it yourself and then entering the second hypostyle hall can you understand or appreciate the rapturous feeling of eternity within this sacred space which gives wings to your soul. The raised and sunken reliefs on every surface, of such intricate design, of such exquisite artistry, leave me breathless. The vaulted ceilings, the corbels, how, as the light is perfect, the gleaming white limestone appears not of stone at all but of soft velveteen, like pure gold spun as cloth, the vivid colors of the reliefs jumping out into mine eyes.

I sit in Horus' chapel, communing with him, telling him of my love, first closing mine eyes and then opening them to gaze upon the living relief images of him receiving offerings from Seti, Isis giving her protection behind Osiris, who sits on the throne. Of the many chapels this one may be my favorite. Yet in the Chapel of Isis, as she shakes the sistrum, she who is all and my guide comes instantly and absolutely alive in luminous colors. Her dazzling face, her arms, her graceful shoulders, her cheeks, her hair, her countenance of serenity: all instantly bring me to Heaven's door.

O Master, O faithful friend, dearest God, thank Thee for these treasured gifts. Greatest praises to Thee.

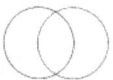

*A*bedjou is a thriving town alive with all manner of citizen: farmers, merchants, artists, craftsmen, and more share this lush sacred place. Seti's temple is much changed in your day; lost are its quay, ramp, and second pylon, plus other accoutrements, but the feeling remains of how it speaks directly to one's heart. Led by a hierophant into the courtyards, I gaze upon them and the town by sunlight for the first time. *Abedjou* is readying itself for the next acts of the Passion Plays, so I wander into the impressive gardens, taking in the flora and meditating by the sacred fountain of life, and then return to the main courtyard, now becoming surrounded by pilgrims and townspeople. I find John in the same tree we sat in the night before and join him once more. He and Father and my brothers spent the night in the humble abode of our ship's captain, blessed is he. And it is clear the thousands of pilgrims have largely camped throughout the entrance to the town and around the temple. Such a scene of Faith is this.

Long it is before the next acts begin. But in early eventide we are treated to the Quest and Lamentations of Isis and Nephthys. Two strikingly beautiful priestesses play their roles as they search for Osiris's body around the temple and in the village. Finally finding him on the riverbank, they issue great cries of lament to the heavens, their faces bent upward and flushed, wet with tears, and the pilgrims join in. I am moved indeed, for a feeling of this magnitude is universal and cannot be playacted. Touched to the depths, I look upon the faces with understanding, for the release of joy will be forthcoming as the Egyptians are nothing if not festal. This is all prelude. Isis and her sister speak many sacred words, yet this is only the beginning.

As night falls, again *Abedjou* is alight with lamps, and the scene shifts to the front of the temple, from which the *Neshmet* bark emerges, the boat Ra sails upon the Nile each night. Carried on *Neshmet* is the dead body of *Wesir*, Osiris. Though his face is not visible, the robes, the *Atef* crown of two ostrich feathers combined with the original *Hedjet* white crown of Upper Egypt, and the crook and the flail in his crossed hands announce it is he. The procession is long and resplendently colorful and impressive as it exits the temple and crosses the courtyards; dozens of priests and dozens more servants of God walk in silent serenity behind *Neshmet*. For king and commoner alike, Osiris promises eternal life; his Resurrection insures it, and all Egyptians are encouraged to journey to *Abedjou* at least once in their lives. This aspect is the sole reason for the great popularity of the trinity of Osiris, Isis, and Horus, and much it teaches me of the true nature of the Initiate's journey.

We are all Osiris.

Yet, what is the mystery of *Wesir's* journey that seekers, Initiates, Adepts, scholars, and your later so-called theologians have all strived to discover? Later men of learning have fumbled, as if in the dark, desperately looking for some seemingly deep secret that they all insist cannot be found. Is it the sheer mastery of sexual energy through the opening and control of the chakras? Is it the deciphering of nigh-limitless arcane symbols? Is it the solution of scientific equations that lead to the meaning of life? As I am showing thee, dearest reflections, it may be all of these things and more. Yet, deeply and truly search thy hearts…It is none of it.

Eternal life is attained through the conquering of fear.

The procession now weaves its way through the outskirts of the town and then turns toward the mountains, crossing the stretch of desert in between and then returns into the cemetery grounds. Next it passes the tomb before it winds up at the Osireion, the olden temple of yore in which the enlightened builders created a sacred space for water to issue in, representing the primordial waters from which all is born.

This done, there is now a grand mock-battle wherein *Wesir's* enemies are slain on the banks of *Nedyet*, the Nile, near the tomb itself. Throughout the scenes we have witnessed of the Passion Plays townspeople have played roles on both sides of the cosmic drama. And then there is a trial of Set before a Divine tribunal.

Attended by a mere thousandfold, by order of the chief hierophant I am included in a ceremony in which the two women who earlier played the roles of Isis and her sister Nephthys emerge in the doorway of the Hall of Appearings. Their bodies are beautiful, their stunning, empathetic faces, too. In their right hands are jars of faience, it appears filled with water, and loaves of bread are in their left hands. Not one sound stirs, and the two living goddesses now bow their heads. Someone near me whispers to his neighbor that the bread is symbolic of the god's body and in some private ceremonies is broken and shared among the faithful. This touches my heart with its high meaning, its intent so utterly filled with Love.

Now she who is Isis speaks: "Come to your house, come to your house! You of *Abedjou*, come home to your house. Your foes are not! O good musician, come to your house! Behold me, I am your beloved sister, your beloved wife, your Mother beloved. You shall not part from me!

"O good youth, come to your house! Long, long have I not seen you! My heart mourns you, my eyes seek you, I search for you to see you!

"Shall I not see you, shall I not see you, Good King, shall I not see you? It is good to see you, good to see you. You of *Abedjou*, it is good to see you!

"Come to your beloved, come to your beloved! *Wennofer*, justified, come to your sister! Come to your wife, come to your wife. Weary-hearted, come to your house-mistress! I am your sister by your Mother, your Mother by our Father, your beloved wife. You shall not leave me! Gods and men look for you, weep for you together! While I can see I call to you, weeping to the height of Heaven! But as yet you do not hear my voice, though I am your sister whom you loved on earth. You loved none but me, the sister, the sister! Now hear my song, my beloved, I am your wife!"

Now she who is Nephthys speaks: "O Good King, come to your house! Please your heart, all your foes are not! Your Two Sisters beside you guard your bier, call for you in tears!

"Turn around on your bier! See the women, speak to us! King our Lord, drive all pain from our hearts! Your court of gods and men beholds you. Show them your face, King our Lord! Our faces live by seeing your face! Let your face not shun our faces! Our hearts are glad to see you, King! Our hearts are happy to see you!

"I am Nephthys, your beloved sister! Your foe is fallen, he shall not be! I am with you, your bodyguard, for all eternity!"

T he chief hierophant, or high priest, comes for me in the middle of the night. Never do I learn his name, for he does not tell me, and I do not ask. But he is kind and wise and clear of eye. Tall and lean like my Father, his voice is much the different as it is a true basso. "Were you asleep, young Yeshu'a of Nazara?"

"No, for I knew you would come."

He has brought me a white robe and a simple golden crown to wear. Quickly I dress as he directs me to remain barefooted.

Through a hidden underground passage, he leads me out of the back of the temple to a small dock, and for what seems an age we travel into the darkness beyond the village in a small boat made of reeds, in the olden manner of the Land of *Khem*. Pitch dark it is, my heart pounding in my ears, and not a word is spoken between us. Sending bits of soul beyond my normal vision, I perceive we are passing through slender canals. The sky is a glittering canvas of life, the thousands of stars so bright, so vast, seemingly so close I feel I can cup them in my hands. Words my Father once said to me enter my heart: *If you believe enough, you can change the stars themselves.*

With my soul I feel ahead and see the waterway will soon widen. And lo! We sail into large pond, the hierophant fairly pushing his oars deep into the water to make shore. As we dock he instructs me to walk ahead, and suddenly I espy a hundred Initiates or more, all in white robes and crowned in gold as I.

My feet touching land once more, all at once many hundreds of torches blaze and the entire area is lit with light, I seeing the women and men Initiates all traveling a path around the pond, some with their heads bowed in solemnity, others dancing merrily, still others making signs in the air. Drums, flutes, and zumarras curry the air with enchanting rhythms and melodies. Yet as soon as the vista is lit alive by the torches, the next moment they go out, as if by one hand, as if they be one torch, and we are plunged into absolute darkness once more. Another moment passes, and the torches come alive again, all is seen, and I am walking the path along with the others. A terrible gong sounds, and the torches go dark once more. This goes on for some time, back and forth, light and dark, the festive music fading as the gong saturates the scene.

Now, in the darkness, upon the pond is seen one very bright light. There is a large reed-raft, and upon it stands… Osiris! The Good Shepherd, the King of Kings, the Lord of Lords, the Resurrection and the Life. Gasp! I look closely, my third eye propelling me to the raft of reeds…It cannot be…It is Father! My dear Father plays the role of Osiris!

Amid exultant cries from the Initiates surrounding the pool, the light on the reed-raft grows brighter still as it floats toward land. His feet touching the path, Mighty Osiris is next placed upon a donkey, his white robe shining in the torchlight, his crown of gold, much finer than ours, sparkling like a magical sun. A great rush of joyous sound erupts as he then rides down the path in victory. Some shower him and the path with white rose petals as he passes, the ground around him becoming glistening piles of Faith.

Then the darkness comes again. Absolute darkness. Excruciating moments pass. And silence reigns, save the rustle of the reeds, the rushes, wherefrom life is born and where souls go to be reborn. Blood is rushing to my head, my lips, mine eyes, my cheeks, and a sob is suddenly in my throat, tears well in mine eyes, for I know what comes. I clutch my robe and twist it in my hand in an attempt to quell the pain. The end is nigh.

Whoosh! The torches are alight again, yet now it appears there are thrice as many, our shadows short and thick with black. Now, in the near distance, King Osiris is being ridiculed, insulted, battered; people are throwing fruit and stones and pieces of pottery at him. And horrifically, he dies, bleeding, yet not before a small group of ebon-robed men hang him on a crooked tree, the blood oozing from his face and hands and feet and torso.

I am weeping now, the tears bursting from mine eyes, once or twice my wails heard, but mostly they dwell and die within, my hands shaking, my head drooped in defeat. Is it truly dear Father up there? I cannot tell, but surely he would not allow himself to be killed in such a senseless manner...Yet it is so genuine.

Yet, too, in moments I transcend my emotions, from abject, selfish, piteous loss, to a feeling of unimaginable joy. They have cut him down from the tree and placed him in a tomb, three priestesses hovering over him. The torches are made to show the passing of three days as the triumphant music builds to a blissful climax. In my Heart I am alone, but around me are people sobbing, clutching each other, others with closed eyes, hands palm-to-palm before their lips in fervent prayer, desperate hope in their very thoughts, in every word they whisper to their god, others stomping the ground with their fists in anger, righteous indignation, furious at their seeming loss.

Yet in my Heart I am alone. There are other Initiates on the fringes who see, this I can discern by my eye of the soul, yet with all my many failings, I not only see, I *know*. The Hebrews call this *The Glory*. And if you peel back the many veils you have placed before your soul's eye, you will discover you also *know*. I have never separated myself from Source. You, too, will find this in yourself, as you begin to let go to the Heart. This is my gift to you, your gift to yourselves, the gift of God within us all. I suffered, more than most, perhaps more than all, and on this night I have seen my dear Father enshrined as Osiris, and then destroyed.

I suffer not.

Lo! A great light emanates from the tomb, the music gaining in pitch and intensity, and a figure of Light emerges. He is reborn! And now a streak of Light, golden and lilac and blue, shoots to the heavens, the music reaching a mesmerizing crescendo of joyous sound, all the notes becoming one.

"He is reborn! He is reborn! He is eternal!" cries the multitude.

Across the pond, though first seen by very few, another raft of reed has appeared.

"Look!" an Initiate screams, pointing to it.

There in a blaze of golden-glory is a seemingly towering Isis, atop her head the horns of the sacred cow with the sun disc between them, one of her most recognized symbols. Holding the Ankh of Eternal Life in one hand, she outstretches her arms in epiphany, the golden light around her growing even brighter. Then it is done. The torches go out, again as if they are one, and in the flash of an instant all is dark.

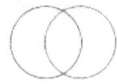

"Young Initiate, tell us of the beginning of the Universe. How did it occur?" a strident voice asks out of the darkness. There is condescension in the tone; he who speaks thinks me incapable of answering.

I stand in the Hall of Questioning, beneath the Temple of Seti the First. Another day of the Plays has passed, with mourning and weeping and recitations of sacred passages from olden oral traditions. Before me an unseen group of high priests asks me questions to test my sacred knowledge, ascertaining if I am fit to pass to the next grade of Initiate. It is enough to unnerve anyone, standing thus before these Masters who use the veil of darkness to inspire uncertainty, fear.

Deep and menacing, another male voice comments with contempt, "This *boy* is doomed to fail. How is it he is allowed to assume this initiation at such a young age? None has passed this test so inexperienced, not Osiris himself." Another voice in the dark quiets him who doubts me, remarking I have shown great knowledge and skills in the Heliopolitan rites.

Yet, amidst my innate confidence, a small doubt festers. I will know the answers, of this I am sure, but already I wonder if I am to be absolutely honest. Should I tell them what I believe they want to hear? Or shall I be completely true to the core of all things? Is there a difference between the two? *There is no religion higher than the Truth*, the words of my Father intone within me.

Say I, "In the *Bhagavad-Gita* it says: *Never have I not existed, nor you, nor these kings, and never in the future shall we cease to exist*. And in the oldest sacred texts, including thine own, it reads: *Without beginning, the Law creates thought and living matter*. Most learned Masters, I say to thee the Universe has always been and always shall be." Now I itch for wanting to continue, as I sense approval from some of these holy men behind the veil of darkness, but others still cling to the gamesmanship of fear the veil provides them. Shall I reveal the whole Truth? There is no question…I shall. "Yet, while this is true, I also tell thee verily the Universe is an illusion, a chimera, like the projection of light on the path in the desert showing us a pool of water, where there is not. One day science will prove this to the small human mind—"

A few gasps escape the darkness, a mumbled condemnation. "He goes too far!" cries the voice of the second Master, who has called me doomed.

Traveling into your time, beloved ones, I see thee and all which exists in the Akashic Record. "Yes, some of you may doubt me or think me a fool, others may not want the utterance to manifest in the world. But far into the future the word hologram will exist in the languages of humanity. From the Greek, *holo* meaning whole and *gramma* meaning message, hologram will be defined as *a three-dimensional image formed by the interference of coherent beams of light.* I tell ye true: the Sacred Universe is a Heavenly reflection of our creation. It is the *Veil of Isis*, a reflection of the True Light. Yet, Masters, even a reflection of the One True Light is of God, for it originally comes from God. Thus God permeates all matter in the Universe...The Law is omnipresent and omniscient and omnipotent. This teaches us the true nature of the Universe and the path of our mission...The Universe of our creation is our work in progress, our heavenly work."

Out of the darkness the disembodied voices murmur approval, I even recognizing the one who has censured me. "Tell us, most young Initiate: why is the body of Osiris cut into fourteen pieces by Set and his followers?" he asks.

"This was a much later addition to the story, Master. It does not exist in the original, yet it does have meaning. It represents the fourteen signs of the olden Egyptian zodiac. Thus it describes the journey of the human soul in physical body, passing through all the sky signs. It also symbolizes the Christ figure being immolated on the fourteenth day of the moon, the same day the people Israel have command to celebrate Passover, as it is said to have been the day of their passage of the Red Sea."

"Why is the phallus the one piece not found by Isis and her sister?"

"As the male creative principle, this part of the story reveals even the phallus to be dependent on the Great Cosmic Mother of all Creation for its existence."

Another voice now demands, "Then tell us why the number of Set's conspirators is seventy-two?"

"Many are the meanings of this number…It is said there are seventy-two names for God, seventy-two angelic realms, that the orbs of the heavens seem to move through one degree of their cycle every seventy-two years. Yet, again, the Truth is plain. The number seventy-two represents the planets, the moons, the asteroids: all the bodies of our solar system. The journey of the beloved Osiris, from the origin of consciousness—Unity—to the seeming-separation of three-dimensional life symbolized by Set's seventy-two, only to be reunified by his Resurrection into eternal life, is in the story well-told…"

I project my soul-vision well into the darkness and enter the thoughts of some of my questioners. Are they ready for what I am about to say? "Yet there is a grave danger in this story. By teaching people through a story that depicts physical life as evil, evil has been and will continue to be the result. By teaching a false creed some call the sin of the world, sin is the result…Surely you can see this."

Once more, my beloveds, I project myself forward in time, well beyond my days, and see the world as it has long been for you and your civilization. "Now the age is born, most esteemed Masters, when the world will come to believe that the Earth is but a rock without Spirit, devoid of life, something to be conquered and controlled by man. And humanity will no longer see the Divinity in itself."

Silence reigns. My curt questioner soon groans, and then with gravity states, "Yes, yes, with the split of Lower and Upper Egypt, many corruptions occurred. Tell us: does the Egyptian religion have as its basis one God or many gods?"

"Master, Egypt is the Mother of religions, and within its fold are many hundreds of gods. Yet at its very core it tells the Truth of the One God. Amun would best represent this; he cannot be known or seen, he preceded all the rest, and was without Mother or Father. Yet each god is in truth a trinity. There is Amun, yet his viewable face is Ra, and his body Ptah: one Supreme Deity from the trinity. Thus, though it appears complicated to the casual observer, each of the Egyptian gods is but a sweet facet of the One True God. Indeed, the beloved trinity of Osiris, Isis, and hawk-headed Horus is symbolic of this. By the love of Isis, the world's first immortal, Osiris, is resurrected to eternity. Yet she did not act alone. It is also by the power of Horus that Osiris achieves immortality. The Divine Horus is shown hawk-headed to announce he is born of Spirit, of his Virgin Mother, Isis. In truth, Horus becomes the mediator between Osiris and man. His earthly birth is wrought from the Resurrection of Osiris, becoming him in the earthly plane, so the myth tells us. It is plain that Horus represents the Holy Spirit indwelling everyone and everything...He and Osiris become interchangeable, as in *I and the Father are One*...Father, Mother, Holy Spirit. Though Osiris, Isis, and Horus were truly Atlantean and not Egyptian, Egypt is the flame which keeps their story alive."

"How is this represented in the cosmos? Tell us of the three wise men."

Suddenly the heavens are seen above us, as if the ceiling and temple are no longer overhead, and every star known to man is seen by our eyes.

"Behold! There is *Sopdet*! The Greeks name her Sothis, She who is brightest. This is the Star of Isis. From their guilt men sometimes now attach false meanings of catastrophe to Her, yet when She first appears the river floods with life. Above Her—" I point to the Belt of Orion "—are the Three Wise Men, Alnitak, Mintaka, and Anilam. They seek union with Her to birth the Holy Child Horus." I now with my hands indicate the entirety of Orion, the Sky God. "Some of the stories say the child is Venus herself; the tales are well-known, and are merely star-lore meant for our understanding of how the cosmos works. Sothis will become known as Sirius, the brightest star in the nighttime sky, and while Osiris is often associated with Orion, I tell thee true: his proper link is with Canopus, the second brightest object beside Sirius. Hence the Canopic Way. Yet the Truth behind the myth is that Horus was Light-conceived, an Immaculate Conception."

For a moment I contemplate amidst more murmurs in the darkness. "…The myth of Osiris is so profound he is, to some, conceived as the Nile itself, the green-faced god, the god of vegetation, bringing water to the land, and like the Eleusian mysteries of Greece, the Osirian Initiate is brought to the gates of death to conquer death itself, so they may become Osiris. In the secret ritual performed on the water a simple Truth was revealed. Osiris is seen riding a donkey; this is symbolic of his being born both of God and of a human. He represents our higher nature, our Godself, yet while in body he is human, as are we all…until we achieve our Ascension. The donkey represents our lower nature."

A new voice suddenly queries, "Why are there forty-four nomes in Egypt?"

"Like thirty-three, there are many meanings attached to the sacred number forty-four. Egypt has at different times had anywhere from thirty-eight to forty-four nomes. Yet forty-four is the true number. There are forty-four chambers in the Halls of *Amenti*; as above so below…It is but a reflection of the heavenly sphere of perfected creation, the Consciousness of God. Beloved Thoth's books number forty-two plus two more which are secret, making forty-four. The name of God amongst the Lemurians was *Yawee*. Verily, this was the name for the multidimensional building block of life one day to be called DNA. Within human DNA are coils carrying information and instructions; these will be named chromosomes. At the original level of absolute Unity Consciousness, we humans have forty-two plus two chromosomes; most of the world's original indigenous peoples will retain this number, while the rest of us continue to explore and evolve and add more chromosomes. Ultimately, the journey leads back to the Unity of God:

Supreme Love and Peace. Myriad are the meanings of the sacred number forty-four."

"From where did Egypt come, young Initiate?"

"When Atlantis was destroyed, it became a place of salvation for the sacred knowledge. In truth, the island lands of Albion are the last remnants of Atlantis; Egypt was like unto a satellite of Atlantis, a colony. Much later in Albion, those who are the Druids built what became the Father of religion."

"And no doubt you know of the great stone circle some name Stonehenge."

"Indeed, Master."

"Who built it? By what method were these massive stones transported from afar and then situated so perfectly upon the land and what is the purpose of the circle?

Beloveds, Hannah has told me of this, as has Uncle Joseph of Arimathea, silently. Yet far back I travel in time to myself witness it, I standing upon Salisbury Plain, the lush green of the land imbuing me with great joy. Out of a golden fifth-dimensional temple come Manetho and Thoth, smiling and inviting me to allow myself to know the Truth of their great works. And indeed I see!

"Beloved Masters, already the stone circle is much more ancient than people believe. Truly the builders were Atlantean, so deep in their knowledge they raised and transported and then perfectly planted the stones by means of levitation. A cosmic portal, it measures the solstices and equinoxes, the upright stones precisely placed within an atom's breadth upon the ley-lines of the planet so all may enjoy the full fruit of the Divine connection to the heavens. Glorious festivals are there staged and enjoyed, and many rituals performed; there is also communication therein with life upon far away worlds. Yet its most fundamental purpose is to enable the process of Ascension."

Now there is silence, a deafening, long silence. Then like a clarion, out of the center of the darkness emerges a commanding voice I know well. "Tell us of the Hebrews. Firstly, tell us of the religion of the Hebrews." It is my dear Father who speaks, praise Thee God for his presence here.

"Verily, the beloved Hebrews have not their own religion. They took bits and pieces from all the others, and made them their own."

"Can ye give an illustration of this, one which is hidden from the profane?"

Oh, dear Father is wise; ever he has instructed me well.

"There is none better than the true identity of the Hebrews' Founding Father, Abram, or Abraham. Many are the stories surrounding this Holy Man of God. Yet look closely; see how the olden Hindu *Brahma* is so akin to the name Abraham. Sarah, or Sarai, was Abraham's wife, and *Brahma's* consort was *Sarasvati*. In northern India there was once also a holy river by that name. Lord Yesu Krishna, or Christna, the Christ, was *Brahma's* Father and guide, and to escape The Flood, together with *Sarasvati* they fled *Haran*, where Krishna had been king. In every sacred text I have read, including the *Bhagavad-Gita*, they came to our lands. Let us be plain: *Brahma* is Father Abraham of the Hebrews. And what is more, born of the long line of Melchizedeks, the Melchizedek who was the King of Jerusalem at this time...was Lord Krishna himself. Though our scrolls identify *Haran* as a stop along the way, the angels inform me that *Haran* could well have been Canaan, and while the Hebrews at times disparaged the Canaanites, witness that they also never invaded Canaan. Whether Canaan was Phoenicia, *Haran*, or it represents a sublime state of consciousness before The Fall, matters not." (Of course, dear ones, I do know what it is, as do you. Search your Heart of hearts, and you will know it once more.)

A bolt of energy pulses through me, from the top of my head through my spine. I feel the lilac-white light come from my Father, he who has played the necessary silent role since our arrival in *Abedjou*. It seems all my past identities never cease to surface in my conscious mind. I have known this on a very deep level; I have experienced some of the memories, yet now, with dear Father guiding me, like a spray of vivifying cold water on my face I know. Yes, most beloved reflections, I was the original Melchizedek, hundreds of thousands of years ago. But I was also Krishna, the Melchizedek who is named the King of Jerusalem before the Binding of Isaac. Until now I have only sensed him as my brother, but all is changed in this moment; another veil is lifted, though many initiations and lessons still come. Dearest, Sweetest Lord, how is it I am so loved?

Say I, "In Joshua it reads: *And I took your father Abraham from the other side of the flood, and led him throughout all the land of Canaan.* It also reads: *And Joshua said unto all the people, Thus saith the LORD God of Israel, Your fathers dwelt on the other side of the flood in old times, even Terah, the father of Abraham and Nahor, and they served other gods.*

"*Terah*, beloved Masters, was another name for Krishna meaning savior, protector; often it will in future be spelled Tara. Indeed, by this we know Krishna not to be the earthly Father of *Brahma*, but his Spirit Father. ...Masters all, even the name of the Holy City of Jerusalem is derived from the Sanskrit *Yadu-Ishalayam*, meaning the Holy Rock of the *Yadu* tribe. Krishna was a *Yadu*.

"Will you tell us of Moses?" asks another voice in the darkness.

Again the question rises up like a snake within me: Am I to reveal the whole Truth, save my identity as Moses, or am I to remain with what is accepted as truth? Once more dear Father cuts himself off from me, trusting I will succeed without his guidance. Such an Adept is he. "I tell thee true, most revered Masters, that there were three men whose stories were together woven to give the Hebrews the full range of wisdom and political authority; our true Moses was Asarseph, born of Egypt...You know well the story. Of the other two men I will not tell thee more, for it is of great importance to the identity of the Hebrews."

"Tell us, then, Initiate, what is your purpose?"

"I seek to be schooled by the great Mystery Schools of the world: the Egyptian, Druid, Hindu, Greek, Persian Magi, and more."

My heart aches now to tell these great and humble men what my Father has always taught me without coddling me. And on this day, in this moment, I do. "Dear Masters, I tell thee true: I wish to make the supreme sacrifice, to first move beyond the initiatory systems which teach of fasting and abstaining and suffering as a pathway to God, the things which weaken our physical and energetic bodies, then to provide the example for all humanity of how to attain immortality through Love Pure, forgiveness…To teach again how to eat of the bread, which represents the body of man, and to sip of the wine, the blood of man, without priestly interference. Long ago it was thus, yet far too many priesthoods since The Fall of consciousness have told women and men that the rituals would only succeed if the priests themselves performed them. This is what has created the wall between people and their souls. Two thousand years it will take, but my example will teach the utter Truth: each must be their own priestess or priest."

A collective sigh emerges from the darkness beyond. "What if you fail?" asks my dear Father. "No one has ever succeeded at this task. Each one who has tried has failed."

"I cannot fail, for my Heart is pure. Learn all of the exoteric systems I will, yet only to see them fall in the service of Love. Upon my return to Judea, as is the way with Essene Initiates, I will ask to teach the teachers in the Temple of Jerusalem. Many have done so, and some succeeded. Ever I will shine the bright Light of Truth on those in positions of religious and academic authority who, by their own fearful ignorance, abuse others and their own power and contribute to the world's quotient of fear instead of fostering Love, Truth, and Beauty…But this is only the beginning. I know each test will be the harder and that I must pass through the Dark Night of the Soul—eternal life is attained through the conquering of fear—and I know I will return one day to Egypt…Yet already I have seen my Beloved, she who makes me whole. Through her I will create in mine own image an immaculately conceived child."

Suddenly a joyous hymn rises in the Hall of Questioning, hundreds of voices strong, such a song of exultant glory it is, and a great light descends from the vaulted ceiling, I seeing the lotus capitals of the columns.

And my Father steps forward wearing the rich purple robes of the Supreme Essene Master, the other Masters gathered around him. "Masters all, may I introduce to you my Spirit-born son, in whom we are well-pleased."

They place me in the Sepulchre, the Holy Sepulchre of Osiris, my body anointed in holy oils and herbs, and the lid is shut upon me. Darkness. Yet, beloveds, I fear not. At peace I am, for I have you in my breast. I know you are here with me. Such joy and strength it gives me to have you here, caring for me, seeing to my every comfort of the soul, you knowing in your hearts that all I do, I do for thee.

For the entirety of my first day within, I summon my Beloved, she who makes me the Christ. I call to her, and she hears; her awareness is pure. Long it will be, says she, before we will truly be one in body and Spirit, yet we may always be together thus, our souls melding into one, each feeling and thought shared. Her fullness, her wisdom, her heart's ability to pierce the veneer of this ritual and enter mine, all inspire me ever to succeed, just as does your Love.

The second day I listen to every one of my Father's words, every bit of advice he has given me I hear again. His recitations and explanations of the sacred mythos and of the wisdom schools saturate me, the many hours passing like minutes. Yet, it is true, dear ones, that by the third day I have moments in which I think the priests will never open this initiatory tomb, that if I am here much longer the demons of insanity may overtake me. The oils and herbs with which I am sheathed are meant to protect my physical and energetic bodies while being in this close space, but their odors and those of the walls around me permeate, the small, well-placed air holes providing just enough oxygen to remain alive. Now I heed the call of Isis; off in some seeming distance her voice sings, and I enable myself through deeper meditation to once more grace the Tree of Life and Knowledge. Thank Thee, God. Ever my praises ring for Thee.

Now it is like a sunburst suddenly envelops me—the high priests have lifted the lid, and I am carefully guided to a sacred pool where I am washed, I gradually returning to normal time and space. The priests are joyous, singing celebratory, transcendent hymns while issuing praises for my successful journey, finally drying me off and dressing me in a white linen robe.

Surrounded by a group of eight, I am led to the Osireion, beneath the central chamber, all parts of which are submerged underwater, save the absolute center, where two staircases rise and meet on either side of an eternal-flame stone altar. With God I commune, as I am left alone, with no instruction, the Osireion pulsating with power all around me. Deeper and deeper I plumb my heart. Pure white Light surrounds me: the holy cocoon, the Cosmic Egg of Peace Manetho once described to me. Such a wondrous feeling it is, this blissful state of being, I blessing every soul I have encountered in my young life, then remembering and blessing those of previous and future lives. So beloved of me are all of you who inhabit my Heart.

All at once I perceive a giant face slowly coming into form above me, a beautiful, perfectly symmetrical face, golden, its countenance of pure serenity.

"Approach my Steps of Illumination, dear Yeshu'a of *Nazara*," it speaks without its lips moving. "My Divine Son has told me of you, as many times has Issa, and Thoth and Manetho. You, beloved of all the ages, have proven yourself worthy of me. Climb my Steps, and I will meet you."

When Osiris beckons, when he lovingly entreats thee, ye follow his path. And so I do, slowly climbing the steps, up into the main chamber, with each one my Heart lighter and lighter, as I seemingly emerge from the water in which the room is flooded. Three steps from the apex I see his form atop the room, suspended in the air like a vision, yet gradually I realize I am releasing from the world, moving beyond it, I for an instant becoming the stars themselves, their light passing through me, like a healing balm of Love. And then I am beyond them. As in body I reach the altar of the eternal flame, Osiris enfolds me in a sweet embrace, and all my bodies: physical, mental, emotional, and energetic, meld into one. What great gift is this!

On this the last night of the Passion Plays the sun shines at midnight. I thought the town aglow when we first arrived, but truly each cubit of every street on this night is bursting with light. No shadow dwells in *Abedjou*. Along the main avenue thousands of torches and oil lamps make festive this celebratory eve, triumphant music rising to the heavens in epiphany, and all are joyous following The Feast. At dawn Osiris was reborn for the masses, a statue of him on the *Neshmet* bark seen floating into the quays of the town. Wearing the feather crown of the goddess *Ma'at*, the statue was then brought in procession to his temple, the euphoric masses following the priests. Purification rituals ensued upon the reinstallment of the god in his temple, and the *Djed* pillar was raised.

Many in the streets talk of the fact that Osiris did not die for them, that he never died at all; there was, in truth, no sacrifice, only the attainment of Love Pure, pure knowledge, pure awareness. They tell of their deep understanding of Ascension, not of Resurrection, for they speak of Horus, Osiris reborn, sure in their hearts they, too, will achieve this desired goal of the soul when their day comes. As Captain Djedi and his crew ready our ship for departure, in my innermost Heart I bless this Holy City, Abydos, this repository of Light, this blessed place so soon become my home.

# Chapter Sixteen
# Sinai

WE STAND AT THE BASE OF Mount Sinai, my family and I, the many crags peering down at me like prying eyes, in full knowledge that I have come to undergo my next initiation: the Essene Rite of Passage. Wondrously I gaze up at the rocky pinnacles, the narrow areas between of green and copse, and the visible dark hollows I know to be ancient temple-caves where high alchemy and regenerative rituals were performed thousands of years before my days as Moses.

By man's ignorance, long thought to be Mount Horeb, the true Mount Sinai is known by you as *Har Karkom*, situated on the Sinai Peninsula, part of a truly ancient trade route in the Negev Desert. What is more, it was originally named in honor of the Sumerian lunar deity, Sin, and the mount is man-made, a living monument to Sin, who equates to the Egyptian Thoth, or even Moses. The word *sin* derives from the Syrian language and means *to shine*; the Babylonians had the similar word *sinu*, meaning the moon, *to shine as the moon*, as the chalk-white Negev Desert shines, as does Mount Sinai itself.

Near the base, dazzling rock-paintings depict the ibex, its horns representing the moon; you may have seen paintings or statues of Moses or Solomon wearing the horns, symbolic of wisdom, not of the devil. As Father and I pass through the internal caverns, at the exact center of the mountain, upon a massive rectangular stone, we view a glistening, white semi-circle disc-stone: the moon. All around it and surrounding the cavern itself are stones of pure ebon, black, like the nighttime sky. In the Age of the Holy Spirit archeologists will begin to piece together the bits of the Sinai puzzle, and their findings will corroborate my words. In Exodus it states: *And Moses wrote* all the words of the Lord, and rose up early in the morning, and builded an altar under the hill, and twelve pillars, according to the twelve tribes of Israel.

No such edifices were ever found at Mount Horeb, yet they have been at *Har Karkom*.

On our journey here together Father recounted some ancient legends, giving me clues as to their inner meanings, and from them I intuit what I may expect from the Sinai Rite of Passage. Ever one to point out that literalists like the Pharisees and the Sadducees fail to see truly, Father more than once has told the olden tale of the Ethiopian priests who failed to open the Ark of the Covenant; they finally brought the sacred vessel to their king, who was pure of Heart. The priests had succeeded in opening all the seals, or chakras, of the Ark but the last. No matter their knowledge and their extraordinary efforts, the final key eluded them. Yet when they brought the Ark to the Ethiopian king and told him of their failure, he merely touched its lid and the Ark opened wide, revealing its treasures. This tale I hold dear, as always the Heart is the key to finding God.

Climbing the rugged paths, occasionally we are stopped by various Essene priests, keepers of the mountain's sacred places, inquiring of Father our business, gazing upon me askance, shocked at my sheer youth. *How can it be, a mere boy such as this will undertake the Sinai initiation?* they ask. *This is folly or hubris or both.* Father assures them all is well.

Yet walking through these craggy trails, while I am with the angels, ever understanding the nature of life and my mission, I do have doubts. In my mind I return to Abraham, or *Brahma*, who clearly came into possession of the Sumerian Table of Destiny. As was true of the famed later Mesopotamian-inscribed tablets I, as Moses, brought down from this mountain, the Sumerian Table of Destiny contained all that humanity had ever and will ever know, yet the information was in the form of symbols. More was revealed in the breadth of a mere finger than in all the Commandments. I as Krishna knew all, my Spirit born son Abraham learned, I as Moses learned and knew all, and I as Solomon knew all. Once more I climb this sacred peak in quest of the Mystery, to learn anew the All. Yet this time it breathes within me because of you, beloveds, my cherished ones; this time an entirely new birth of humanity comes.

Because of you.

As dearest John of the River is my forerunner, I merely am yours.

Far below us my family now rests in a monastery; too, many of the caves long ago used for regenerative purposes are now repositories for some of the ancient records, and dear Mother has promised *Savta* Anna to study while I undergo the Rite of Passage into the Essenic Order of Melchizedek. And as Father and I emerge from the inner tunnels of the mountain and reach a sacred temple-cave, I am sure of my sacrifice and my success. A priest guarding the cave and the rough trail leading to the highest, most remote crag instructs me to recite a most solemn vow of secrecy and to swear an oath of allegiance to the holy order.

Turning his back without a word, Father departs. I am then blindfolded and led high up the mount and placed in the middle of a sacred circle; herein I will spend the next four days and nights, without food and water, open to the elements: a hot blaze by day and like blistering ice by night. Suddenly I feel Osiris's Sepulchre to be a cozy holiday.

Off to one side a small fire burns within a stone lined pit; there is scarce little wood to be found here to feed it, but mine eyes espy some promising bits of branches and twigs. There are bushes aching for water, dried up vines, and the wrinkled remains of berries. Easy it is to believe death lives here. Yet I first bide my time by walking back and forth through the sacred circle, tracing patterns of the Flower of Life, Metatron's Cube, and the Tree of Life and Knowledge. This gets me through until nightfall. But by midnight, I feeding the fire the best I can, the wretched cold is seeping into my bones, and I hear both real and imagined creatures scurrying through the paths, some in primal battle, the hungry cries of wolves around me, and the calls of night-owls and birds of prey above, and I gaze over the cliff wondering if I would be better off jumping to my death, the cold cutting into my skin, my lips, my hands and feet. Yet I do not, for you are in my Heart, beloveds.

The indigenous people of the world call this sort of ritual a vision quest. When one is committed to their tribal traditions, they undergo such a test; thus the reason so many have wandered off into the desert to find God, creating their own Rite of Passage. Yet this is an especial one; it calls to me, this place. Once thinking I had unveiled all of my prior-life memories, more rush into me now, in the forms of knowledge, wisdom, and places and people and emotions and thoughts. I nary have been without any of these, but what I am learning here transmutes all, transforms my very essence.

Tonight a red scorpion nears me by the fire. So tired I feel I may fall asleep at any moment, my first instinct is to kill him. Crawling his way right beside me, one would not fault me for doing so; his sting can kill. Yet in him I see the Love of God; God within him breathes. To him I speak in dulcet tones, give him the name Ezekiel, meaning God gives strength, and honor him by allowing him to share in the heat of the fire.

And I hear his voice. He tells me of his many gifts and travels and the problems he has had to conquer in order to survive. We are not so different, he and I. He reminds me to call upon Ra, the Sun God, to find him in my abdomen so I may warm my bones, and by day to travel in my thoughts to a cool spring, so I shall not wilt.

By the second and third days I am dreaming of being with my Beloved, as a man is with a woman; this comforts me, but I also feel shame for thinking thus. I smell her skin, her flower-like essence, and feel her sweet caress, her body against mine, and all at once I am transported to be with her. Her lips like sweet cheery wine, I surmount my fears once more and return to the wretched Mount Sinai, this prison of mine own reflection.

Yet all is forever changed, for I see only through my Heart's eye, the eye of the Soul, the Spirit's eye. Night has fallen following the third day; what little shrubs and bits of grass are left to throw onto the dying fire are not enough to warm me. Yet the owl speaks to me; when in the beginning his hoot had merely annoyed me, now he sings a song of pure joy. I know the song to be the same; it is my place in the Universe, my perception which has changed. Whereas the eagle hovering above had at first brought fear into my breast, now he tells me he is my dearest friend. More, I now fly with him; I am upon his wing flying over the world in freedom, he telling me all he has learned.

Dearest, sweetest, most bountiful God, ever I thank and praise Thee for this wondrous gift to learn of myself and You and all Creation as One Life, one indescribable breathing quintessence of Love.

Suddenly every single thing is luminescent, literally filled with pulsating Light: every pebble and stone, each bit of dirt, every sere blade of grass, every bit of animal dung, even the shivering and shriveled elm without a leaf radiates such beauty my heart feels it may burst. The air itself sparkles, like a bejeweled, infinite ocean of stars it shines. And indeed, I see God within the bush, showing its beauty to all the world: azure, green, golden Light pulses like a magical rainbow.

"Now you see, young Yeshu'a," utters a Voice both sweet and indisputable. "Many times before you have heard me, only now more clearly, more cleanly do I sing, as you have come to yourself. As Moses and Solomon and Melchizedek you knew, yet now it is not to you to write the words or draw the symbols; you are the Flame. You are to breathe the Truth, to walk among men as a living example of God within them, within all. There is no journey more honored, more holy, more beautiful, more loved...or more fraught with danger. For by my grace you dare to show humanity what it really is."

I am dumbfounded. "Yet, dearest God, how can this be so? Have I not sinned on this quest? For I have thought to jump the precipice, as it seemed the easier than to withstand one more minute of one more initiation, and I have dreamed of the sweet pleasures of the flesh? ...Tell me: how can it be I am gifted this sacred mission of Love when I fail so miserably?"

"Firstly I would tell you, beloved son, ever you have been able to see me in all things; it has been within yourself you have in moments denied me. All the wisdom you know; your mind remembers the words well. And verily your Heart is open and strong. The veil you have now shorn is the result of this Rite of Passage. Never again will you need to learn the lesson. Yet still ye doubt, for the thought of sin has entered thy mind."

Say I, "Surely, dearest God, for in thinking of ending my life, of allowing the passions of the body to enter my thoughts, have I not sinned?"

"Yeshu'a, when you learn to truly forgive yourself, then will you know the world is truly without sin. Yes, there is a moral code one should live by; all cultures have this. Yet the only sin is your mind working to keep you from absolute union with the Divine, my Divine Radiance. Indeed, you sin when you break one of the Commandments, but only if you allow your mind to involve you in it, if you adopt the attitude of negation. Many is the man or woman who, having reached the state of pure bliss, has committed an act considered sinful, even murder, yet it was the implementation of the Divine Plan; in such circumstances many forces are at play in the developments of all the souls involved. Knowing this, one can see these moments do not negate or delay these enlightened ones in their union with my Radiance. Do you understand?"

"Indeed, I do."

"Remember: the utter absence of fear guarantees supreme safety, while the presence of fear may well manifest what is most feared. ...Upon this mount, when you feared the birds of prey or the howling wolf might eat you, believe me, the thought entered their minds. Yet as soon as you returned to your true state, once more they were your friends, as you came again to know and accept that you created each other. Of course, it is more complex with humans, but *The Law* still holds. So, forgive yourself; every single human being has thought of ending his or her life, believe me. And young one, allow yourself to feel what it is to be a man; rejoice in your sensuality, in your feelings for the beautiful Magdalen. Like the Egyptian *Ta Wer*, Magdalen also means tower, the Tower to Heaven. It is not sinful to feel the beauty of the fulfillment of the flesh; it is only sinful if you let your mind negate that beauty, to transmogrify it into something it is not. If you remain in my loving embrace, seeing the beauty in and necessity of all things, it is impossible to sin. Now and forevermore you will know the world is without sin."

"Yes, I see! I see!" cry I as the stars shine down upon me a Love so inspiring as to vanquish all darkness, all doubt, all fear. "Great praises to Thee!"

"In your circle you have been tracing patterns of Sacred Geometry. Already you know Sacred Geometry entails the use of ratios found in nature and throughout the Universe; the most important of these is the Golden Mean. If you look closely, the measurements given in Exodus of the Ark of the Covenant work out to a width to height to length ratio of 1:1.666, very near the Golden Mean ratio. Too, the measurements of the lid, or what the Hebrews call the Mercy Seat or *Kapporeth*, also calculate to a 1:1.666 ratio. The Hindus, Egyptians, and Chaldeans also had this knowledge, as of course did the Lemurians and Atlanteans...Obviously, the dimensions given for Noah's Ark also calculate to this sacred ratio, as does the Earth and the human body. The world's great artists and musicians often use the Golden Mean in their works. Dear Manetho has informed you that the Kabbalists and Pythagoreans deciphered all the measurements of Noah's Ark, and that within this Sacred Vessel of Consciousness there are three levels of eleven sections each, making the sacred number of thirty-three. Do you recall what important Truth this reveals?"

"The Cosmic Axis, the *Axis Mundi*, is the spine, with thirty-three vertebrae...The Truth is the Ark is Man!"

"Indeed, beloved one. But there is more. Noah's Ark is also the Universe, for the Universe is but a representation of perfected humanity; they are one and the same. The story of Noah and his ark is a cosmic parable concerning the repopulation of planets at the outset of each new cycle, the Grand Cycle which on Earth is measured by the Precession of the Equinox. Sheba revealed to you that the Ark of the Covenant will one day be represented by your Mother, the perfected womb of creation, as, in truth, all is Christ. Now, listen closely, young Yeshu'a: what I say to you is that the two arks are truly one; they are but symbols of the same thing."

The radiance in all that surrounds me is growing in pitch and power, the brilliance golden-white in hue, filling the sky with warm, pulsing luminescence. A Love I am only beginning to truly understand is revealing itself to me. Yet, verily, it is I who open my Heart enough to receive it.

"You are at the doorway now, beloved. And only you have the key. This is the power I thee give. You may open the door when you answer the question of all questions. It is you who have asked it, and I have given you the answer. With all we have discussed, tell me: What then *is* the Universe?"

For a moment I think, knowing it is God who waits. Then I think without thinking, a state of being now fast become first-nature with me, knowing that my Heart will know, knowing I am the seat of wisdom, inviting in confidence all the angelic forces that guide my every step, craft each of my epiphanies, and form my very words before they escape my lips. Dare I say it aloud to God? "...Dearest God, the Universe *is* Consciousness!"

"I Love you."

The Voice has ceased.

Did I hear God speaking from the bush? Was it that I heard God in the trees, the air, the rocks, or the stars? Within each spoken word was a pulse, a pulse born of the Holy Stream of Sound and the vibrant codes of visible and invisible Light.

God spoke through everything, including myself. And to me God revealed all.

Great God, how I Love Thee!

Exultant, I travel outside of my body, my consciousness within both my etheric twin and my physical self. From above I see myself, atop Mount Sinai, within the sacred circle, and I see myself in all my lifetimes, both on Earth and throughout the Universe. Now I journey through the Milky Way, mingling with the stars, with the Light-dust of Creation, and then to the Pleiades, a most powerful form of blue Light-dust; here I will in future study its complex forms of male-female energy. Throughout the cosmos I travel in joy, partaking of the infinite elements of our Creation, inviting the sweet ambrosia of enlightenment to enter my Grail, the Holy Cup of Consciousness which exists in the very center of our brains.

But it is of my family I think most; ever they call to me, as I to them; thus I return to Sinai, into the tents of the monastery, and greet them as they eat their midday meal. See me they do, and rejoice at my coming. In my physical body I hunger, yet, by sharing in their meal, I, too, am given a sort of sustenance, an energetic sustenance; atop the mount my physical body, though weakened, is given relief. And I now return to it in full and offer my praises and prayers and meditation to God, until my dear Father and brothers arrive before dawn, to guide me down the long trek of the mountain.

Entering the monastery, upon seeing my dear Mother, I rush to embrace her, sweetly kissing her cheeks, lips, nose, ears, eyelids, and forehead, each many times, she caressing and stroking and soothing me like a newborn child. I bury my face in her breast and speak softly of my Love and gratitude for her presence in my life. She gives me water and purrs and rubs healing balm into my sunburned skin.

My Light-conceived cousin Mariam is now also here, having arrived with her parents, Rebekah and Simeon, since my trial began. My childhood love more beautiful than ever, she approaches me with her hands covering her Heart, a single tear coursing her cheek. She who shared so much with me, taught me so many things, and helped me through my early trials is now my great friend. "Our Lord blesses you, Yeshu'a; you shine with Light. From the coasts of Gaul your sweet cousin Sara sends her tidings of great joy. How she misses you and holds dear the memories of youth you share."

Lovingly I look into her emerald eyes, seeing the woman come forth from the child: such strength of purpose, such steely resolve, such Spirit. And I, too, hear Sara's voice, she who led me atop the *benben* in my early days in Heliopolis. "Blessings upon you, dear Mariam. Sara graces me with her song." Gazing upon this beloved Daughter of God, and she upon me, already we know our fates are intertwined. Mariam will be a most important teacher of *The Way*, and mostly from afar Sara will be the same.

Turning to view our family, holding my Mother's hand, say I, "A thousandfold blessing upon us all. I have come of age. And we have found favor with God and with man, thus Peace and Love be with us. Now it is time for me to begin God's work, for I have found the Temple of God within me, thus God prepares for us the Feast. Let us to table so I may break bread and give to you each a piece before I nourish mine own body."

# Chapter Seventeen
# Remembrance

DEARLY BELOVEDS, IN MY HEART each one of you dwells, thus ever am I in yours, for, in truth, they are the same; there is but One Heart. I hear each of your voices sing your song in your own special Key of Life. Each of your prayers I hear, as indeed they are mine. Every sorrow, every joy, every triumph, every betrayal, each emotion felt to the core is known by me, and thus now by you.

For you are the beginning and the end. Every day you have known, and every night never forgotten. Deep in the well of your Heart is your Love for me, for I am here, with you, and you shall never leave my side. This you promise. Though the world seems to teeter on the brink of destruction, though darkness appears ready to devour all light, though each day seems to bring closer the edge of the cliff of the world, I tell you the opposite is true. Never will you die; never will the dream end. You are never alone. And the dream has only just begun. Because of thee.

You have designed it thus so that you may release all your earthly cares and proceed into the fullness of what most people still call God; without this initiatory act, it cannot occur. So, beloveds of my Heart, bless it all, Love it all, forgive it all, and release it. If you fail to do this, fear not: all will be well, yet you will be obliged to do so anyway. Many of you do not trust your own shadow; thus how can you trust others? Yet you must. The longer you delay, the more difficult it will appear to be.

Radical trust is now required of you. There is no longer a choice. Until now you have been able to live your day-to-day life as you always have, believing you could somehow pull through. And the illusion tells you that you can. But it is false.

From now on, if you make everything you do be about God and you respect people's private lives, all will be well. No longer can you live as you once did. It simply is not possible; God will not allow it. Each of you must cede control; stop trying to control anything, except thyselves.

The original meaning of the word meek was *great power under rigorous control*. So, those who inherit the New Earth will be those of *great power under rigorous control*.

Do ye Love God? Thyself? Thy loved-ones? Thine enemies? Then upon thee God now bestows this sacred duty: Radical Trust. Of everyone and everything. Through it all I am with thee; ever I am by thy side, so ye may dare to be loved, my cherished ones.

Obviously the world did not end on December 21st, 2012. Many misinterpreted the Mayan prophecy, and from ignorance believed it spoke of the End of the World. Yet, as I have shown you, it is not the end of the world but the beginning of a new one. What you are experiencing are the painful birth pangs of Heaven being reborn on Earth, and the old rules no longer apply. In truth, they never did. While many still believe in the End of the World, many more believe the world will continue on as it has done, in worse and worse forms, and cannot conceive of Ascension, personal and planetary, and that any of what I share with you in these pages is possible; it is still easier to believe in evil than in God. Verily, this is the reason for existence: to grow beyond three-dimensional time and space, to embrace God within yourself so that you suffer no longer.

Listen deeply thy Hearts, beloveds. Can you hear me? I know you can. My Faith in you is unbounded, my Love for you infinitely pure and everlasting.

As you rediscover your Divinity, you will find each of you is uniquely seeded with the Gift of God, and that your unique connection with God is a dedicated waveband that you alone are wired to pick up and to use with Love as its source of power. Even if at first you find it difficult to hear beyond yourself, eventually, with pure devotion you will reconnect with your I AM presence, with God, when you have truly dropped the Veil. Yes, finding God within you is an act of Grace; God bestows this upon you. But it is up to you to bring it to full flower so it may bear fruit.

At this very moment when so many are changing their diets, the true, hidden reason for this is that in the future God will no longer accept the consumption of animals, vegetables, fruit, or other Earth-life by humans. While I do not suggest you do this, it may surprise you to know that already many people are living on Light; they have not eaten in twenty, thirty years, and drink very little water, and they lead full, active lives. This demonstrates the gradual return to the pristine state of Heaven on Earth, as in the days of Lemuria. And over the past two decades many thousands of souls have ascended into higher states of consciousness, into the higher dimensions. They have become Light-beings. The Mayan calendar names December 21st, 2012 as the end date, or the beginning of the Age of the Holy Spirit, the Aquarian Age. But in truth, the process is an organic one, and it began in earnest twenty-two years ago when, after millennia of work, the rebuilding of the Christ Consciousness Grid was completed, thus making Ascension more accessible.

This means many things. Firstly, it means every act based upon greed will no longer be tolerated, as money and the systems designed around its acquisition steal from others, the whole, and thus God. Whether it is one country from another, one corporation from a weaker one, one person from another, those who seek to gain will learn the oft painful lesson that Love gives and gets no gain. Each decision based upon the acquisition of wealth, power, possessions, all the desires of the ego, will instantly be met by strict resistance and, ultimately, failure, as God will no longer permit it. It also means in each interaction, if balance is not met, if one fails to forgive, issue sincere regrets for transgressions, take responsibility for their actions, or think of others before themselves, Consciousness will make certain those who do so will feel loss; God will be sure the balance is met. Those who withhold what is due will suffer want, and, at this moment in time, acutely, until they truly undergo that initiation, which, in turn, will reverse the process and strike the balance. There is no escaping it. With something as basic as money, easy it is to think the world will continue to live by its false creed. Yet, in truth, at a precise point in time, it will no longer be endured. The world is as you dream it, and if you dream of a world that existed in the past and are a part of seeking its continuance, if you do not change your thinking, beware. You will be obliged to meet your Divine I AM presence, and if you resist your Ascension, you may soon find yourself starting over. Beloveds, is this what you want? Knowing you, truly I think not. Every single one of you I know, and those who play that game are testing God to the extreme, have little Faith, and seek to deny God and themselves and those around them Love. God does not play games.

In your culture you have erected many walls based upon fear that you must destroy before you can walk with God, before you can achieve flight, before you will arrive in the fifth dimension; I assure you, my beloveds, many are already there awaiting you with Love. If you were taught to see evil, ask your Heart about it; your Heart knows all; it will tell you there is no evil. If, for instance, you believe homosexuality is wrong because it says so in your Bible, and as a result you find it a repugnant lifestyle, let me assure you I have never found this to be so. Love rejoices wherever it is found. I have known many so-called gays in all my many lifetimes, including in Palestine, and I found them to be some of the most loving, caring, sensitive souls. In the ancient world all were welcomed and celebrated regardless of their sexual orientation. On a societal level, the projection of aberrance onto these wonderful souls originated with the early Roman Church Fathers, who, like many people, were obviously threatened by their own feelings of sublimated sexuality, of the submerged currents of sensuality within themselves. In truth, we are all attracted to each other, no matter the gender. And in the Aquarian Age of the Holy Spirit transgenders occupy an especial place in my Heart, as they have learned to balance their yin-yang in a most remarkable way. Beloved of me they are.

Likewise the projection of evil onto the number 666. I tell thee true: All numbers are sacred. How can a number be considered evil? Three hundred thirty-three plus three hundred thirty-three makes six hundred sixty-six. How could all those threes and thirty-threes equate with evil? Many false meanings have been ascribed to the number 666. To some, the original Beast was Nero, and the number equates to Nero. False. To others the Beast is Man, sinful to the last, or at the very least 666 equates to his lowest nature.

From the mountaintop I cry: Any spiritual system that says you are a sinner, were born a sinner, will always be a sinner, is selling a false creed based upon fear.

I will now share with thee the true meaning of the number 666, and why it eventually was sold to thee as the personification of evil. Once again, it has to do with our DNA and our intimate connection with God, our collective Godhood. And beloveds, it also relates to how we allowed ourselves to become disconnected from God by the Church Fathers, beloved they are of me. You must forgive them.

Throughout time the Third Eye was known to be a sacred mark on the temple of man. Then, seemingly all at once, in the West it became the mark of the Beast, an evil mark, as it leads to the pineal gland, the gateway to God. Within our multidimensional DNA are twelve interdimensional, interactive layers, each layer corresponding to a dimension. And there are four groups of three layers each; these represent our DNA magnetic balance. The first group houses layers one, two, and three, which, added together, total the number six. The second houses layers four, five, and six, which total fifteen, and, from the number fifteen, one and five equal six. The third group has layers seven, eight, and nine, which add up to twenty-four; two and four equal six. Six six six. And the fourth group houses layers ten, eleven, and twelve, which total thirty-three, the master number you know well (and also adds up to six). Beloveds, long this information has been known, much longer than can be by most believed. Many are the scribes who have told this secret to a disbelieving, ignorant world, and to thee I now share this most beautiful Truth: Learn to ask questions, especially of things said to be evil, for the Truth is often the opposite. The secret of 666 is that it proves we are God, that God within you dwells.

Now, ask your Heart if this is so, and it will tell you. From your Heart nothing is hidden. And, too, you will know Beloved John did not write the passage in Revelations stating the anti-Christ is represented by 666. This was a later interpolation by the early Church Fathers. In truth, what Beloved John revealed in Revelations had been transmitted many times prior, most especially in the original Sibylline Oracles, without mention of that *dreaded* number.

You should also know that 666 has been made to appear evil by certain powerful men due to its correspondence to the nuclear composition of carbon-based life; carbon-based life is composed of six electrons, six protons, and six neutrons. So complete was this ingenious plot to reverse the Truth that we have come to believe that all carbon-based life, including ourselves, is evil. Dearly beloveds, do you understand? Then you may forgive. Because if we but shine the Light of Love onto it, we can see that we owe a debt of gratitude to the Roman Church Fathers for giving us such a clever, tantalizing puzzle to decipher.

For indeed there is more. The triple six also signifies the three mathematical base-six (and twelve) calculations of our dear Earth. The first six is time, resultant of the Earth's rotation, upon which we so heavily rely. The second six indicates the magnetic compass system of three hundred sixty degrees, another extraordinarily important aspect of our lives on Earth. The final mathematical base-six (and twelve) system is gravity.

And there is still more. The three sixes signal completion, as throughout it the sacred number nine is found. Six plus six plus six is eighteen; eight plus one equals nine. And every other mathematical equation, including squaring it, calculates to nine. Through the agents of Love and power under rigorous control, nine is the number of the balanced completion of the Soul's journey. Beloveds, you are told I expired in the ninth hour, that I appeared nine times after my Resurrection, that nine is the number of the woman or man who achieves the Divine Will. The Freemasons cite nine as the number of human immortality. It is also the number of the Divine Hierarchy, symbolized by nine choruses of angels. Too, Saul of Tarsus names nine spiritual gifts of God: Faith, wisdom, knowledge, the gift of healing, the ability to distinguish spirits, prophecy, the ability to speak in tongues, to understand them, and the gift of performing miracles. Saul also numbers nine gifts of Spirit: Love, peace, patience, joy, kindness, goodness, self-control, gentleness, and trustworthiness.

The compass is also a circle of nines. Each of the eight forty-five degree points adds up to nine. In addition, the opposite headings of each of the eight added together also equal nine: for example, 360 plus 180, 90 plus 270, 45 plus 225. Simply put, if one travels in one direction long enough, they will eventually find themselves standing in the place they left. The path becomes one line circling the globe. Thus, its meaning as a direction must be considered by both its magnetic headings, as it has no beginning or end.

If you see truly, my cherished ones, without rancor, without judgment, with nothing save Love, you will plainly see there was a plot, as always, to keep you from discovering your Divinity as did I, and in that the sacred number 666 plays an important role. In truth, while much is made of my Immaculate Conception, the process of Immaculate Conception occurs every day in nature. We humans can achieve it by accessing the deep knowledge of the Earth, much of which is within those sixes, nines, and the Golden Mean.

As did I, you can ever find a way to condemn the behavior of those who, perhaps, subconsciously seek to keep us in bondage, while not condemning them as human beings, as souls. There are subtle ways of doing this. And gracefully, beneath this you may discern their mission is actually to fabricate the labyrinth by which they are tested to find their Divinity. God bless us every one. While the majority of humanity is now beyond this, and cries for freedom from oppression, clearly there are still many wonderful souls who need to bleed in order to find God.

In prayerful-meditation spend one hour daily with thine enemies. Invoke the Violet Flame of Love and surround them with its healing light. Every thought, emotion, and act of Love you send out into the Universe is instantly felt, and will alleviate suffering. Verily, all the world's problems would be solved in twenty-four hours if enough of you put forth enough Love-energy.

This is most important because, though the world did not end on December 21st, 2012, the year 2013 marked a terribly challenging new beginning. Surely, over the past two decades, you have been noticing the intensifying effects of the Earth changes taking place. There are terms like climate change and global warming that are manifestations of ignorance. Yet you also know about the cycle of the Precession of the Equinox and what it means and how this cycle is unique. The last few centuries of industrialization have certainly contributed to the severity of the birth of the New Age, but fear not; you have planned this perfectly. Much talk is spent on the melting polar ice caps, especially in the Arctic Circle. But do you realize four billion tons of methane lurks beneath rapidly melting Antarctica, roughly equivalent to what lies beneath the Arctic Circle? The release into the atmosphere of a combined total of eight billion tons of methane represents a massive amount of gas twenty-five times more powerful than carbon dioxide.

And it will happen quickly, beloveds. The last five ages of mass-extinction of life on Earth were resultant of the sudden release of polar methane.

I tell thee true: 2015 and 2016 will be a watershed of rapidly increasing challenges to tenable life on Earth. And it will be up to thee to grace thy body and thy eternal soul with the necessary Power of Love to come to thine Ascension, to ascend as does the Earth into higher states of consciousness. As ever I will be with thee, yet forget not that this is an aspect of etherization, and that, amidst it all, the systems and institutions of controlling humanity will continue to crumble before thine eyes.

There is nothing ever to fear. You have planned this perfectly. God has given you all you need to survive, indeed even to flourish, in a paradise of which you have until now only dreamed. This is one reason why so little reincarnation has been occurring over the past thirty years. The New Children come from other parts of the Universe to help you in your time of need, to gift you the example of unconditional Love, to teach you how to use the Sacred Inner Skills and all your Divine magic lovingly.

Walk with me. Take my hand. Be with me. Accompany me to the mountaintop, my cherished ones; I have shown you *The Way*.

For you are the beginning and the end. Every day you have known, and every night never forgotten. Deep in the well of your Heart is your Love for me, as I am here, with you, and you shall never leave my side. This you promise.

Never doubt, never fear, never lose one ounce of Faith. Forests there are aplenty, and flowers of gleaming, delightful hue, animals of pure, gentle, stirring love, and life so beautiful as to grow thy Heart, in Heaven on Earth. Even as you finish these pages and await the next, soon they will come, with even more insight, more wisdom, and more Love with which to imbue yourselves. To Judea, England, India, the Persian lands of the Magi, Greece, Egypt, the Holy Lands, and beyond this world we will together travel.

And by my side my Beloved will be.

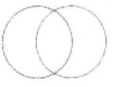

In this most inspirited age, as I assist in all your endeavors, I with thee share the passing of my dear Mother. She who is loved by so many, she who brought unimaginable joy to so many hearts, whose Love affected deeply so many dear souls, has in an act of sublime grace passed over into God's loving embrace. Ninety years she gave the world bliss and Love and wisdom. And I am purely joyous. This is the great gift she and God bestow upon me. Filled with grace, I celebrate her every instant I breathe, and rejoice in her ever-living Spirit. She it was who gifted me this life so I might gift you the same and thus complete my missions. She it was who entered once more the Secret Chamber of my Heart and gave me the precious gift of unconditional Love, of the bluebird of joy, of Divine wisdom, of the sight to see the good in all humanity. She it was who first told me I returned to Earth to help humanity once more, to burnish every single thing into the Light of God. She it was who gave me a voice to sing thy praises, hands to heal the sick, ears to hear prophecy, a mouth to speak infinite tongues, patience to await you, a mind to understand all, and a Heart strong enough to fill all thy hearts with everlasting Love.

Plumb deeply thine own Hearts, gaze into thy loved-ones eyes, and ye shall find her. Call upon her, and she will be there. She will hear thy words, and impart her wisdom and solace and joy. Ever she is with thee. And she has risen.

Let go and let God, and surely ye shall find, yet seeketh only through thy Heart, for therein the Kingdom of God truly resides.

When you are with God, there is no suffering; when truly you know the Power of Love, there is never lack of any kind, only the abundance God surrounds you with each and every moment. The Truth does set you free. And though you may not see her standing before you, believe me, she is there, any time you need her. As the beloved Matriarch of this blessed world, each of you holds a special place in her Heart, for she is the Dove, Spirit born anew, the Holy Spirit indwelling everyone and everything.

As ye do with God, deep in the dazzling silence, with nothing save gratitude and Love call her in prayerful-meditation, and listen with thy Heart. Hear ye she will, and abide by thy Love. This I guarantee. All her beauty will rush into you, and then shall you know she lives forevermore. And your Love she will return to you ten thousandfold. For she is all three Marys rolled into one.

Rejoice in her Eternal Spirit, as it is yours.

You are the beginning and the end. Every day you have known, and every night never forgotten. Deep in the well of your Heart is your Love for me, as I am here, with you, and you shall never leave my side. This you promise.

I have shown you *The Way*. Now it is your turn.

You are all the ones you have been waiting for.

# Afterword

BELOVEDS OF MY HEART, in reaching this point of my story, truly your own story, you signal your preparedness for what in future is to come. Simply, the fact you were drawn to this book and have devotedly read its words is a loving affirmation of your readiness to enter the Queen-Kingdom. As you awaken and continue to discover and embrace your Divinity, much more you will learn by reading the next portion of our story because your heart is open to receive. Be joyous in thy coming. Long I have awaited thee, but my patience has not once been tested, as, like you in your Heart of hearts, my Love is pure. You inspire me; your Light is unto that of a thousand suns, yet it is your single-Hearted devotion to rise forevermore that stirs the Eternal Flame. So close are you to reaching the mountaintop, and all is happening just as it should.

There are those who do not want our story to be told, to reach the Heart of Humanity, beloved of me they are. There are also those so bathed in ignorance they do not *believe* it, who cannot allow themselves to *believe* it; even some religious folk still deny God. As they do in uselessly trying to prevent the Light of God from entering the world, some may attempt to stop the publication and circulation of our story by projecting onto it any form of fear that occurs to them. Some will call me a liar, a charlatan, a madman; with vicious vehemence others may say bits and pieces of our story can be found in preexistent texts. Acknowledging one is Yeshu'a to a messianic culture invites all manner of insult and projection, and is even fraught with peril. At the very least, some noble souls will seek to denigrate me. All are equally beloved of me.

Firstly, I will say this, dearest reflections: Little by little, wonderful people who have never had experience with the art of creation are learning there is nothing new under the sun. It has all been written and painted and sculpted and composed before. While many in your culture still cannot tolerate the fact that creativity is a direct link with God, artists resonate and connect with the Divine Mind, and glean from God a refined expression of Its beauty. Even if in some cases aspects of it appear dark and are not to your taste, it is still the reflection of God's Glory karma-lizing its way to perfection. And everyone from Homer to J.K. Rowling has been accused of plagiarism, ever by those who do not understand or accept Reality, who deny the omnipresence of God and how the Sacred Universe truly works; *The Story* is as old as time. Bless them.

I also tell thee true: This is not a channeled book. There is no outside influence dictating our story to me. It comes directly from Source, and bears the stamp of the precise words and images of mine own reminiscences, mine own memories, a humble candle of *The Way*. I leave to you what to feel in your heart about it, as that is the reason for the telling: to Light thine own special *Way* to God.

Beloved Ones, thy Divine Flower is opening, petal by petal, and with each passing instant ye step closer to God, thy radiance a most beautiful sight to behold. Thou art so blessed. Thou art *The Way*, the Light, and God beams upon thee eternal Joy.

If ever you should doubt me or that these are my words, call my name; with nothing save Love and Joy and Grace, call my name, and I will be there, as indeed I always am, and ask me. Then, like the lovely trill of the whippoorwill, the murmur of the stream, the call of the sweetest breeze, if you listen closely, you will hear my voice, confirming all you have heard and read and seen is true.

I Love you.

# Coming soon

### Book Two

THROUGH AN ANCIENT FOREST of pine and oak you walk at dawn, the trees scraping the sky, a rising lilac mist still obscuring the view of what beckons ahead. The last calls of the nightingale ring through the air, plaintive reminders of what you sense you may lose: your innocence. Yet, too, from the uppermost branches the owl coos his eternal wisdom into thine ever hopeful ears: verily, your innocence awaits you, the Great Secret long lost to the human soul, now increasingly revealing itself to you every single moment. What lies behind you, what you wrongly perceive as your innocence, is, in truth, suffering, pain, guilt, shame: every illusion you have ever foisted upon yourselves and then clung to as substitutes for true Love. So skillful have you become at perpetrating this illusion, you are only now just beginning to sense it as the Light of God pours into the world. Before you, what lies ahead, what you seemingly fear, is Love Pure.

Beloveds, look within, deeply, and you will know what I say is true. Though many souls have long been awakened, how many of these reverse-truths do the majority of you still cleave to in your lives? *Seeing is believing* stands as a brilliant testament to that of which I speak. Truly, believing is seeing, for without profound belief that in time transforms into Divine knowledge or gnosis, one cannot see. Another is blowing out the candles on your birthday cake and making a silent wish; only then will it come true. No, dearests. The opposite is true. You must speak your wish aloud, with pure intent for all the Universe to hear; only then will it come to pass, and only if you seek to better the world and uplift humanity by its manifestation.

When you learn how to ask for what you truly want—Love, God—you will find it.

How hard it is for so many of you to release your cultural conditioning. You must bless it all and Love it all, but you must release it, for verily they are adept little games you use to keep yourselves from God.

Here ye are now, standing before me. How glorious the sight of thee is. How joyous I am to see thee, ye beauteous, awakening souls, ready to embark on the next stage of thy journey, the journey all Love makes. How I have awaited thee with such loving patience. Finally you waken to the dream.

And how many have been vilified for claiming they were me: from Sun Myung Moon, John Lennon, and Krishna Venta, to David Koresh, Arnold Potter, and Bahá'u'lláh? Is it possible you do not believe I inhabited them, as I do you? Are you one of those, out of arrogant religiosity, who projected their own insecurities upon them? For I tell thee true: they were me. Within each I breathed.

Increasingly more of you, women and men, are coming to know yourselves as Christ, or Spirit; there are many names. The Children of Light rise. The transformation of Humanity begins. And scripture speaks of thy coming, calling you false prophets, and warns against following you. Yet, beloveds, to all I say: Only follow your own heart. All are invited to the feast. Everyone is a prophet. In such lovely ways each of you is becoming me.

I am you. And I cherish you.

As you now waken to the dream, in the morn, walking through this Sacred Grove of Consciousness, the rising mist is the veil you have placed over your soul's eye. At any moment you can release it all and be with me. I have shown you *The Way*. Now it is your turn. No one else can walk your walk, no one else sings in your Key of Life; no one, least of all myself, will ride in on a white horse to save you. Once ye finally become who ye truly are, thine own savior, grand miracles Magdalen and I will perform, but only because you perform them with us, as One United Essence.

In this Aquarian Age of the Holy Spirit I again have fulfilled many missions, largely unknown to humanity, and also hidden, protected from the profane so they would have their full intended impact. As a child in Africa, by a tribal chief I was entrusted with a crystal that held the especial, ancient souls of a number of tribes who were the keepers of their knowledge. Indeed, one of the tribesmen recognized me and called me Issa, as the Hindus and Persians did two millennia past. Not even to my family was I to reveal this sacred trust. And, as the tribal chief prophesied, when a man, I participated in a ritual ceremony with many others, from all cultures, during which I dropped the crystal into a deep hole leading directly to our Mother's belly, thus helping to bring female and male back into balance in this world. So far had the female been pulled into the male way of life that many such ceremonies were required to rebalance the energies of this beautiful planet.

How we have desecrated the Heart.

Born on the Autumnal Equinox, as she also was over two thousand years ago, and having birthed me nigh-on the Vernal Equinox, as she did over two thousand years ago, my dear Mother of this life informed me of my sacred duty, so beloved of me she is. Yet not once have I considered myself special, singled-out for Godhood, though there have been many who believed this of me or that I thought thus. O dearest Father and Mother taught me so very, very well. In truth, perhaps unknowingly, each of you has performed missions of equal import, each circumstance, encounter, and resolution subtly crafted to re-create Heaven of Earth. In thine eyes I see naught but the Light of God. It is to thee I sing my praises of thy great works. For all I have done, I have done for you, and you have found the Truth in yourselves, beloved of me you are. All life is special.

To those across this world who are ready, who can withstand and interpret the intensity of my energy, I appear in Lightbody, bilocating, trilocating, even quadrilocating. They see me appear in their homes, gazing upon them caringly in their rooms, and we commune, for theirs are most profound missions of Love. Sometimes I appear as a child, others as a loving brother or Father, and I am known for my humor and joyousness. Others hear my voice, as I hear theirs, and their missions are just as pure. Still others have a thought come to them, a Heart-thought that may transform a situation, a relationship, a condition; they then act upon it, for beyond the Veil they know I have placed the thought there, as they recognize me within themselves. Others come across me in the guise of a homeless man, a once-battered woman now become like Magdalen: a co-messiah, an old man, bent like the twig of the elm, with nary two coins to rub together, a thief become a saint: all dispensing wisdom like it be penny-candy from their pockets. And by the exchange, those upon whom the wisdom is bestowed, they, too, become The Christ. Which of these are thee, beloveds? You are all the beloved Children of God, and the sight of thy glory fills me with such joy. In such lovely ways you are becoming Christ, and changing the world in the doing. By your own methods you are realizing that the Tree of Life and Knowledge is upside down and your true roots are in Heaven, not in the Earth.

Sometimes my travels take me to distant galaxies and planets, as, indeed, the coming of our Lord requires the coordination of all members of humanity strewn throughout the Sacred Universe. How joyous your cousins and brothers and sisters on other worlds and in other forms are for your wakening. All eyes of the Universe are trained upon you in Love. Many long ages they have awaited thy coming.

Beloveds of my Heart, upon this day I now write each of you inch by inch is coming to Love Pure, learning every moment the Great Mystery. The Universe is opening up in an entirely new way, never before seen in all the ages of time. It can be convenient to believe you know not what comes, to think it impossible the Light of God pours into the world, that Spirit and matter are one in the same. So long you have lived the illusion, through so many lifetimes, you cannot see The Reality. Such is the traumatizing affect of the disease of dualism. Of all the peoples of the world, of all the cultures and belief systems, it is hardest for you, for you have not been able to conceive of it. Even the difference between my original tongue of Aramaic and the Greek, from which much of what you believe derives, is stark, and deeply exemplifies this. For in the olden languages like Aramaic dualism did not exist. The intrinsic, incontrovertible Truth of Unity with God was implicit in every word and phrase and parable. Come the later translations into Greek, and then of course into Latin, the languages of men, and all the accompanying interpolations, the great change occurred.

All over this world today are people who know and live the Truth, who know the future, and create it by the knowing; they see truly, through the One Eye. Until recently most of them were Indigenous people, who have never been disconnected from Source, from God. They deny not, they fear not, they fool themselves not. And truth be told, there is a woman who soon comes. Still at this moment she learns the Mystery, for she is quite young, yet already she has participated in some of the most important ritual ceremonies of the age, of which I, too, have taken part. The glorious mantle of guardianship of the Earth has been transferred to her. Yes, I know her name, but I will not speak it; she comes from the lands wherein today resides the Kundalini. Daily we educate her all the more.

And when she finally appears, she will say the same words I have many times given thee: *You are all the ones you have been waiting for.*

For what comes will be leaderless; you can no longer render unto Caesar. And as you fulfill your Ascension you will discover truly Divine society, wherein all are cared for and money exists not and no one is taxed and children teach the teachers, and all daily enter and imbibe of the Temples of Illumination and the Temples of Healing. Here in the gleaming multihued forests the sacred unicorn resides. Yet there is governance in the fifth-dimensional realm; there are systems of barter made fun for all, and every breath is made Holy. This you shall know by me to be true.

Still your Heart. Ask your guides to take you there, call upon Adama, your sublime Divine Father. Ask that he impart in your dreams the lessons necessary for communion, and so you shall commune. And I, too, will be there; many call me by my Ascension name, Sananda. Yet, dearly beloveds, do not make it be about me...but about you.

And call upon my dear Mother. She now leads a Holy Host of Angels on your behalf, and will come to soothe you and impart her wisdom. Ever she will hear your words. In your Heart her voice resides, if you can but still it enough. If you know the Truth of God, if you can release your sorrows like the dove, if you can find the ability to not cleave to her or me, you may even be able to observe us as we visit you in the physical realm, so beloved of us you are.

And as you continue to learn about my life, by mine own words, you may begin to discern that to comprehend it truly you must come to know the difference between an illusion and a vision. Forty-four more years did I live after my resurrection, and, as is true today, from afar I spoke in a blended voice. There are passages in your Bible which speak of the women being fearful after my seeming passing. Yet truly it was the men who feared, and by the year thirty-nine A.D. my dear Mother was already bitter by what my male followers were teaching, how it was the opposite of what I taught and demonstrated, and by how they fought amongst themselves for power, beloved they are of me.

There is no need to condemn them or the church created in my name. However, there is the need to understand it, for only by so doing can you move on to the future in full knowledge of what is true and what is not. Myriam of Tyana once said it so very well: *It is time for what has been silenced to be heard. It is enough! It is enough! IT IS ENOUGH!* This the Egyptian alchemists called the Opening of the Mouth, and in your Aquarian Age of the Holy Spirit it is essential it is done. By all of you. For, as you delve deeper into my story, increasingly you will recognize it is your own, and along the way are many surprises which at first you may not accept or understand, but in your Heart of hearts you will know to be true. How I Love thee. In thy courage, thy Spirit, thy Beauty and Faith, how I Love thee. Discover the reasons for your fear, identify them, become angry if you must, know them all to be illusions, and then release it all in Love. Then consciously you will *know*.

I await you.

Our story now takes us to Qumran, Akasha, Mount Carmel, Jerusalem, the Druids of Albion at Avalon, the Hindus, the Persian Magi, the Pleiades, and much, much more. And with each step you will find it is your own feet that walk this Path of God, this Divine trek to Truth, Love, and Beauty. In you I have never once lost Faith, for you are my dearest reflections, in whom I am well-pleased, whom I Love without measure in my bottomless Heart.

Serenely walk through the ancient forest of oak and pine, gazing lovingly upon all the splendor around you. Invite the beauty to enter you, and listen with your Heart: Life is asking you to participate; Life wants to be loved, and as you stroll amidst the treasures of Consciousness you will soon know it is time to release and finally accept Love Pure.

The lilac mist is rising.

Fear not. I have shown you *The Way*. Now it is your turn. You are all the ones you have been waiting for.

# Chapter One
# Home

GLAD IS THE SUN UPON THE sweet purple hills of Galilee. And joyous is my heart as our caravan makes for Mount Carmel. Since entering the Samarian lands north of Judea increasingly mine eyes have taken in the splendor of familiar terrain and sights, and beyond Joppa I sent bits of soul ahead to see dear *Savta* Anna. On the morn we left Mount Sinai, I told her of our coming, and now my soul's eye sees her far ahead, amidst the succulent multi-terraced vineyards of Carmel, picking grapes and wildflowers and speaking with the angels.

Like a sprite I jump from the wagon and rush into the wilderness, silently telling my parents to fear not; I will now send my body through the interdimensional tunnels of time and space, and surprise with delight my dear Grandmother. Though I have not yet mastered all aspects of bilocation, I can successfully project my physical and energetic bodies into different locations and behold all there is to see, and be seen by all with eyes enough to see. Father has promised to continue my teachings so that I may speak and hear, have the sense of smell and touch, and remember all which transpires. Many more years it will take, yet I will then be a true Master.

Beneath an oak tree I stop. Nearby, a small stream courses through the fertile ground like a joyous serpent of life. Atop my right shoulder perches Hannah, the lovely Phoebe Savta gifted me in Egypt. Originally come from Albion, my Savta Anna's true homeland, Hannah has taught me many beautiful, wondrous things. Many believe the Phoebe to be indigenous only to the Americas, but Hannah has told me her family has long thrived in Albion, the abundant rain the isles receive, and their plentiful bogs and lush forests conducive for the insects upon which they mostly survive.

She gaily flutters her lilac-gray wings, her golden-orange breast heaving with delight, her eyes bright and beating in anticipation. "Anna! Anna!" she sings in her soul-voice. "Dear Yeshu'a, she is near!"

"Yes, lovely one of my heart. Do you see her, far ahead in the vineyards? Is she not the most beautiful Grandmother, so ageless, so eternally young and fine? Her song is like the most exquisite poetry."

Says Hannah, "Indeed, she is. Yet, lest ye forget, as I have been teaching thee the way of flight so ye may soar like the bird, also remember her sense is so very keen. If we are to surprise her like an enchanting gust of wind come from my native isles, best we keep our thoughts pure and silent. Come, I will with thee travel through the dimensions so that we may remain here and also be there. She will be most pleased!"

Beneath the oak I bring my hands together palm-to-palm before my heart, the sun shimmering through the branches. With great praises I call upon the angels to take us to Carmel, keeping a close eye upon my physical body here in the wilderness. Great balance and focus is required; yet, too, I must equally *let go and let God*. Hannah is still and sure as she sets her beak softly against my neck.

Our vision is clear as crystal. Many miles ahead *Savta* Anna is now wiping her brow with a cloth, resting after picking wildflowers. Beside her, on a simple wooden bench, is a basket filled with purple grapes. Off in the distance behind her looms one of Carmel's yurt temples. Softly she begins to sing the love-song of Inanna, from ages long past, and my heart smiles, for I know as well as she that once the Sumerians sang it to me.

We are passing through the pastures now, and the forests, Hannah and I, both of us keeping our physical and energetic bodies attuned to both locations. And all at once we stand before Anna as she leans over picking up a fallen cluster of grapes. So bright our light shines, she starts as if hit by a premonition, and turns to see us, her most beloved bird and grandson. A smile ear-to-ear comes upon her face, a dazzling blue light shining around her. She is truly the faery feather queen of Avalon, light as the air itself, and we are not astonished to see her feet leave the ground for a moment, joyous at our arrival. So expert is Hannah, she wings over to her and rests upon her arm, and looks back at me, I then signing two fingers over my heart, the symbol of Love, and suddenly a beam of lilac-white radiates from *Savta* Anna's third-eye and nestles with mine. What great joy is this!

"We cometh!" I cry. "I could not wait any longer!"

"I know, dear Yeshu! God is with thee. And I await thee with great joy."

Suddenly it is as if I am whisked up into Heaven; a great light has pulsed all around me, and now I am surrounded by the many souls of my family, of our family, the family you and I share. As one they enfold me in a sweet embrace. There is a voice I at once recognize, as it is the Voice of the All, yet it is also Anna's voice and Mother's and Father's. Great love there is within it. And I am given visions of my near-future missions, and especially of the two John's: John of the River, whom I will assist in Qumran and at Carmel, and Beloved John, whom I will guide and instruct at Carmel, who will become my protector, my envoy of peace, and my devoted translator; so many are the roles of Beloved John. I am also gifted a vision of Seth of Damascus, of whom I but briefly spoke in my previous pages. Already Seth is an Essene master, older than I, and mostly he will remain hidden, for his knowledge is of such purity that he must remain beyond the fray of what comes, beloved of me he is.

My arms have become wings, my body feathered, my sight so powerful I gaze into the Eternal, free of veils of any kind. And all at once again I am in the vineyard, dear Hannah now back on my shoulder, and we issue our farewells to Anna. My Father's work is begun. Each initiation I have survived and passed, and though much there is still to learn, I now know it is to me the gift is given to teach others, to lead my brothers and sisters out of darkness. So full is my heart, I see each of thee coming of age, as once did I, thy hearts aching with joy, blessed be thy names.

Dear God, thank Thee for this great gift of Life.

When two days hence we arrive at the base of Mount Carmel, I find Anna walking in the pastures. Running up to her, I raise her in my arms, kiss her cheeks and lips and temple, and we dance through the barley, the Chime of God ringing in our ears.

**M**uch you may hear of my dear Mother. Yet it is naught to what she is in life. With our return to Galilee, the name itself meaning *circle*, often I find her at the Well in our humble village of *Nazara*, engaging passersby and all who come to draw water in conversation. Known by you as Nazareth, our town has grown since I was a boy, and it is soon clear to me that Mother knows everyone. Even those upon whom she has never gazed know her well; this may to you sound impossible, but believe me, dear reflections, it is so. If someone needs food, water, shelter, money, their clothes mended, directions, or a mere smile from her gracious lips, instantly she knows it and dispenses it with joy. She is in me, dear Mother, and from her I learn so much. With such pleasant fervor she discourses on politics: the differences between the Sadducees and the Pharisees, their corruption and that of the Sanhedrin and, of course, the Romans. Yet the twinkle is ever in her eye, for between the words, so adept is she, she is speaking of God. And even those who are not consciously aware come away with wisdom and a sneaking feeling that they have been awakened. And then there are the narratives of the mythos, when above all she shines for all to see, as in this she is openly speaking of me and what she knows best: God.

Once while sunning on the brow of a nearby hill, when a group of Nazarenes approaches the Well and asks Mother what will come of the growing discord in Jerusalem, I see a pure smile light her face like the sun. "Fear not, brothers, sisters, for one day soon the Teacher of Righteous comes, born of a virgin Mother, of the Holy Seed of God, and through his works the Path will be lit for all to see. By this very well he will meet his Beloved." Her azure eyes glint like the Eternal Flame of which she speaks, for she is the herald. Yet, too, as my lessons with the Essenes continue, it will be Mother who grows concerned by the swiftness of my course, while Father will become increasingly sure.

O Mother, how I love thee.

Late one afternoon an Essene artisan rushes into our humble home on Marmion Way, out of breath, clearly shaken to the core. I know not his name but his face is familiar to me. Issuing his sincere regrets for interrupting our home, he asks after Father. "One of my masons has been badly hurt."

With eyes closed, my dear sister Martha informs him, "He has been in Sepphoris but now returns through the fields." Lovingly she fondles her vial of whores' tears upon the twine around her neck. "He will with Yeshu'a come to you when he arrives."

The man, both tall and stocky, looks upon me as if I have appeared suddenly from the air. I smile quietly, silently assuring him it will be so. Like many of the outer groups of Essenes, he is a good, simple man who once sought refuge from the tyranny of our lands merely so he might ply his craft, care for his family, and contribute to a community whose sole purpose is to serve God. They are our lifeblood. And in this worthy artisan I recognize a face I will see again when I am a man. He sees light around me; this I intuit, and to his soul I commend his vision of caring for his workman.

When Father returns, we at once set out for the man's home, traveling through tiny settlements east by north of Carmel and *Nazara* until we reach the outskirts of Rumah. Everywhere Father takes me with him, and as we are a family of healers, Mother and my sisters, too, have their healing missions, visiting the leper colonies and the poor who have not coin or goods to pay a physician. Under dear Father's tutelage I learn firsthand many forms of healing that will inform my life in so many ways. As a small child of just two or three years it was instinct; when I witnessed suffering, without thought instantly I joined with it to remove its root cause. Whether the result was emotional or physical, all at once my heart sought the sufferer and healed the problem. Now I am in essence relearning how it is truly first-nature with me, how to ever live through my heart and allow it to govern me. Yet, too, from Father's gracious knowledge I am being schooled in all aspects of the various forms of the healing arts.

As we cross the small threshold into the artisan's home, Father clasps arms with him and offers his praises. "Blessings, Jacob," he says in his softest voice. "Greet Yeshu'a, my son. He will assist me. I have also sent for Jedediah to join us."

This perplexes Jacob; he does not appear to understand. "Gracious Father, I am most grateful for your assistance." He nods to me and puts his hands together, palm-to-palm.

"Tell us what has occurred."

"It is Isaac, one of my finest stonemasons; his left arm has been very seriously cut." He indicates an area extending from his wrist to his elbow. "A slab of marble slipped suddenly from its casing, jolting another mason, and his chisel sliced Isaac's arm. It bled badly...We have applied ointments and placed herbs on it and tightly wrapped it, yet he is expiring. I fear for him. Much blood he has lost."

At this moment Jedediah from Carmel arrives. In my previous pages I briefly spoke of him as we set out for Egypt. He is a gentle, loving soul, a priest who promised to teach me many things numinous.

"Blessings unto all of you," says he, a genuine and empathetic smile upon his face.

"Where is Isaac the mason?" Father asks Jacob.

"In the barn. Come."

As Jacob leads us out of the house and across a field to the barn, Father speaks softly to me. "You understand, my Spirit-begotten son, that Jacob has knowledge of our ways yet does not understand them. You and Jedediah will stand on either side of Isaac to balance the energy, but this is not strictly needed; you will truly be shielding Jacob from what transpires. Anon you will do this on your own; do not forget that most do not comprehend healing, and are rapt by it or fearful of it, and you must protect yourself from becoming seen a witch or miracle worker. Often the journey of the true healer is to instill the Love of God and then to move onward, not forming attachments. Almost inevitably the relationships change upon the successful resolution of a healing; you can be seen as a freak or a god to be worshipped...Many cast stones at all that glitters. Such is the nature of Love in this world. Rare is the soul who truly understands."

Dear Father gazes into mine eyes and, like a serene prophet, declares, "I tell thee now, Spirit-born son, a day will come when you will be angry, disappointed, and frustrated that people will be more interested in your healings and other seemingly miraculous acts than in raising their God-selves out of their human-selves, your true mission. Lest you forget: your healings and other acts of God are merely means to an end: to shine a bright Light upon the Path to God, to bestow upon others the ability to find the Light in their own souls, to become Spirit, so they may raise themselves to the Glory of God."

In between the words, he is informing me what he will do, and how my Mother and sisters will continue my training to be in constant interaction with the angels and my guides.

Jacob lights an oil lamp after we enter the barn, his long face solemn with concern. In the center upon a raised pallet, surrounded by masonry tools and bales of hay, is Isaac, two women ministering to him. As we approach, they give way. Isaac's face is pale, he shivers and sweats, his brow creased in worry.

"Blessings upon you, my son," greets Father softly as he takes Isaac's hand into his. "We are here to help you."

A melting smile emerges on Isaac's visage. "Thank you, dear Father of the Essenes."

Jedediah now stands directly to the left of the body, and I to the right, as Father bends over Isaac. Jacob is to the rear, chewing his nails, whispering to the women.

Removing the wrap, we see the injury, and I almost gasp: the cut is deep; a bit of bone is visible. And Isaac shows great courage: attempting to stop his shivering, biting his bottom lip, and giving freely his damaged arm.

Silently Father speaks to me: *Yes, dear son, the injury is serious. By morning this man would die without God's assistance. Yet, you have seen; he is willing to receive. He is already accepting the healing. This is how we work. For those who are not willing to receive we can do nothing. Now witness: I place my left hand on the opposite side of the arm, palm open, while with my right I place my forefinger and middle finger upon the incision. Remember: we live our lives in a state of semi-meditation; thus, when the time comes, we can reach a deep meditative state with ease. With my two hands I am forming a circuit, an energy conduit between the two hands. Our guides tell us what is to be done, and we do not question them. Each healing is unique, and requires a special approach, yet, too, there are fundamentals that repeat themselves. As you continue to learn anatomy, through your guides and the angels, soon you will find there are no limitations involved in healing, and, using your one eye, you will even be able to travel through the inner body to see what lies within. God's Love can heal any disease, any ailment, even broken bones, as you did as a child, yet often one must journey into Akasha, the Book of Life, to find the root cause. Isis will teach you this. Now, dear son, we will call upon our guides and the angels to supply pranic healing energy to sew the wound together. This we do with pure intent, Love Pure.*

Father, Jedediah, and I commune as one around Isaac, summoning the power to flow through us, through Father's hands, and give great thanks to God for this most precious gift. Slowly and surely Father traces his two fingers over the incision, from wrist to elbow, his deft touch directly on the skin, sealing the wound with God's energy. Only a moment or two pass. Next, I hear the call of the angels to apply a special healing gel to the wound, an etheric balm not visible in the three dimensional realm. Then we are to purify the blood of any infection, flush the adrenal glands with pure healing energy, and, lastly, supply pure healing energy to the entire body.

Certainly three or four moments have elapsed. Father heaves a small sigh as an almost imperceptible smile comes across his face, and we inspect the wound anew.

"Isaac," Father says. "Look what gift God has bestowed upon you, for it is you who have done it."

With a tinge of color back in his face, Isaac raises his head and turns his arm, and his eyes bulge. A thin red line is all that remains of the once-mortal wound. It is perfectly sealed. And Isaac issues his profound gratitude to Father.

Jacob and the two women approach to see what has transpired, and they are shocked to see it, Jacob finally falling to the ground in grateful prayer for the saving of Isaac.

On this day Father teaches me a great lesson. We thank our healing guides and the angels and God for what has been done, for we are merely instruments in their cause to uplift humanity. Surely we infuse ourselves with the knowledge, with God's Love, and increasingly more we can achieve through this ever-growing base of understanding, but truly it is God and the patient who are the healer. Conventional medicine does battle with disease, in an *us versus them* approach, and sometimes even succeeds, whereas the healer becomes one with whatever the problem is: Loves it, blesses it, forgives it, and releases it, and thus transforms it…if the patient is willing to accept, to receive. My dear Father today demonstrates to me his love for Isaac, for the wound itself, to such a degree that God rushes in and heals them. Father sees the sacred in everything.

What great gift is this, to witness one of the very acts of Love for which I will become known, which will in part propel me to my destiny. All of this I do for thee.

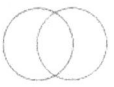

"Your relationships with your guides are like any other in this life," remarks dear Mother. She of the chestnut hair, ebullient spirit, gleaming azure eyes, and blazing heart speaks with soft certitude. "Thus you must be there for them. Attend to them. Be present for them. The more you consciously do this, with love in your heart, the more they will be there for you."

Salome, Martha, Esther, Mother, and I sit in a sacred circle we have created behind our humble home. As you know, God is everywhere, in everything. Yet to bring God in to a place one must create a sacred space. Martha is especially adept at this. On the day I was born, she wove a mighty sacred circle, dancing like an animal possessed around the room, great intent in every step. Beloved of me she is. Here she has counseled that we bless and make holy the four directions and the above and below and middle Earth, inviting God to participate in our exercises. Ever she is learning, dear Martha, and intuiting and growing. As she stepped out the circumference of our sacred circle, in her hands she turned over her little crystal spheres, a gift from Anna the Prophetess. She is scarce without them, in her trusty pouch or in her hands.

Salome, she who will be cherished, is much the different. Her way is silence and stillness; a mighty, mysterious river courses within her. And Esther is perhaps most like Mother, a galvanizing, truly motherly presence, caring for all.

Sister Salome declares, "Dearest God of all living things, hear our love and praises for Thee. ...Let us now sit in prayerful-meditation, sisters and brother and Mother, and await the calling of our guides. Ever we have heard them, yet Mother is indeed wise—we must be present for them, as we are for each other and our companions, and our conversing will be all the more pure."

Beloveds of my heart, each of you has guides. Often they are your ancestors, dearly departed family members, or loved-ones with whom you feel an affinity, and they are also those of especial skills and arts with whom you also resonate. Too, you may have animal advocates and nature spirits who also help guide you on your path in life. Of one thing you may be certain: they ever have your best interests at heart, seeking only to uplift you in your experience of existence and God.

Yet never forget: your beloved guides often do your bidding. If too much you are out of balance or seek to break the boundaries of privacy in people's lives by having them tell you these things, you alone are responsible for what transpires. Indeed, you also may not receive Truth. Make your wishes highly purposeful, meaningful, of pure Love-intent, of God; *turn your gaze inward and upward*. Seek to know and to be with God, to be given the gifts to help humanity. And cherish your guides for their presence in your life. For, indeed, they are your personal angels. As they guide you, you must guide them.

In deep silence, call upon them again and again for their loving guidance. It may take time, but I assure you they will make themselves known, for they are always with you. You may also ask if any spirit-being present is, in truth, your guide, and if they are not and you feel negatively influenced, I also assure you they will lose interest, by way of your inner knowing, and depart; heed only the angels of your best nature. At first you may perceive your true guides as just a thought that enters your mind: a bit of advice or wisdom or intuition, a direction, or a warning. But if you continue to abide by them, setting aside time each day, at dawn and dusk and as you lay your head down to sleep, soon you will discern their voices, learn who they are, and to some they will eventually appear in Light. And before long you will be at all times in conversation with them, as God is everywhere at once. Yet even this is only the beginning.

On this day we commune with them for some time, and then share what we learn. And anon I hear the voice of Rachel, a Child of God who hails from the area east of the Plain of Gennesaret, the Greek word for the original Hebrew *Chinnereth*, meaning *Garden of Riches*. The town of Gennesaret sits atop a lush hill on the northwestern shore of Lake *Chinnereth*, known by you as the Sea of Galilee: the Great Heart. As Rachel has been visiting her uncle's family in nearby Besera, I have befriended her since our return to Galilee. She is a brilliant young woman, six summers older than I, with many gifts to give the world, but she has become filled with self-doubts, for barely can she see. The news of my skills has already permeated many souls in our land. My childhood healings, our family's recent return from Egypt, my journeys with Father to help others to heal themselves: all have ever so slowly become known. Now as I commune with God, offering my gratitude, praises, and love, and speak with the angels and my guides, a lovely voice emerges in Consciousness.

It is Rachel, she of the golden hair, of art and painting and the written word, of stories from time out of mind: *I want my vision, my sight! It was robbed from me as a child, and I can abide it no longer. Great dreams I have, yet I must have my sight to achieve them. Help me!*

Though from the wilderness it is a cry, her voice is beautiful, like the lilting song of the lark. And in this moment my personal rendering of the Serenity Prayer enters my heart, given me by the angels: God, gift me the grace to accept the things I cannot change. And grant unto me the power to *change the things I cannot abide*! Think not, beloveds, that the Serenity Prayer originated with Reinhold Niebuhr, for it has always existed, and, like all art, was written by God.

I will help Rachel gain her vision, of this I am sure. She is accepting of the healing. And already I am receiving the information that will assist me. And by her journey to find her God-self, her Divine I AM presence, she will become one of my most important companion-teachers, one of the one hundred forty-four.

Out of my body I now travel in my violet soul and become the dove: the white bird of Peace and Love and Ascension, traveling to Rachel's home: Capernaum.

Difficult it may be for you to envision Palestine as it is during my days here, for it has long since become a nigh-barren wasteland, the earth itself crumbling and washing away from so many centuries of misuse and rain. The multi-terraced vineyards, the luxuriant orchards, the rich, green foothills, the fertile valleys of Samaria, the dense forests of the northlands: all this and so much more are in your days gone. Yet truly this is in ancient times *a land flowing with milk and honey*: the grassy hillsides home to grazing goats, sheep, and cattle, gifting us milk, and honey in the form of plenteous flora and bees: flower and woodland, pasture and vegetated, grassy terrace, lush flatland and hills and valleys and mountains, and all manner of sacred animal thrive here.

The circle that is Galilee is cut into two parts: Upper, or Northern, Galilee, a mountainous region wondrous in its clime and people, and Lower, or Southern, Galilee, wherefrom I hail. As is true of highland country dwellers, Upper Galileans are fiercely independent, anti-orthodox; in Judaic terms even anti-ecclesiastic. The plentiful streams and rivers, its fertile soil, its heavy dew in the dry, hot season, the hearty disposition of its people all contribute to a diligent peasantry. The Talmud states: *Galileans are more anxious for honor than for money*. Nowhere is this more evident than in Upper Galilee, its northern region edging toward Mount Hermon, the Mount of Transfiguration, two rivulets emerging at its feet, at Dan and Caesarea Philippi, which then combine to form the River Jordan.

Lower Galilee is much the different. Its midpoint roughly between Capernaum and *Nazara*, here reside the lush valleys, the abundant springs, the foothills I cite as crowned in violet hue. The pastureland is verdant, the region prosperous, our foodstuffs, including our fish, renowned throughout the Roman Empire and Persia, the Plain of Gennesaret near Rachel's home flush with date palm, walnut, olive, and fig orchards, yielding ten months out of the year. Of life here I have given thee many visions: of the keeper of the vineyard, the fox dashing to his lair, the industrious carpenter, the flourishing farmer, the shepherd of the lavish flocks of sheep, ever at home on the hillsides, the exultant glory of the spring-born blooms. Here we nestle between the heights of Mount Hermon and the tranquil valleys of the Jordan, and between the desert and the sea, and attract all manner of traveler from Persia and Mesopotamia, Greece and Rome, and Gaul and Africa. Along the Sea of Galilee are nigh-twenty towns, inhabited by some one hundred fifty thousand people, and situated at its northernmost point, Rachel's Capernaum serves as a wayfarer stop: for statesman, merchant, diplomat, pilgrim, scholar, and camel-driver alike.

At its southeast edge, Lower Galilee borders Samaria at Jezreel Valley, part of the vast area known by its Greek name: the Plain of Esdraelon, the Carmel range to the west and the River Jordan to the east. Jezreel means *God sows*, and derives from the name of the clan who ages long past founded a city of the same name there, atop a hill at the southeast border. The southwest rim is called the Valley, or Plain, of Megiddo, after an ancient city once located there. The true meaning of the Greek word Armageddon is *the Plain of Megiddo*, erroneously believed by many to be the spot where the End Times battle between good and evil will occur. Because this region is a flatland corridor nearly surrounded by rocky prominences, battles have long been fought here, since the days of Deborah's judgment under the palm tree and *Barak* bringing his hearty Galileans to battle *Sisera*.

East by north I wing to Capernaum, for I am the dove. With each passing instant my heart flutters anew at the sights of gorgeous Galilee. O'er Garis, Bethmaus, Taricheae, and Gennesaret I fly, finally settling atop a palm overlooking the limestone synagogue only recently discovered in your age. Heaving my white breast in delight, I gaze upon the beauty of Rachel's Capernaum. Likely you are familiar with the many later stories of my visits to and connection with this city, that it was home to Simeon, known by you as Simon Peter, the Sons of Thunder—James and Beloved John, sons of Zebedee—Andrew, and even Matthew the tax collector, and that I performed many healings and miracles here: curing the paralytic and the Roman Centurion's servant, the miraculous catch of fish, the coin in the mouth of one, the multiplication of loaves of bread and fish, the stilling of the storm. In your New Testament Capernaum is mentioned sixteen times, and it is said I here performed twelve miracles. Yes, Capernaum eventually becomes a base of mission operations for the issuance of *The Way*. And in some manner these acts did indeed occur, but are vastly misunderstood by most, and greatness is wrongly bestowed upon me because of them. Of all this I will say but one thing: all the many errors of interpretation made about the Bible are born of the folly of the mystical books being seen in literal terms, as referring to places, times, people, and material things, instead of being correctly regarded as containing only eternal truths about things spiritual. I and my partners of *The Way* brought the Mystery out into the world for you, and within your Heart, even if you do not consciously understand them, the sacred Eternal Flame is alight, hinting of the deep inner meaning of these things. Search within yourselves, my beloveds; your heart knows all, and will reveal all when you find the key and open its door: when with Love Pure you ask of it to be loved.

Speaketh with me now and tell me it is so.

With all this, I now tell thee true: my link with Capernaum began with sweet Rachel, through the healing of her vision, through the perfection of her spiritual sight, with a woman who, like my dear Mother and Magdalen, though nearly blind, saw more than all my male so-called disciples, save one, beloved of me they are. For forget not: Beloved John, Thunder Brother, in time saw all, and gifted it thee in his Revelation come from the Holy Spirit: that the perfection of Man and God is born of the Woman, Clothed with the Sun. This perfect prose foresaw the true significance of the prophecy of Immaculate Conception to be the final redemption of the Universe: Maria, Sophia, Mari, Meri, Mary the Virgin, born herself immaculate, shall conceive the perfection of man, the Son of Man. Yet, beloved reflections, it is not I of whom it speaks; that is a false creed born of the hubris of religion. No, dearests of my Heart, the Son of Man is not one man, one human, but one hundred thousand times one hundred thousand humans: the sum of humanity, who shall in the final hour overcome the limitations of matter, and the suffering that is the result of the materialization of Spirit. And the agent shall be Love Pure: the Woman within all of you. As it was in the beginning, so shall it be in the end.

In such lovely ways, each of you is becoming Christ.

The son of a U.S. diplomat, Pietro de la Luna grew up in Africa, Europe, and the United States. He has also lived in England, the U.S., and France and traveled widely as an adult. He received BA degrees in music and history and has enjoyed a successful music career. He has also written articles for various progressive organizations.

Pietro is a devoted healer, and works with healing circles around the world. Working with his healing guides, he has been a successful conduit in curing various forms of cancer, bipolar disorder, angina, Parkinson's Disease, Lyme Disease, blindness, tooth problems, ulcers and stomach disorders, and physical injuries, as well as many other conditions, ailments, and diseases. He has also been a successful conduit in dissipating severe weather events. Working with Light—5th, 6th, and 7th dimensional energies—Pietro is a quantum surgeon, and is purely dedicated to uplifting Humanity and the world.

A pure empath, he has the gifts of prophecy, healing, deep intuition, telepathy, clairvoyance, clairaudience, clairsentience, fifth dimensional tweeting, and extraordinary positive influence to shape the world. Pietro combines all the sacred inner skills and transforms them into higher skills. And he is actively engaged with Spirit, the angels and archangels, and people across the world preparing for Ascension, creating Heaven on Earth—loving conduits in opening quantum-divine portals from British Columbia, Alberta, and Mount Shasta, to Peru, Chile, Hawaii, Australia, and New Zealand, as New Lemuria is born.

Pietro is a member of Inspiration Life, a global group of visionaries who by example inspire others to find inspiration within themselves. In the upcoming book by Merry Hall entitled Vision, Passion, Mission: The Head, Heart, and Hands of Evolutionary People, he will be featured as a visionary, lighting the path to the New Illuminated World. He is also a newly contributing writer for The Magic Happens, a distinguished webzine whose mission is to stimulate the imagination: Humanity thriving out loud.

In divine partnership Pietro is working with shaman and author of the exquisite Silver Wheel, Golden Elven Queen Elen Tompkins, birthing and raising Avalon, the New Illuminated Avalon. Invoking the ancient Lemurian wisdom of and with the Elven elders, and with our star family and many devoted souls, Elen and Pietro burnish Avalon into the realm of visibility, returning to the heart of vision.

Visit Yeshu'a at www.yeshuamagdalen.com

# READERS' PRAISE THE YESHU'A SERIES

### Uplifted and Healed Me

"The energy transmitted through these words uplifted and healed me. Thank YOU!"

Heidi

### Delighted To Find This Soul Aligning Treasure

"If you remember who you truly ARE, you will love this series as Yeshu'a dances through the past and present. If you wonder who you truly ARE, these books could defi nitely trigger feelings that resonate and assist you in your remembrance. Pietro de la Luna has a magical style of writing that lends one to experiencing oneself in the story he weaves. I was so joyous as I started reading, knowing Pietro and others know and remember what I already intuitively knew. Perhaps his tale will inspire joyous alignment with you as well? At the very least, Yeshu'a is delightfully entertaining while at the same time magically uplifting. Enjoy it in meditative bits or front to back as it suits any preferred reading style. Thank you, Pietro, for sharing your bright light!"

M. Hazlewood

### The Missing Parts of The Greatest Story Ever Told

"Yeshu'a is an astounding journey. It's not just the events in the life of Jesus in the years before his public ministry, but a voyage into his innermost thoughts. I read these books with the feeling that the author had been there himself witnessing the events, the detail is so intimate. We learn about Yeshu'a's family and his closest friends, his teachers in Egypt and in the Essene community at Mount Carmel. And about his past lives, of which he has full memory. These are novels to be sure, but it feels like the truth to me. Any seeker of wisdom will find deep satisfaction in this series, written in a soft, melodic poetry that transports the reader into another dimension of feeling. The author says, "You are all the ones you have been waiting for." This series is the one I've been waiting for. Can't wait for Book Three."

Donald Sosin

## A Beautifully Written Masterpiece

"Such a beautifully written masterpiece, it is as if I am living within it, transported back to the moments, watching all that happens as a sacred witness, the sights, scents, and sounds etched upon my soul. Mr. de la Luna has renewed my spirit. He demonstrates poetic courage in chronicling his vision."

Rachel

## Say Yes To Yeshu'a

"This series is an amazing and eye opening account that is so much bigger than you could ever imagine. A must read. If I had one wish for the world it would be for everyone to experience the life of Jesus as the author expresses it. What a gift to the world!!!!"

Katelyn

## I Truly Enjoyed Reading Yeshu'a

"I truly enjoyed reading Yeshu'a. I love books that make me feel as though I am a part of the story. Yeshu'a pulled me into itself from the first chapter. I recommend this series to all who seek a different viewpoint than what we have been taught of the life of Jesus."

Linda

## An Affirmation of Humanity's Potential to Save the World

"In today's world we are encouraged to fall to the feet of Pope, preacher, guru, philosophers, politicians, kings, queens, movie stars, and so on and so on. Pietro de la Luna's poetic series, Yeshu'a: The Hidden Life of Jesus, gives us a refreshing alternative interpretation: "YOU are all the ones you have been waiting for!" The series portrays Yeshu'a's deep respect for the Humanity he serves, encouraging that which is holy within us all to flourish. It also reveals love for the Divine Feminine, as the female participants in Jesus' life are lovingly fleshed out more fully than in the standard gospels. We found these books to be a blessing and believe you will too."

Burl and Merry Hall

## The Gift of Truth

"I want to thank you from the bottom of my heart for the gift of truth. For quite some time I have wanted to read the real story and at just the right moment the Yeshu'a series was offered to me. A thousandfold blessing upon you. In Light and Love,"

Patricia

## Divine Truth

"Beautiful. Thank you for your Divine Truth."

Michelle Lightworker

## Made My Heart and Soul Sing

"Truly and utterly beautiful! Made my heart and soul sing."

Princess Kelly

## Thank You For This Precious Wisdom

"Wow! You speak to the heart of everything. Thank you for this precious wisdom and for sharing it with the world."

Suzka

## Beautiful, Enlightened Masterpiece

"Beautiful, enlightened masterpiece of understanding our true nature, our higher Self, our everlasting soul, the straight purity of our Heart, beloved Brother Pietro, indeed you are, because you are highlighting the Path we have to follow in order to become our better selves, exactly, good for us all, and highlighting the power of the feminine principle shows your great understanding of our inner dwellings and Human psyche, necessary in order to progress for the better of ourselves and society as a whole! Also a visionary and prophetic view makes you not only a great storyteller, but also a great enlightened humanitarian and profound teacher of our time, worthy of great attention in order to progress Humanity on a beautiful living Earth, elevating ourselves and therefore society."

Murray

## Precious Words

"Precious words. Thank you, Pietro. You are indeed a great inspiration to mankind. I appreciate you."

Maliza

## Thank You

"I am speechless. Thank you."

Parya

## Beloved You Are

"I Love your eternal soul, Pietro, precious and beloved you are. You make the cosmos dance with great joy."

Violet Soul

## Beautiful

"Beautiful, beautiful, extraordinary, wise! Thank you. Love & Blessings,"

Lightning Bearheart

## Fresh Water For The Thirsty Soul

"Heartfelt thanks for what you share and express in your words; they are as fresh water for the thirsty soul. The brightest blessings be with you always. Lovingly grateful, i AM."

Maria

## Beautiful Message

"Thanks for this beautiful message of INSPIRATION & WISDOM."

Michaella

## So Perfectly Depicted

"So perfectly depicted, and just the way I have also felt all to be. Thank you for sharing your Love in just Being, the beauty of Absolute, Infinite Beingness."

Pamela

## Thank You

"You are Pure Love, Pietro. Thank you for inspiring us to be also."

Mari

## Sublime

"Pietro's work is sublime and so true to Yeshu'a's words. I shall learn from Pietro as his presentation inspires so beautifully."

Peter

## The Strength of Rose

"The strength of rose, I feel this in your writing. Such peace I gain, soul brother, from your words. Blessings and my gratitude,"

Greg

www.ingramcontent.com/pod-product-compliance
Lightning Source LLC
Chambersburg PA
CBHW071619170426
43195CB00038B/1431